UNDERGROUND*

Serving the Lord as
Chief of Smuggling Operations—
for Secret Church Leadership
Training 1983–1990

AL BAANNA

*Refers to church activities that are not allowed by anti-Christian governments, so must be done in secret.

Emmanuel Publishing

Underground: Serving the Lord as Chief of Smuggling Operations—
for Secret Church Leadership Training 1983–1990

Published by Emmanuel Publishing
ISBN (print): 979-8-9922103-0-9
ISBN (ebook): 979-8-9922103-1-6

Copyright © 2025 Al Baanna. All rights reserved. No part of this work may be reproduced or transmitted in any form or by any means, electronic or mechanical, including photocopying and recording, or by any information storage or retrieval system, except as may be expressly permitted by the 1976 Copyright Act or in writing from the publisher at Emmanuel@swharvest.org.

Titles from Emmanuel Publishing may be purchased in bulk at special discounts for sales promotion, corporate gifts, and ministry, fundraising, or educational purposes. For details, contact Emmanuel@swharvest.org.

Scripture quotations taken from the (NASB®) New American Standard Bible®, Copyright © 1960, 1971, 1977, 1995, 2020 by The Lockman Foundation. Used by permission. All rights reserved. lockman.org

Photos from Al and Betty's photo collection.
Graphic of papers and wood background © vlntn, stock.adobe.com.

Editorial services by Misti Moyer, MistiMoyer.com
Design by Monica Thomas for TLC Book Design, TLCBookDesign.com

Printed in the United States of America

Dedicated first of all to the Lord God who has blessed me with an absolutely incredible life in His service, and to Betty, my God-given wife, who served faithfully alongside me until her passing from this life in 2013.

Also dedicated to Dr. Alex Maianu, the founder of our original mission organization, and to all the faithful servants of the Lord I've been blessed to work with around the world—many who have served under persecution and difficult circumstances of all kinds.

TABLE OF CONTENTS

Foreword 7

PART ONE

Introduction 13
Chapter 1   God Called—We Answered 17
Chapter 2   The Big DC-10 25
Chapter 3   Eastern European Communism 31
Chapter 4   The Lord Loves Little Children 39
Chapter 5   Visiting God's Servants Behind the Curtain 42
Chapter 6   Praying with Joy! 50
Chapter 7   Take-Aways from 1983 Vision Trip 56
Chapter 8   Major Decision Made—Smuggling Job Accepted 63

PART TWO

Chapter 9   Our Dream Becomes Reality 75
Chapter 10   Cloak and Dagger Days 1983-1990 81
Chapter 11   At Home in Vienna 1983-1991 97
Chapter 12   Visiting God's Servants—Poland and Hungary 104
Chapter 13   World and Personal Events Challenge Our Spirits 111
Chapter 14   Everyday Life in Vienna November 1986 to
             February 1987 116
Chapter 15   Springtime in the Village of Wiener Neudorf ... 124
Chapter 16   Betty's Solo Trip to USA 132
Chapter 17   Grace Church—Vienna 136
Chapter 18   Eastern European Travels Continue—1980s 139
Chapter 19   Fear and Strong Christians 148

PART THREE

Chapter 20	Eastern European Revolutions Brewing	157
Chapter 21	New Role for Us	165
Chapter 22	Impressions from January Visit to Romania	173
Chapter 23	Bugs Still Thriving—First USSR trip	180
Chapter 24	Betty's Cancer Battle Begins	189

PART FOUR

Chapter 25	Beginning a New Year	205
Chapter 26	The Tower Calling—March 1991	210
Chapter 27	Trip to Soviet Union—May 14-26, 1991	215
Chapter 28	Back in Wiener Neudorf After USSR Trip	232
Chapter 29	Summer in USA	237
Chapter 30	Beginning Our Move—Austria to Latvia	239
Chapter 31	Heroes in Latvia—New Ministry Role	257
Chapter 32	First Christmas in Latvia	261

PART FIVE

Chapter 33	Beginning a New Year—1992	269
Chapter 34	New Opportunities Under Way	279
Chapter 35	What Do I (Betty) Do All Day	289
Chapter 36	Medical Care in Finland	295
Chapter 37	A Walk Through the Woods to the Store	302
Chapter 38	Springtime in Latvia	308
Chapter 39	You Must Continue!	316
Chapter 40	Afterword 1993-2024	323

About the Authors 329
Acknowledgments 338

FOREWORD

In His divine benevolence, God has graciously bestowed on mankind His eternal message of glory and redemption. This message is historically communicated in the Bible. Joshua 1:8 unequivocally declares: "'This Book of the Law shall not depart from your mouth, but you shall meditate on it day and night, so that you may be careful to do according to all that is written in it; for then you will make your way prosperous, and then you will achieve success.'" How true those words remain to this day.

The Word of God directs man to an appropriate understanding of salvation from the condemnation of sin. When Adam and Eve ate the forbidden fruit in the garden, their act of disobedience ushered sin into the world and the soul of man. This transgression required a perfect Sacrifice for sin. Only God Himself can pay for man's sin.

This payment was accomplished by Christ's death and resurrection on the cross of Calvary (John 3:16). The personal atonement for every human being can only be accomplished through a personal surrender and acceptance of Jesus Christ as Savior and Lord (John 14:6; Acts 4:12).

Concerning Jesus Christ, John the Baptist loudly heralded these words in John 1:29: "Behold, the Lamb of God who takes away the sin of the world!" These clarion words of spiritual salvation and comfort have inspired millions throughout history. Nations have been transformed and multitudes have experienced the forgiveness of sin and the peace of Christ in their lives.

Sadly, not all nations or tyrants are willing to submit to the truths conveyed in God's eternal and authoritative Word. They vigorously resist and vainly try to stomp it out of existence. Why is this so? It is because sin has blinded them. They foolishly think they can defeat an omnipotent, omnipresent, and omniscient God. How tragic!

Al and Betty Baanna, led by the Spirit of God, objected strenuously to this denial of Scripture and basic discipleship materials by Communist nations. Europe has habitually endured tumultuous periods. God has frequently either been "pushed out" or "religiously legislated" as directed by the ruling powers. Neither situation honors God.

During their younger days, this godly young couple answered the call of God on their lives. They joined with other likeminded believers. Their objective? Smuggle God's Word and discipleship materials into the hands of Eastern European and Russian believers. Their passion for the Word of God took second place to no one or anything.

This book is a remarkable story of both Al and Betty's blessings and struggles. Throughout a number of uncharted years, they endured great inconvenience and danger. But, in spite of all the obstacles, they succeeded in bringing God's Word across unfriendly international boundaries. Consequently, both believer and unbeliever alike were blessed.

The title of this book is: *Underground: Serving the Lord as Chief of Smuggling Operations—for Secret Church Leadership Training 1983-1990*. It is a living testimony of God's faithfulness and providence. The reader will find that it proves inspirational in the chronicling of those tempestuous years. It is our fervent prayer that God will fervently bless and direct those who read this amazing testimony of perseverance. Through it all, God's grace is clearly manifested. To Him be all the glory!

–Dr. David Wold

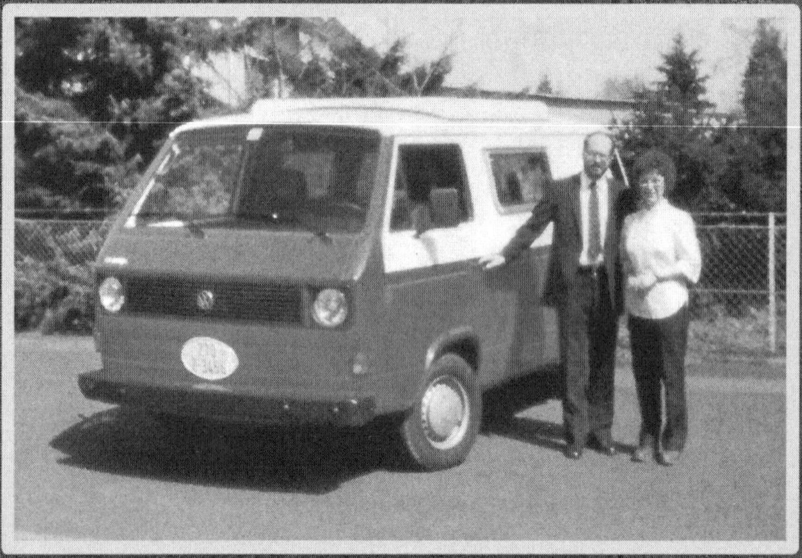

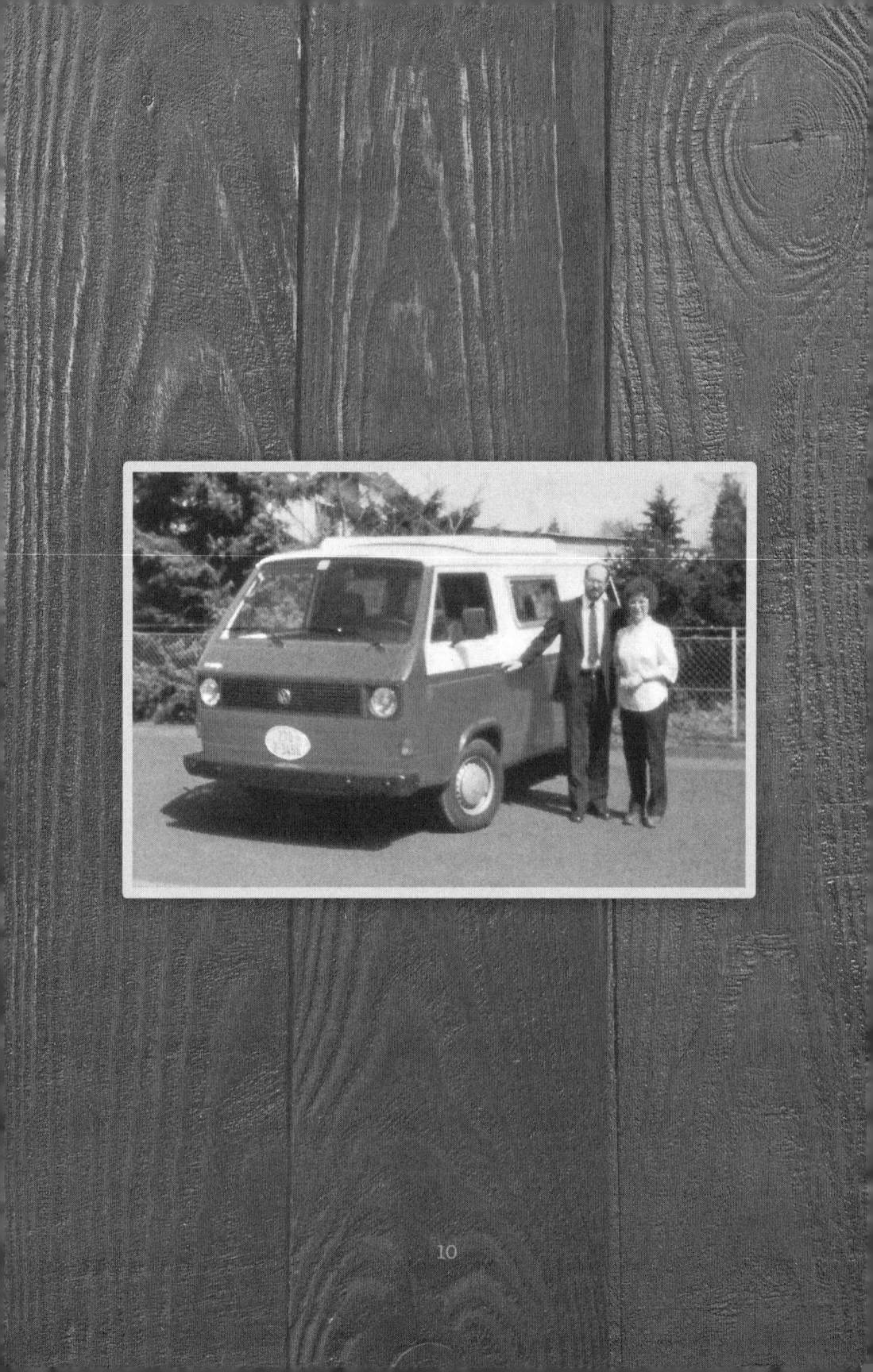

Part One

INTRODUCTION

UNDERGROUND: Serving the Lord as Chief of Smuggling Operations

Few people have had the challenging responsibility of serving the Lord as Chief of Smuggling Operations.

I had the privilege of serving in that role during the 1980s, working behind the Iron Curtain in the Soviet Union and the then-Communist countries of Eastern Europe. Modern-day Americans cannot imagine life for the people in those countries at that time. Conditions were so bad. The Soviet Union was on the verge of coming unglued, and the Eastern European countries were ripe for revolt.

The Communist governments of these countries totally rejected God and His Word; instead, they saw themselves as the ultimate authority over their people. Consequently, anyone teaching that the God of the Bible was the Creator and ultimate authority over all

Al — 2023 photo

needed to be silenced. They attempted to severely limit all aspects of Christian life and values, and in some cases, their plan was to totally eliminate Christianity. "The kings of the earth take their stand and the rulers conspire together against the Lord and against His anointed" (Psalm 2:2).

Consequently, those who participated in our church leader training during those years faced many harsh difficulties. They were subject to arrest, imprisonment, interrogations, beatings, torture, and injections with "truth serum," which caused the victim to tell everything they knew about their underground activities. In this way, the authorities could learn who was illegally "indoctrinating" them with the teachings of Christianity. We therefore protected them—and ourselves—by using aliases. They knew us only as Mike and Leah Hanson. That made it more difficult for the anti-Christian authorities to connect us with the massive ongoing work we ended up joining—the underground training of Christian church leaders.

By the late 1980s, a series of revolutions in Eastern European countries made the smuggling and underground distribution of our seminary materials into those countries unnecessary, as we were able to work openly. Consequently, we were re-assigned to work in the Soviet Union, where I was to serve as the Biblical Education by Extension Co-Coordinator for the Soviet Republics of Estonia, Latvia, Lithuania, and Belarus. We then obtained Soviet visas to move into the Soviet Republic of Latvia in 1991, just as these four republics were all in the process of becoming independent countries.

Why did I choose to invest many hours into the task of writing this story?

First and foremost, Betty wanted to leave her family and friends the story of her relationship with the Lord and her experiences in serving Him in very difficult situations with a lot of personal challenges. For that purpose, she kept hundreds of journals with thousands of pages describing our lives and ministry experiences during these years.

However, God took her from her earthly life in August 2013 before she had a chance to complete the project of preparing these notes for sharing. Therefore, I asked God to enable me to do it in her stead.

It's my prayer that family and friends, and especially the younger generations, will be encouraged and inspired to serve the Lord wholeheartedly, like the many church leaders we encountered behind the Iron Curtain that were prepared to serve Him fully in any and all situations.

Betty's 56th Birthday — Riga, Latvia

A common theme we saw again and again as we met with these church leaders, whose lives were threatened by God-hating governments, was the message of Matthew 10:28, "'And do not be afraid of those who kill the body but are unable to kill the soul; but rather fear Him who is able to destroy both body and soul in hell.'"

Since this book is a memoir, by definition it's based on our memories and understanding, which may, in some cases, be faulty and incomplete.

While the greater part of the content of this book is from Betty's journals, another sizable part is from prayer letters we wrote over the years to our prayer and financial partners in our ministry. For security reasons, I've chosen to carefully limit stories about people or places in areas where persecution may now be, or could end up becoming, a serious issue. For this same reason, I've chosen not to use full names for the people we worked with.

It was not my intention for this book to carefully record a detailed piece of church history; others are better qualified to meet that challenge. My intent is simply to glorify God by sharing something of His love and grace and power in the lives of many of His devoted servants, including us, Al and Betty, two very ordinary, simple, shy, unsophisticated farm kids from the middle of nowhere in the American Upper Midwest.

As I began the process of reviewing our old writings and old photos that pictured our lives from the beginning, Psalm 139:16 came to mind:

> *Your eyes have seen my formless substance;*
> *And in Your book were written*
> *All the days that were ordained for me,*
> *When as yet there was not one of them.*

This verse reminded me that God knew it all beforehand, and our early "pre-Christian" years and all the hard things we experienced along the way were all part of His plan to prepare us, not only for our earthly service, but even more importantly, to prepare us for spending eternity in His presence. The story we share is all a part of His work in our lives that we may be "conformed to the image of His Son" (Romans 8:29).

I chose the New American Standard version for all Bible references in this book. When I became a Christian in 1979, I went out and bought a New American Standard study Bible and began memorizing many verses. To this day, in 2024, this version is usually the one that comes to mind when I want to remember or share a Bible verse.

Since we didn't begin our service for the Lord until middle age, I've included the story of our early lives prior to God's call to serve Him unconditionally however, wherever, forever in About the Authors.

Chapter 1

GOD CALLED— WE ANSWERED

For we are His workmanship, created in Christ Jesus for good works, which God prepared beforehand so that we would walk in them. –EPHESIANS 2:10

Shortly after receiving God's free gift of salvation in Christ Jesus in 1979, I (Al) began to sense a clear and powerful calling to make an unconditional commitment to serve Him—not to a specific place or ministry, but to an open-ended wherever, however, forever. This was a very scary decision to make! I spent many nighttime hours alone in the dark on the living room floor for months struggling with this. Finally, I gave in and agreed with God to make such a commitment, trusting that He would use it for His good purpose and recognizing that I was totally dependent on His grace to do whatever He had planned.

Now I needed to share this decision with my wife. Would she think I was crazy? Would she refuse to go along with this scary decision, which could totally change our life as a married couple? So, with a little fear and trembling, I shared this decision and commitment with Betty. She gently explained she had been struggling with the same challenge from God and had made the same decision as I had. She had also been afraid to share for fear that I wouldn't accept it. So with this decision firmly made by us as a couple, we were ready to move forward.

In God's perfect timing, He brought an escapee from Romania to the church we had just joined in our home city of Fargo, North Dakota. Dr. Alexandru Maianu had escaped his country because of persecution and threats on his life. He had suffered greatly under the oppression of Communism, to the point of seeing his own son killed by those opposed to his Christian work.

Dr. Alexandru Maianu

Alex sought the Lord long and hard before making the very dangerous decision to escape. He had to leave all of his family behind, not knowing if they'd ever meet again this side of heaven. But he had this burning desire in his heart to spread the gospel in Romania via Christian radio and literature, and to do that, he needed to go to America, so he was willing to take the risks. His ministry, Emmanuel Ministries International, was named after his son.

By coming to America, he believed he would have the opportunity to provide teaching via radio and Christian materials for the many church leaders in Romania who were oppressed by the anti-Christian government. To say that his plan to escape was risky is an understatement, for had he been caught, he knew he would have been imprisoned.

When Alex came to our church and shared his story, along with his dream of providing Bible training and Christian literature for his countrymen, it was as though the Lord simply dropped this opportunity into our laps. Al and I were SOOOO excited! That excitement and enthusiasm was very quickly dimmed, however, by almost everyone we talked to about the possibility of our serving with Alex in Eastern Europe. Everyone, including Alex himself, was skeptical of our being able to hold true to what appeared now to be "the impossible dream"!

Al began the process of preparing for missionary service by planning to enter seminary, but quickly ran into an unexpected roadblock. Some years earlier, he had completed all the required university courses to complete his degree in business management, but now he learned that some paperwork needed to certify his graduation had been left incomplete. As a result of requirements for graduation having changed in the meantime, Al was required to return to school to take three more courses to complete his Business Management program. As it turned out, there was a Bible college in the same city as Al's university, so I made plans to take advantage of the situation by enrolling in the Bible college.

Al then went ahead and quit his job as a company general manager, and I quit my office position at a construction company, which meant we were now fully dependent on what we could realize from the sale of our home and belongings. With all this going on, there were plenty of tensions between the two of us as a couple. Many were the times the prophetic words of family and friends would come back to us, reminding us of their concerns that our marriage would not be able to withstand all these pressures.

With some feelings of sadness, we put our lovely home up for sale and prepared to move. It was truly the nicest home I'd ever had the privilege of living in, so even though we were convinced that God was leading us to other things, it was still hard to give it up. The human side of us does not just go away once we commit to the Lord, but it does become a lot easier to view material things as mere stuff. We were challenged even in that area, though, when our basement flooded due to heavy downpours, destroying many of our irreplaceable photographs and mementos, now gone forever.

We had no trouble selling our house, and in a short while, we found ourselves packing up the last of our belongings and heading out to a town in northern Minnesota, where we would both be attending school.

Back to School

So, at middle age, off we went to our respective classrooms, feeling excited and blessed in the Lord's confidence in choosing us to serve Him. However, some people laughed at us for making what seemed to be a ludicrous decision. I believe some even called us "fools." We still weren't sure how He was leading. We did, however, sense that God wanted us in foreign missions. Our interests, our circumstances, and our counsel from the Scriptures all seemed to confirm what we were sensing.

Needless to say, going back into the classroom after being away for almost thirty years was a scary time for me. It turned out, I had no need to fear, however, since I loved school, was a good student, and soaked up the teachings of my newfound faith like a dry garden needing a good watering. My classes revolved around the study of the Bible, but they also included subjects such as biblical counseling and learning how to share my faith with others. I had exceptional instructors who made studying the Scriptures seem like digging for diamonds in a diamond mine.

How I treasured those days of becoming more familiar with God's Word. His Word is so rich in truth, and I just wanted to learn it all in one day.

I also secured a network of doctors and physical therapists that were able to give me some relief for my ongoing back pain, but it was still very difficult for me to keep from thinking about it all of the time. In God's special providence, we were introduced to a massage therapist who came to our city from Germany and turned out to be a special gift of comfort to me from the Lord. Along with him giving me much relief, we were also able to tell him about our Savior, and Al led him into a saving knowledge of trusting our Lord. God's "arrangements" are so marvelous!

During this time, we continued in earnest to learn whatever we could about serving in Eastern Europe. Our time in school took on a much different light now that we felt we had more direction. Al finished his studies and graduated with high honors, and I completed my studies at the Bible college with high grades and a readiness to put to use that which I'd now learned.

I came to love many of my instructors as well. Mrs. A, my favorite instructor, deeply inspired us and helped me, personally, along the way to forgetting all my heavy sins of the past. It's difficult to put all the old self behind, but that's what the Word tells us to do. If we continue carrying along all the ugly old baggage in our attempts to serve the Master, then we get so bogged down that it hinders us from being used effectively. Mrs. A truly was a gift from our Lord.

"Outlandish" Call to Serve as Pastor

After completing our respective school programs, it was to our amazing surprise that one evening the elders of our church came to our apartment and asked Al to pastor the church we were presently attending. Our current pastor was leaving, and they needed someone to take over the shepherding of this church. Al and I looked at each other in bewilderment as we let this soak in. Suddenly, we both began to laugh! It seemed as outlandish to us as God's promise of giving Abraham (age one hundred) and Sarah (age ninety) a son seemed to them at first (Genesis 17:17; 18:12).

Given our inexperience and lack of training, it appeared as though God was making a BIG mistake. We were very new believers, with no "normal" preparation whatsoever in this area, so it seemed pretty ridiculous for us to even consider an appointment like this. We declined the offer. God perseveres, however, and how thankful we are that He does. Al eventually ended up assuming the responsibility of pastor for this church, and it was the best "schooling" we could ever have hoped to have for the ministry God had planned for us in the years to come.

The people of this church took us in, accepted our ineptness, wrapped their spiritual arms around us, and encouraged us in every way possible. Both Al and I were very shy introverts who found it hard to speak in front of groups. But these dear people gave us so much acceptance that it was truly easy to learn, grow, and develop. This experience turned out to be invaluable in the years to come. Along with the invaluable pastoral experience we gained, it also gave us credibility in our soon-to-begin ministry of training pastors and other church leaders.

Once Al accepted the Bemidji pastorate, he bought a copy of Haddon Robinson's well-known book, *Biblical Preaching*. He began reading it from chapter one as he began preaching through the book of Ephesians over something like five or six months. My anniversary gift to Al that summer was a copy of John Stott's book *The Preacher's Portrait*, which was very helpful in learning more about all aspects of serving as a pastor. From there, things began to move quickly. Little did we know that God had plans for our soon-to-be established mission organization in Fargo, ND, to translate those two books into the Romanian language. Al would then be responsible for getting them smuggled into Romania and distributed to all the church leader study groups around the country. Later, he personally used these books in other languages in other Communist Eastern European countries and in the Soviet Union as part of the

Communicating God's Word Seminary Textbook — Romanian Version

Communicating God's Word course we did with church leaders in that part of the world. (Al was honored to have his hands serve as the model for the hands of the modern-day preacher on the course book cover.)

While serving as a pastor in Bemidji, MN, we continued discussions with Alex and had him speak at our church and other local churches. The vision trip that had been only a dream for some time was soon to become reality. "'Therefore, plead with the Lord of the harvest to send out workers into His harvest'" (Matthew 9:38).

The next step, then, was to announce from the pulpit at Christmas 1982, that we would be leaving the pastorate at that church and would be planning a vision trip to Eastern Europe in early 1983. Our prayer was to be allowed to minister among the people of Eastern Europe and to enjoy a closer walk with our Lord.

We know that God is able to do exceeding abundantly beyond all that we ask or think (Ephesians 3:20, 21), and He has wonderfully done so in His response to our prayer.

Things seemed to progress quickly. We began to plan a six-month vision trip for early 1983 to visit Alex's family and other underground Christian worker contacts in Romania, and as the expression goes, the rest is history. The remainder of this book will unfold the story of His work in our lives as we served Him in international ministry.

Like Abraham going out on faith by God's direction (Hebrews 11:8), knowing not where he was going, we placed ourselves in His hands, stepped out, and never looked back. We have never since regretted that decision for unconditional service that we made together in 1981.

There was a song that was popular at this time, which began with the lines, "I have decided to follow Jesus; No turning back, no turning back; Though none go with me, I still will follow." This became our theme song for the rest of our lives.

Chapter 2

THE BIG DC-10

Answering the Call Leads Us to Eastern Europe

It was a bittersweet time of saying our good-byes to family and friends, but never did we sense even a speck of resentment over our leaving the USA for a virtually unknown life ahead of us. In fact, our families—perhaps not fully understanding what we were hoping to do in Europe—were totally supportive.

Thus, it was on an April day in 1983 that the big DC-10 lumbered along the tarmac as we prepared to take off from Minneapolis. The trip was long and tedious and was hard on my (Betty's) already distressed back. Anyone suggesting that travel abroad is so wonderful needs only to talk to us, and we'll quickly dispel any ideas they might have of long-distance travel in economy class being a glamorous experience.

Our first stop in Europe was London. It was all that we'd read about. A heavy cloud cover, cold, windy fields of lush greenery, and yet a nice change from the Minnesota winter we had just left behind. Our bodies were screaming for rest, but first, a hot bath and a nice "spot of tea."

The next morning was Easter, and we were privileged to attend the service at All Soul's Church—associated with John Stott, whose writings on evangelical Christianity we had studied before leaving the USA.

However, before we left our little room for the Easter service, we were treated to a full English breakfast of eggs, ham, stewed tomatoes, and baked beans, all done up beautifully on a table decorated with fresh daffodils.

Our next stop was Germany, where we stayed with friends who graciously helped us buy a VW camper van for our upcoming travels in Eastern Europe. The camper was outfitted with the bare necessities of a fold-out bed, a camper-size refrigerator, gas stove, and a table. There was also a pop-up area over the stove that allowed us to stand up while preparing meals.

Al & Betty with VW Van — April 1983

While waiting a week for our camper to be prepared, we thankfully had time to adjust to jet lag and prepare for our new and very different life in Europe.

Our new friends in Darmstadt took us to visit some missionary friends of theirs who had been serving the Lord for some time. Marianne was a German who married an American, so she remembered all too well what the years of WWII in Germany were like. Our conversation with her was thirty-eight years after the war ended, yet she couldn't speak of those years without having her eyes well up with tears.

Sitting there in that upstairs apartment, looking down over this typical German street, took my thoughts back to what it might have been like for people like Corrie Ten Boom and Anne Frank. My imagination served me well, and I could almost see the Gestapo coming down the street and hear air raid warning sirens filling the air. I prayed that my Lord would never allow me to forget what these dear people suffered. I'd known so many blessings in America, and I asked to be kept sensitive and wise in ministering to the needs of those who had been less fortunate.

Soon, we were saying good-bye again as we prepared to depart from Germany. We had been with these dear friends only a short time, but they had taken us in with such warm hospitality, all out of their committed love for Christ. It was difficult to leave.

Next Stop, Vienna — God's Providence

It was a rather dark, cloudy morning when we crawled into our van, which was now our home, our transportation, and our office. The autobahn was totally intimidating to us, with their being no speed limits and cars traveling up to and over 100 mph.

How we prayed that God would surround us with His protective care. Coming from very quiet, slow-paced communities back in the USA, where traffic was slow and sparse, our nerves were frazzled by the end of the first day. We began to wonder if we'd made a mistake. We missed our new friends, we missed our families, and things seemed so unclear for our future days.

Looking at things now in retrospect, it's so clear that God was indeed ahead of us, preparing for our arrival in Vienna, Austria, but, of course, we did not know that at the time.

Living in a small van where one could never stand up without bumping one's head became extremely aggravating at times. We had no personal space; privacy was nonexistent, so there were many times I thanked the Lord for giving me a husband I enjoyed spending time with. Even so, it would have been nice to get away even into the next room sometimes, but that wasn't possible in our circumstances. We didn't even have bathroom facilities in our van, so we had to stop at gas stations and campsites. Many of them were crude, dirty, and vulgar, and I couldn't wait to use them and flee as quickly as I possibly could manage.

The week we arrived in Vienna, we stayed long enough to visit a Sunday morning church service. Many were the times we praised God for directing us to this church, since it gave us a critical contact for our future ministry. I was in the ladies' room when I was asked to help a young woman by holding the door, which had a malfunctioning lock, while she used the facilities. Don't ask me why I struck up a conversation with this woman, since I was not really an outgoing individual. In addition, to do this in a strange country where I didn't speak the language very well was surely the leading of the Lord.

To my surprise, it turned out that this young woman spoke English very well and really needed the very help we could supply. She was moving from one apartment to another, and she needed help in transporting her belongings. Since we had a van, it was easy for us to say yes, so we drove over to her apartment to help her.

In the process, we were introduced to her blind friend, Mike, who was helping her also. We began visiting, telling Mike how we happened to come to Vienna. It wasn't long before we realized this was a divine appointment, which only God could have arranged. You see, it was Mike who then invited us to go with him to visit an organization housed in a large building—hereafter referred to as the "Big House"—at the edge of the Austrian forest. Since Mike was blind, Al escorted him in.

Considering our limited knowledge at this time, we sometimes referred to this as a case of the blind leading the blind.

Because of the secretive work they were doing in training pastors and lay leaders behind the Iron Curtain (the very type of work we felt God was calling us to), no one was allowed entry to the Big

The "Big House"—Our Office Building in Vienna

House except those working there. Mike just happened to be one of those special people! He worked there as a translator, so he was able to take us right in the back door, where we were then introduced to the director of the organization. We were warmly welcomed and trusted with the work that this wonderful organization was doing. The orchestrations of the Lord's leading are totally amazing, and we saw this kind of thing over and over again, but this was one of the most spectacular.

Being fairly new believers, this was such a faith builder, to see the Lord arrange for us to meet up in Vienna, Austria, with the very people who might help us with insight, contacts, etc. We listened with rapt attention as they shared their vision with us.

The most important issue they shared was the desperate need for teaching for church leaders, so they could then reproduce leaders to grow the church. The governments in these Communist countries were afraid of the power believers had in the faith they lived, so they kept all Christian literature and teaching from them as much as they possibly could. For the believers, it was a serious offense to be caught with Christian literature.

This work in Vienna was a cooperative effort of a dozen or so Christian mission organizations working together to provide Bible education by extension in these circumstances. Over the years, there have been a number of names for this organization and its offshoots, but we'll refer to them as Biblical Education by Extension or BEE World in this book. The challenge came in successfully smuggling the planned two million seminary textbooks into these countries, and then secretly distributing them via an underground network to hundreds of groups all across the Soviet Union and Communist Eastern Europe.

After discussing Al's background involving international business and pastoral experience, they mentioned some staff positions they needed to fill. They suggested the smuggling and distribution job might be a good fit for him. We laughed at this possibility but agreed to visit with them again after we returned from our planned vision trip around Eastern Europe.

Before leaving Austria, we needed to buy a purse for Al. Yes, you read right; men here in Europe all carried purses—not as big and bulky as what women use, but a purse, nonetheless. It was a necessity because of all the formal papers (government and travel documents) we needed to have available for all border crossings. For a staunch, manly Norwegian from a very conservative part of the USA, this was no easy adjustment. But we knew that in order for us to "blend in," it was a necessity, and interestingly enough, Al became so accustomed to it that it became one of the most missed items of European culture once we returned to America.

Chapter 3

EASTERN EUROPEAN COMMUNISM

A Different Way of Life

"Come with me!" was the harsh command from the no-nonsense female Romanian border guard as she led me away for interrogation and a body search. While her colleague led Al away into an adjoining room, she directed me into a large room adorned only with a couple of straight-backed chairs, a small wooden table, and a huge picture of the Communist Dictator Nicolae Ceausescu hanging on the bleak walls.

My heart was pounding so hard I was sure I appeared guilty in spite of our attempts to make sure we were "clean" as we began this trip into Romania, one of the most difficult countries in the Eastern Bloc. Clean meant we had nothing incriminating about what we were doing or who we were meeting with on us.

In the years to follow, I often compared the border guard's harsh command to follow her into a spartan room for interrogation to Jesus's loving command to Peter and Andrew, "Follow Me, and I will make you fishers of men" (Matthew 4:19), which was the decision we had made several years earlier for ourselves.

The threat of harsh interrogations and thorough searches of our bodies and vehicles became a regular part of life for us in the

1980s. It was always a frightening time for me when we pulled up to an Eastern European border crossing with its barbed wire settings, guard dogs sniffing at our van, and the cold harsh looks of the armed uniformed guards in charge.

Crossing into Romania was especially difficult. We apparently were suspected of smuggling Bibles or Christian literature into the country each time we entered, as they took our van apart piece by piece for a thorough search. They removed all the interior panels and dug deep into every crevice and cranny of our vehicle from front bumper to rear bumper. To add insult to injury, they made us put it all back together again ourselves. They also helped themselves to the food and other gift items we were bringing in to share with our contacts.

We prayed each time for God's protection and provision to get us safely through the Iron Curtain. Would we say something stupid in our nervousness? Did we forget some contact information left out in the open in our van or on our person? Did we just plain look too guilty for the guards to let us pass? My hands kept busy as I did my cross stitching, trying hard to calm my nerves. It was always a good distraction for me, as well as for the guards.

They were curious and interested in the handwork I was doing and had a lot of comments, which were apparent even to our untrained ears for these strange languages. Before long, though, the harsh questions would begin. "What do you want in our country?" "Who will you be seeing?" "What are you bringing to our people?" "Do you have guns?" "Are you carrying Bibles?" Our hearts would pound so hard we could hardly hear our interrogator. Only God could protect us each time we crossed a border into the Communist countries of Eastern Europe and the Soviet Union. We commonly prayed, "Lord, you've made blind eyes see; now we pray that you will make seeing eyes blind."

Eastern Europe Vision Trip 1983

It was a warm, sunny day in mid-May when we departed from our comfortable campground environment in Vienna to make our first trip throughout the Communist Eastern European countries.

First, we entered Hungary, where we saw a lovely countryside, with rolling hills and farmers making their hay by hand, cutting with hand-held scythes, and hanging it on lines to dry. Houses looked large, but we knew that houses and barns were typically combined into one building, thereby conserving heat from the animals to keep their homes warm and making it more convenient to care for them.

Then, after traveling through Yugoslavia (a few years later broken up into seven separate countries), we entered Greece. Stopping in Thessalonica, we waded out into the Aegean Sea and reflected on the Apostle Paul and his work in this area. Church buildings have been unearthed here dating back to the fourth century.

In Athens, we stopped to view the Acropolis. This magnificent complex is HUGE. Then there was Mars Hill, where Paul gave his sermon of challenge (Acts 17:26-32). What courage it must have taken to do that in the midst of all the scholars who spoke there.

The next morning, we had to be at the pier by 6:30 a.m. to load our van onto the ferry for our journey across the sea to Turkey. It was a beautiful morning! The rain we had the day before had refreshed everything and things looked so much better. However, at first, they weren't going to let us board, saying they didn't have room. Thankfully, an English-speaking employee intervened for us, and they consented to let us onto the ferry. The trip was long and tiring. I ended up feeling sick for a good part of the way. I had an emotionally difficult time as I barfed most of the way. If you've never been sick in a bathroom that's literally swaying back and forth on the waves, you're fortunate. I really felt rotten!

Then, to our surprise, the ferry stopped to unload all the passengers and vehicles on the small island of Samos, about twenty miles from our intended destination on the Turkish coast. How did we get the rest of the way? Well, Al found someone who spoke English, and he said he had a friend with a fishing boat with the name *Diana* painted on the side. He could take us across in the morning. After spending the night on the dock, the next morning, we were nearly shocked out of our wits to see this very small fishing boat named *Diana!* We were extremely skeptical about crossing the sea on this small boat, but it seemed to be the only choice we had.

Al pulled up alongside the boat, and a man on board looked at our van and pointed to the boat with a questioning look. Al nodded, "Yes," and the man emphatically shook his head, "No!"

At that time, another man approached (apparently the owner of the boat), and he started shouting orders. The next thing we knew, they were placing some planks from the dock to the platform on the back of the boat and motioning us to drive up onto it. Once loaded, we debarked from the harbor out into the open sea. They then realized our van wasn't centered on this small platform and was causing the boat to tilt. They instructed Al to maneuver the van more to the center of the platform to correct the tilt of the boat, a pretty scary proposition on this tilted platform bouncing up and down on the waves, but we really had no choice.

After centering the van successfully, the trip to the Turkish coast was accomplished, but the Muslim boat owner spent the two-hour trip kneeling on the floor of the boat and going through his prayer ritual again and again. Perhaps he was as frightened as we were with this situation.

Once safely on shore, we had to satisfy the customs officials who suddenly appeared over the hill. After inspecting our van and our documents, they allowed us to drive over to the archeological site of Ephesus, where we spent several hours exploring. With virtually no one else around, this was one of my most memorable

Visiting Ephesus Ruins — 1983

experiences of all the biblical sites we visited in Greece, Turkey, Italy, and Israel. I especially remember the white marble road leading down to the harbor.

One of our early discoveries is that driving in southeastern Europe bears no resemblance to driving in the United States or even Western Europe.

The red and white camper van which we had purchased in Germany at the beginning of our travels had generally served us well. However, its low-powered engine kept us from taking advantage of the scarce passing opportunities while driving through the often mountainous terrain. Consequently, we spent many hours crawling slowly along behind horse-drawn wagons and slow-moving trucks and buses.

Many of the Eastern European highways were extremely narrow two-lane roads, with no shoulders and surfaces so rough that we felt like our teeth were being jarred loose at times. If the road wasn't going uphill around a gentle curve, it was usually going downhill around a sharp curve. Usually, 90 percent of the traffic seemed to be buses and trucks, all blasting out enormous thick black clouds of sickening black diesel smoke as they labored uphill at ten to twenty miles per hour.

Since most of our driving had been on such roads and in big cities, we experienced nausea, burning eyes, dizziness, and headaches from constantly inhaling thick diesel fumes. It appeared that the European drivers were very much affected by the fumes as well, because they all seemed to be suffering from double vision. Where we saw two narrow lanes, they invariably seemed to see three, or even four lanes. The dotted white line down the center was the passing lane—from both directions!! It doesn't take a lot of imagination to see why a day on the road left us pretty well worn out.

Finally, it seemed that most of the campgrounds where we stayed had one very similar set of rules. The rules were that all loud talking, pounding in tent pegs, all door-slamming contests, and all dog-barking contests were to be concentrated between the hours of midnight and 5:00 a.m. At that time, all noisy activities were to be brought to a close so that the camp roosters could properly usher in the new day with their crowing routine. In short, sleep was very limited.

All in all, if we had considered only our own immediate comforts and interests, we would have packed up and gone home to the good old USA already. It usually took much more than just a good sense of humor to make it through each day. It seemed like the weather was either terribly cold and wet, or terribly hot and dry. Many of the "luxuries" we were used to in the USA, like laundromats, hot water showers, telephone directories, useable toilets, and toilet paper, must have been illegal in many areas. At any rate, they were very hard to find there.

As far as our "workday" was concerned, we had been warned that everything there would take three times as long. Our experience had been that this first time around everything was taking five times as long as we had anticipated. (Keep in mind that this was before cell phones and laptop computers.)

Above all, there was the perpetual presence of the military and the police constantly watching everyone and stopping us to carefully check all our papers—one by one—and questioning us as to where we'd been and where we were going and why and when, etc. Most officials and "public servants" were not very pleasant to deal with.

In short, some mornings while having our breakfast of bread and jam in our van for the umpteenth day in a row, we remembered how nice it was back in Bemidji, Minnesota, to linger over an occasional leisurely breakfast of Perkin's cake and steak with a full pot of hot coffee to enjoy.

The longer we traveled within the Eastern Bloc, the more difficult it became. Our soft, Western bodies weren't at all accustomed to the many changes we encountered. The lack of hygiene, the impurities of food and water, and the stress-related days and nights began to take their toll on us. Also, we were constantly looking over our shoulders for the secret police, as well as the military, whose job it was also to secure foreigners and help control the people. The sum total of all we faced these days began to wear on us, including the attempts of our spiritual enemies, who never hesitated to further attack our dragging spirits.

Finding campsites for parking our van in the evenings was quite a challenge too. Many sites were so dreadfully filthy and had only the crudest of facilities for bathroom needs. The sharp barking of the large numbers of wild dogs in and around the camps at night was such an eerie sound, to say nothing of their being dangerous in their starved mode as they hunted for some food from the campers. We were being severely tested.

Other challenges began to take their toll on us. Many were the times we suffered from food poisoning and became dehydrated from the vomiting and other less pleasant symptoms of this malady, but we found it nearly impossible to find water that was safe to drink to replenish our bodies' dire need.

The needs of the people we saw every day in this prison country of Romania, where Satan had the leaders in his hold, were more than I could even express in words. But it was the children who really broke my heart. Day after day, and village after village, as we traveled, it was the same sad scene.

Chapter 4

THE LORD LOVES LITTLE CHILDREN

"Leave the children alone, and do not forbid them to come to Me…" is what our Lord said in Matthew 19:14, but oh how grieved He must be to see these little dirt-encrusted kids with their ragged, ill-fitting clothes, and out-stretched hands as they approached us foreigners in hopes of something to lighten their daily struggle to exist.

While stopping for our noonday break of canned sardines and bread in the mountains of Transylvania, I (Betty) saw this little blonde-haired urchin across the road, struggling with her heavy buckets of water, which she had just drawn from the village well. With a burden far too heavy for her young shoulders, this little wasp was trying hard to bring home part of the family's supply but ended up spilling more than she could manage to get home.

Then, as her eyes caught us sitting there in the shade of the roadside trees, her little face took on a glimmer of hope, and I could see the battle begin between her shyness and her desire to approach us. In my conviction of all we had (our fish and bread now held a new appeal), I suddenly lost my desire to eat and employed my best charms to entice her over to our van.

She was so apprehensive and scooted off for support from her brother and sisters. Within moments, with three supporters and

Children in Transylvania Mountains — 1983

a very mangy looking mutt, she appeared from behind the tall fence across the road. They didn't dare to approach us, but just stood there with their sad, appealing eyes glued to our every move. Every encouragement on our part to lure them closer failed, but we quickly rummaged through our dwindling supplies to find something that might brighten their faces—drawn and far too heavy with the burden of life for their young years. How I wished we had brought more things with us! But we did pull together some candy and gum, and their little eyes, so dull and listless, instantly took on a new shine of delight and gratefulness as we placed the goodies into their hands.

Later, in the center of a large, bustling city, out of nowhere came these two little scraps of neglected humanity in front of us with hands open and eyes pleading, competing for our attention. As I looked at the little feet coming through the holes in the front of their far too small shoes, my heart broke and my tear-filled eyes made it hard for me to find the treats I had in my bag. As the light changed for us to cross the street, one little girl quickly tugged on my arm and, with a radiant smile, placed a crushed and soggy wild plum in my hand in grateful exchange for the treats I had given her.

One of the saddest sights we witnessed were all the handicapped and poor lined up outside the gates of a downtown church. People with deep, open sores, deformed limbs, missing body parts all exposed eagerly to the passing public in hopes of receiving alms. There was one little girl—about seven or eight—sitting on the cold, hard cement in all her filthy rags with her arm bandaged and tears streaking down her dirty face, looking for a handout. Her eyes were staring off into space as though she neither cared nor intended to go on living. I still see that haunting look in my mind's eye and wonder if she was really disabled and alone, or whether her parents forced her to do this to gain money for the family.

How can a loving God allow this to go on you say? But you see, it's not the desire of our loving Lord that these children be neglected. He grieves even more than we do over these unfortunate little ones. But He has given man the free will of choice, and the choice of the leaders in these countries had been to follow a godless ideology which led to callousness beyond compare. But He has also given us a choice: Will we choose to follow Him in loving our neighbor or not?

Time after time, I thought about how these little ones must look so much like the ones who approached our Lord during His time here on earth. His heart was touched, and He placed their welfare before so many of His other concerns, pleading with His followers to care for and love them.

Chapter 5

VISITING GOD'S SERVANTS BEHIND THE CURTAIN

Challenge to Fear Only God

We were now in Romania, where we didn't normally give ourselves the privilege of worshipping openly with believers, but no one here knew us yet, so we risked going to this church in Sibiu. The women were all seated on one side of the church and the men on the other. It was very rigid and traditional. Many women were wearing scarves on their heads, believing in the concept of "head covering" (1 Corinthians 11:3-16). Their hymnals were covered with paper to help preserve them. Very few had their own Bibles, and those few Bibles were very old and well worn.

The pastor noticed our presence right away and asked Al to share a greeting. Then Pastor B. asked us up to his apartment during a break in the service and asked Al to preach when the service continued! Much time was spent in prayer. Al was sitting with the pastor, and I sat with his wife. Al gave an inspirational Bible message to this packed church of about three hundred people. I knew he was apprehensive, since he hadn't prepared for this, but the Lord used his willingness and spoke powerfully through him, which we saw happen time and time again.

I had a young woman, Simona, come up to me during the service and interpret for me. I came to feel very close to her before the day ended. I prayed she would have the courage to continue serving the Lord in this environment. She wanted so much for me to give her the words to some of our American hymns and was totally baffled that I didn't know all these beautiful songs by memory! There was much emphasis placed on memorization because so very little was available in print. They never knew when even the few Bibles they now had would be confiscated. I saw six people using one copy of music in the choir, but most of them knew the words anyway.

After the service, the pastor invited us up to share a meal with his family. We were served a simple, but delicious meal, and enjoyed such sweet fellowship with these folks, whom we'd just met hours earlier. The bond between believers was sweet and strong. We felt the love and joy exuding from them as they were given the privilege of providing hospitality in the name of their Savior. We parted with hearts full and minds reeling from all the things we wanted to remember.

The pastor looked so weary. They were terribly overloaded with work. Some had up to fifteen churches to serve! Romania had thirteen hundred Baptist churches, with only one hundred sixty pastors. The government allowed only five students in seminary each year, trying desperately to choke out the church in every possible way. God is greater, however, and the number of active believers was increasing rapidly, in spite of the oppressive authorities.

That evening, we returned to the church we'd visited in the morning. Again, Al was asked to speak. We had hoped to sneak in this time and just remain unnoticed. We had been out walking around in the sun all day. Hot, dusty, and tired, we weren't prepared for this immediate attention. Al was whisked away with the pastor again, but this time, I panicked when I realized his tie was in my handbag—it would be improper for him to preach without it! I was able to pass it to him so he could take the pulpit in proper order, but I could see he was pretty frazzled. It was a hard lesson for us to learn to always be prepared to preach when entering a church. People were so hungry for any news from the West, and they especially appreciated a word from their fellow Christian brothers and sisters who were praying for them. The fellowship and teaching were sweet, and the lunch afterwards was very interesting!

The pastor's wife once again served us, and a number of others, a meal after the service—a nice meal of cold cuts, goat's cheese, and what looked to be plain cheese, but turned out to be slices of congealed lard! I tried warning Al before he took too large a piece but wasn't able to head him off, so he had the "privilege" of partaking of this unusual delicacy too. There was plenty of bread to help us get it down, but this wasn't the only time we were surprised with unusual items on the menu in the various homes we were invited to.

It was hard leaving Simona. She and her friends were all so eager to hear about America and our way of life there. I spent a lot of time pondering the events of our day as I slept in our van that evening.

Pastor B. preached his message that day from Matthew 10:28, which says, "'And do not be afraid of those who kill the body but are unable to kill the soul; but rather fear Him who is able to destroy both soul and body in hell.'" That spoke loudly to Al and me as we were now looking to do dangerous work with the persecuted church. His message that Sunday seemed a confirmation from the Lord, Himself, that this was His plan for us, and we were not to fear the authorities who opposed God and His people. God used Pastor B.'s message to help prepare us for all that was to come with being fully engaged in underground work and the scary challenges that presented.

Whenever I began feeling sorry for myself, I would always try to remember that we were here because we chose to be. The nationals had no such choice. The privilege of meeting our fellow believers rejuvenated us. They looked so weary and worn, but were always—ALWAYS—so delighted to welcome us into their homes, and treat us to the best fare they had available, most often sacrificially. They would sit and visit with us while WE ate, but never take a bite themselves.

However, God also encouraged us with special gifts when we most needed to see His hand during our most difficult days. Betty tells the following story about a day when that was true:

The Wedding

Climbing out of our VW van parked at a campground on the outskirts of Bucharest, we found there was no hot water at the campground, so we didn't linger over getting cleaned up. We pulled on old drab thrift store clothing so we could blend in with the crowd as we began our discrete search for the address of the underground contact we planned to make that evening.

"Oh Father," I prayed, "I want so much to be obedient to your call on my life, but does it have to be here in Romania on Julie's wedding day." Now only a third of the way into our six-month vision trip to Eastern Europe, it simply wasn't feasible for us to return to the US. Air fares to and from Eastern Europe were prohibitive, especially on our tight budget. This happened to be the day in which our daughter, Julie, was getting married back in America. Nothing about our daughter's wedding day went the way we would have envisioned it. In the first place, due to scheduling issues, we were eight time zones away in Bucharest, Romania, when Julie walked down the aisle of Calvary Baptist Church in Fargo, ND. I felt miserable, but God knew my aching heart.

As we walked in downtown Bucharest to scope out the address for the contact we were to visit that evening, we heard this beautiful church music. We peeked into the entrance of the sanctuary, and a wedding was in progress! The church shimmered with a riot of

Wedding in Bucharest

color—ornate icons and statuary, priests clad in stately ceremonial garb, and lavish bouquets of elegant flowers.

As we stood in the doorway looking in, the beautiful music we'd heard from a block away now wafted down from the balcony at full volume. The aroma of incense mingled with the smell of candle wax.

"Come in, come in!" the family motioned. Though they spoke no English, and we spoke no Romanian, we were warmly welcomed into the church to share in the festivities.

There was the bride dressed in an exquisite old ivory-colored lace-trimmed wedding dress, possibly a family heirloom, with an elaborate headpiece and veil. At her side, her new husband, dressed in a white suit, gazed lovingly down at his bride, obviously marveling in disbelief at his extraordinary good fortune.

As we lingered by the door, the family reiterated their welcome to join in the celebration. They served us sweets and fruit punch and some of their hard-to-get chocolate, treating us as honored guests. My heart experienced such mixed feelings: sad, because I was missing our daughter's wedding, but exhilarated because the Lord in His goodness provided another wedding for us to be part of. It was a very unique day of special assurance from God's hand.

Visiting the C's

Having located our intended contact's address that afternoon, we returned to visit them that evening after dark. I don't know why, but it seemed that almost every time we needed to do this, it was raining, cold, dark, and gloomy. After carefully scanning the area for police, or others who might have been watching, we proceeded to find the place where we were to meet our contact. However, the old woman at home told us that Mr. and Mrs. C. were gone, attending their worship service. We didn't feel real comfortable with this explanation as we weren't sure we could trust this woman, but stayed a time, hoping our contact would come home.

When they arrived, they quickly secured the locks, closed the curtains, took the phone off the hook, and checked to see if we'd been followed. They lived in constant dread of the police coming and needed to exercise extreme caution in meeting with their contacts. Mrs. C. shared some of what it was like to live with the shortages and the ever-present threat of their persecutors, but when she spoke of her Lord's faithfulness and the protection He provides, her face shone with a radiance that made even these grey surroundings seem bright and beautiful. Oh, that my faith and courage would be so strong and so dependent on the Lord's strength.

Mrs. C. prepared a lovely lunch of cool vegetable soup, with a light cream broth, hot and crispy breadsticks filled with white cheese, and stewed apples for dessert. I'm sure they had spent many hours to gather up enough ingredients for these dishes, but they counted it all joy and a deep privilege to serve. It was a very humbling experience for us. The family was made up of doctors, dentists, biochemists, and professors in environmental controls. However, rarely were these professionals permitted to work in their learned fields; instead, they were made to take much lesser positions with bare bones pay for their salaries. It was a way for the authorities to demean people, to oppress them to the point of despair.

Most believers here thought only about 2 percent of the Communist Party members were actually committed to their beliefs, and the rest just went along with everything for the sake of convenience. There was no logic to their ways. They ousted the Christians, who were the hard workers, honest, dependable, etc., and gave the best jobs to the party members, who were lazy, dishonest, disloyal, and didn't have any sense of work ethic, but only collected their paychecks at the end of the week.

Before leaving these dear folks, they gave us a bag of pears, apples, cake, homemade jam, and a lovely, embroidered scarf to take with us. We knew these gifts were given sacrificially, with joy and love. How humble we felt! Yet we were the ones they revered, kissing our hands, hugging us, and treating us with great respect. The only courtesy and chivalry one would encounter here was from the Christians.

Suffering became even more unbearable for those believers who had applied for immigration but, for a variety of reasons, were made to wait. Life became quite miserable for them. The children in school would find themselves being "volunteered" for manual labor work projects. Those with higher education were made to take menial positions, having nothing to do with their particular vocations, but having to do double, or more, shifts of work that no one else wanted.

We spoke much of the literature available in these countries. At each stop, we discussed the various needs, things that might be encouraging, like stories of those living for Christ under great difficulty. We would pray and sing songs together; we shared the faithfulness of our Lord and Savior together through the poem, "Footprints." These were blessed times of fellowship and learning, no matter how bittersweet. We always left feeling renewed and refreshed in our spirits and ready for further battle. Their examples of faith, hope, and fearlessness fused into us with vigor and vitality, for which we were always so grateful.

There were so many controls ruling the lives of the people. They would run into things like all the red tape involved in making purchases, provided there was money to do so. To buy a car, for example, the money must first be deposited in a bank before they could even have their name placed on the three-to-four-year waiting list. These were things we, as Americans, knew nothing about.

Long lines for food become the normal way to shop. If there were items available, then people queued up well in advance and stood for hours just to get something as simple as a few rolls of toilet tissue. The stores were so dark, it was hard to tell if they were really open for business unless one saw a line forming.

Chapter 6

PRAYING WITH JOY!

The Romanian pastor's tired face immediately brightened with joy as he replied, "Yes, we will pray on our knees!"

It was late at night and time to conclude our visit with another man of God in one of the Communist Eastern European countries. My suggestion that we pray together brought this memorable response and led to the precious time of prayer that followed.

It had been a long tiring day for us as we walked many miles around a strange city while praying for the opportunity to safely visit this Eastern European pastor. Now God had graciously allowed us to enjoy several hours together. In the privacy of his home, he had opened his heart to us about the body of Christ in his country, its strengths, its weaknesses, and its many needs. I was moved when he confided that they prayed every day for the church in America. In turn, we were thankful that we could tell him of many brothers and sisters in Christ in the West who were praying for them and wanted to know what they could do for them.

As we knelt and prayed together, we realized a special closeness to each other and to our Father in heaven. It was a meaningful reminder that those who belong to Christ in Eastern Europe, in America, and in all countries around the world are all part of the one true Church; that is, the body of Christ. When He returns for us, we'll all be together, forever, without the barriers and challenges of our earthly lives.

As he prayed in his own national language, I understood few of his words, but I clearly sensed his joy in speaking directly to God, our Father, as a little child lovingly and trustingly speaks with his earthly father. To this man, prayer was not a dull duty, but a precious privilege to be treasured and enjoyed. It was obvious, as well, that here was this man's source of strength that made it possible for him to give sacrificially of himself for the flock entrusted to him. To him, prayer was not a luxury, but a necessity.

Reluctantly, we had to end this special evening in time to catch the last bus, so we left his home about 11:00 p.m. As we walked along the silent, totally dark streets under a threatening sky, we realized after a mile or more that we were absolutely lost! As we turned and tried a different direction, we prayed that the ever-present police patrols would not see us and question us as to what we were doing so far from downtown so late at night. Thankfully, a lighted bus stop with people waiting soon appeared, a welcome sight. As we boarded the last bus of the evening a few minutes later, it began to rain.

Then, as we stepped off the bus into a torrential downpour (with no umbrellas), we had to stumble and splash along on foot in the darkness through muddy fields for the last mile to our hotel out in the countryside.

The astonished desk clerk stared at our soaked and muddy clothes, and my torn stockings from a tumble I'd taken in the dark. With mouth agape, and not a single word, he handed us the key to our room. We hurried for the lift before he could come to his senses and ask any questions. It was a hilarious sight, I'm sure; however, at the time it just didn't seem very funny to us at all. We were sure we'd end up being interrogated before we reached safety, but the Lord in His goodness saw us through a very tense situation.

The next morning, we decided to treat ourselves to a breakfast at the hotel. We ordered some sausages, eggs, cheese, and rolls. The waiter leaned secretively over my shoulder and said in whispered tones, "We have some sausages, but you wouldn't want them!" Thank You, Lord, for once again sparing us a bout with food poisoning from bad meat by urging this young waiter's heart to warn us. We saw time and time again how our safety could be explained only through providential care. We skipped the sausages and settled for the bread and jam.

Visiting Dr. Dan

Dr. Dan was another Christian leader we visited as we moved from city to city. He was not home, but his college-age daughter, Christine, answered the door and invited us in. She told us how she and her friends had already been questioned by the police because of their Christian faith. She'd accepted that there would be more times of questioning in the future. She told how her father, Dr. Dan, had just driven six hundred kilometers to visit with a brother in Christ who recently was released from prison, so he could learn what prison was like for him. Our impression was that he felt it was inevitable for himself as well. It was only a matter of when.

Later, when we visited with Dr. Dan, he expressed, "What I do for my Lord is so little in comparison to what He has given me." He cherished the fellowship with believers like us who came to them from the West with aid and encouragement and good teaching. He said it helped him to keep going.

There was still a great need for medicine. He shared the story of one patient who had stomach surgery, and only aspirin was available afterwards for the pain. He specifically mentioned the need for medicine for those suffering from rheumatism and migraines. Another need he mentioned was powdered milk for infants, as safe regular milk was not available. (Milk from local cows was considered seriously contaminated by the fallout from the Chernobyl nuclear plant.)

Bibles were still a desperate need—especially the larger ones with print the older ones could read. No one had glasses, so the larger print was important.

Before we left, he told us the safest time to come to visit him was during sports events. Everyone attended, and police were busy watching also. Many took their TV to the hills near the Hungarian border in order to receive Hungarian TV signals. The worst time to visit was when government officials were visiting their city. Then the whole city was crawling with police.

Traveling on to Bulgaria

We were on our way out of Romania and heading towards Bulgaria. While we had no problems at this border, they did search our van very carefully. We found a campsite for the night, which wasn't too bad, but the mosquitoes were fierce that night. They really feasted on me, so it was hard to sleep.

The Bulgarian terrain was lovely—rather like Minnesota—but the ever-present Communist red star hovered over all the signs and war monuments. The faces of the people were grim and hopeless, with women working the fields by hand. In the midst of this poverty, the only construction we saw was that of more war monuments. The land appeared to be far more unspoiled than that of Romania, and much cleaner. The crops looked good, with many apple orchards and wheat and corn fields. Roses grew in mass profusion and were planted between highways as well.

As we passed through the villages, we saw most babies and toddlers wearing hand-crocheted outfits. The windows of their homes were "curtained" with brown paper. Donkeys seemed to be the favorite animal for both working the fields and for transportation.

We stopped in one of the villages around noon and picked up some bread, still so hot we could hardly hold it. Yummy! We tried hard not to think about the lack of cleanliness in preparing and handling these items.

We needed to go downtown to find a map, which would hopefully assist us in finding our contact. So, we hopped on a tram that was packed about as tightly as any we'd seen. The trams were so old and worn they had trouble staying on the tracks. We soon learned, however, that maps were at a premium here. Actually, paper in general was at a premium. We searched through an entire department store without success, so we went out into the square to rest a bit.

One was always entertained by the flower peddlers, along with those selling corn-on-the-cob, freshly roasted peanuts, and whatever wares they could do without. The women were especially interesting with their bottle-dyed red hair, probably one of the few ways they could have color in their lives. Finally, we stopped at a little tiny kiosk and found a map. Praise the Lord for this success!

It was a blessing to find the map, since now we were able to go to our contact. It began raining just as we got off the tram, but we didn't have far to walk to the church. We entered the building—unnoticed, hopefully, or so it appeared to us—and sat down, preparing to worship. The people gathering were all ages, but one thing was common: they all looked very poor. No affluent members were in this group. The old white-haired pastor slowly made his way to the pulpit. The whole congregation came to their feet, while the pastor dropped to his knees for prayer before beginning the service. We were surprised at the dynamic nature of the service, since he seemed so docile, but God's power obviously was infusing him.

Finding someone who spoke English in Bulgaria was very difficult; however, God, in His providence, placed a young African man next to us, and as I glanced at the Bible in his hand, I noticed with great delight that it was printed in English! We had prayed for God to lead us to an English-speaking Christian contact who could brief us on the state of the Church in Bulgaria. *Is this the one you have for us, Lord?*

When the service ended, we took a chance and approached him to ask if we might have a few moments of his time. He was very cordial and willing. We walked to a nearby park where we felt more comfortable to ask him some questions. We learned he was in this country as a student and had been attending this Baptist church regularly.

We returned to the same church that evening—in the rain, of course. Al was asked to share greetings from America and had the group sitting on the edge of their seats as they listened intently to encouraging words of our Lord's promised return.

I believed we got the information we needed from the African student, so felt it was a successful time of learning about the state of the Church in Bulgaria. That night, as I listened to the raindrops falling gently on the roof of our van, it was as though God were patting our heads and saying, "Well done." We had now completed our contacts in the East and looked forward to returning to Vienna. I didn't realize the stress we were under until we were finished, and the load seemed to lift. It had been a hard couple of weeks, but soon, we'd be heading on out. That was the difference—we could leave, but they couldn't.

Chapter 7

TAKE-AWAYS FROM 1983 VISION TRIP

The next morning, we started out for the border with Yugoslavia. The roads were very rough, but lots of new construction was taking place. The terrain was peaceful and pleasant, with lots of rolling hills and lovely green meadows. Our border crossing into Yugoslavia went smoothly. The guards barely looked in the van and gave us no grief. One never knew how it was going to go—that was the stressful part.

It was amazing how much better Yugoslavia looked to us this time through. Guess it was all very relative. Since the other Eastern Bloc countries were so much worse, this looked good now. People weren't quite as bold here in coming up to us and wanting to look over our van. It was quite a spectacle in the other countries. As we observed the many shacks along the road, we were quickly reminded of the severe poverty in these socialist lands. We pulled over to have our lunch, which we often did; however, the many heaps of garbage left by those before us made it less than appetizing. All this went with the system. When there is no motivation (or vision), things die, and it soon becomes a society where people just don't care.

Most of our driving that day had been on washboard roads, offering no more than two lanes. We shared these roads with wagon teams, bicycles, and many who were simply walking. We stopped

Slow Traffic in Yugoslavia — 1983 Vision Trip

at a crude vegetable and fruit stand and were happy to find some tomatoes and a watermelon. That would go a long way in making our evening meal more appealing.

It had been a long, hot day of driving, so the showers in our campsite felt very inviting. Many were the times when there was no hot water to shower, but tonight, we were blessed.

The clouds were hanging low over the rugged peaks, almost as an ominous warning of what lay ahead for us. Leaving Yugoslavia, we crossed their border control with ease and no incident. However, when we arrived at the Austrian border station, it was a totally different story. All we could understand was the guard's strong statement of "zurück" (go back). He said it with such finality that we were alarmed. With all our finesse and limited German, we tried diligently to learn what the problem was, but to no avail.

All we understood was that there was no way they were going to let us into Austria. We comprehended enough to realize it had something to do with the legal registration of our van. We understood it was useless to try to get into Austria, since the guards had made up their minds, and there was no way they were about to reverse their decision.

With heavy hearts and confused minds, we drove back across the border into Yugoslavia. If they were wondering why we were re-entering their country so soon again, it wasn't voiced, and we surely weren't going to try to explain our plight to them. I was all ready to load our van on a train and have it shipped back to Vienna, but God, in His graciousness, gave Al the wisdom to try entering into Austria through the Italian border.

This meant more than another day's driving going southwest, where we hoped to cross into Italy. From there, we could try re-entering Austria from a different border crossing. It took Al some time to explain before I understood how vital it was for us to get out of the Eastern Bloc and into a less rigid environment, where we could more easily work at solving this problem.

So, we drove back into Yugoslavia and headed south, continuing to drive for several more hours before fatigue overcame us. We stopped at a campground. The events of the day had taken their toll, and we were both drained and so very weary. Many portions of Scripture came to me during the night, along with many possible reasons for God allowing this to happen.

As if a pail of cold water had been splashed on my face, the thought struck me that perhaps we had become too nonchalant in our prayer times. Not asking God for His involvement and assistance? Had we become mechanical and assuming in our requests for His care? I couldn't help but believe that this whole miserable incident was, at least in part, related to our growing attitude of taking God's protection for granted.

After pouring out my heart in utter repentance to our loving Father, I thanked Him from the depths of my being for teaching me this valuable lesson about Himself, for showing me how much we needed Him, how little we actually controlled, and that our battle with the fleshly nature and our tendency to rely on our own strength was not over yet. It is an ongoing battle in which we need

His help to conquer, knowing we can maintain victory only through the Spirit and our cooperation with Him. As the night wore on and dawn began to seep through the dark sky, we finally fell asleep in the comfort and knowledge of His love for us.

After spending time in prayer the following morning, we left the camp, traveling toward the Italian border. We again asked God for His will to be done and, if it pleased Him, to allow us safe crossing over into non-Communist turf. As we left Yugoslavia and crossed into Italy, the guards barely gave us a second look, merely waved us on through. *Thank You, dear Lord Jesus, for bringing us this far.* I believe we learned our lesson. Never again did we approach a border without doing so with hearts tuned completely to the Lord's bidding.

Now safely in Italy, we still had the Austrian border to cross. With our hearts in our throats, pounding so wildly we were sure the guards could hear them, we approached the border station gate. Thankfully, this time the Austrian guards just waved us through without further questions. I couldn't believe it! Could it actually be so easy? I kept looking for more guard stations where we might be stopped again, but praise be to our Heavenly Father for His unfailing love! We were now safely in Austria, and all we had to do was reach Vienna, where we could then investigate the issue of van registration.

The drive from Italy to Vienna was gorgeous and a chance to fully appreciate the wonder of God's creation in its awesome splendor. We also appreciated seeing a beautifully ornate church in the midst of nearly every village, indicating incredible honor and reverence to our God, even though we suspected many didn't know the saving knowledge of our Lord and Savior.

Key Takeaways from Our Summer 1983 Vision Trip:

- **Fear only God**—important lesson brought home to us by Pastor B. in Romania
- **Don't neglect to pray sincerely**—lesson we learned the hard way in Yugoslavia

- **Need for church-based leadership training in Communist countries**—expressed to us in visits at each stop as we traveled from England to Germany to Austria, and then meetings with church leaders in a number of Eastern European countries where anti-Christian governments attempted to suppress Christianity
- **Boldness in witnessing**—our excuses for timidity in witnessing for Christ in the USA didn't hold water (see newsletter below that we wrote to our support team back in the USA after meeting with persecuted church leaders in Eastern Europe)

"Wiped Out Excuses"

If I had to pin a title on this newsletter, that would be it! The Lord has taught us through our Eastern European contacts that our pet excuses for not being bolder and more effective witnesses to the gospel of Christ just don't hold water. Excuses such as "I don't have the proper training," or "She might be offended," or "I can tell he isn't interested anyway!" All these excuses can be made to sound good if we really work at it. However, we had to re-examine the validity of our excuses as we listened to a young man from Eastern Europe tell of his life as a new Christian in a very hostile environment.

Converted at the age of seventeen, he experienced the loneliness of being a Christian in a peer group which had been saturated with atheistic teaching and taught that Christianity was only a ridiculous superstition held by old ladies. He had no Bible school training, no Christian bookstore in his neighborhood, but he had his New Testament, his love for Jesus, and a desire to tell others about Him.

On the job, when his fellow workers took their frequent "smoke breaks," he would bring out his New Testament and read, praying that others would want to know about his faith. When he traveled on public transportation, he would be seen reading his New Testament and looking for opportunities to share the Good News with curious passengers who would likely laugh at his faith and make fun of him.

Then he found himself as a draftee in the army, where it was the duty of his military superiors to break him of his belief and dependence on a God they claim does not exist. This period of "testing by fire" became increasingly more frightening and difficult as he faced higher ranking and more determined inquisitors.

Then he remembered Jesus's words to His disciples from Luke 12:11, 12, "Now when they bring you before the synagogues and the officials and the authorities, do not worry about how or what you are to speak in your defense, or what you are to say; for the Holy Spirit will teach you in that very hour what you ought to say." He concluded that he, too, would depend on the Holy Spirit for strength to endure and for the words to answer their hard questions.

As he trusted in the grace of God, he experienced a peace that defied description, and he answered their questions with words that were more than he alone could have mustered.

As he told his story, I thought to myself, "How can we excuse our timidity in much less dangerous circumstances? How could we not trust in that same grace to see us through our 'difficult' situations? How could we pretend there was so little we could do with our 'limited' resources?"

In short, under scrutiny, all of our excuses prove to be not only weak, but invalid. The truth we had to face was that we were too often concerned about possible negative responses and how people might view us.

This same truth was presented to us again only a week later when visiting committed Christian workers in another Eastern European country with relatively fewer restrictions on Christian activities. We were told that the people in this country were generally very open to the gospel of Christ.

We asked what the main difficulties were in reaching these people.

The reply included a reference to the "sleeping church"; not concerned enough about lost humanity to make sacrifices of comfort and security; not willing to jeopardize their children's chances for education and a good job; not willing to invite problems with the government authorities by being too visible.

As they described this problem of the comfortable sleeping church and its excuses, I thought silently and sadly to myself, "If these are all worthless excuses in an environment such as Eastern Europe, how much more worthless are our excuses in the West?"

Reminders like this can be painful, and we are tempted to fall back on our excuses again, saying, "But Lord, but, but, but..." and again we come back to saying, "Yes, Lord, we have no excuse." Again we thank Him for His grace that saves us and enables us to live out our lives in His care, seeking to serve others while we prepare for eternity in His presence.

> For I am not ashamed of the gospel, for it is the power
> of God for salvation to everyone who believes....
> For in it the righteousness of God is revealed from
> faith to faith; as it is written: "But the righteous
> one will live by faith." –ROMANS 1:16–17

Please pray that we might always remember these lessons learned and, by the grace of God, practice them boldly in our lives.

Chapter 8

MAJOR DECISION MADE—SMUGGLING JOB ACCEPTED

October 1983

Back in Austria after our introductory travels around Eastern Europe, we were now ready, practically and spiritually, to prepare for the next steps. Our first few days back in Vienna were taken up with the practical things of life—laundry, grocery shopping, and picking up the mail. It was always a relief when we could skim the mail and find no emergency situations.

Our most critical need before going back to the States to plan our next steps was to meet at the Big House with the leadership of the mission organization we had met with earlier in the summer. They had suggested some possible positions we could fill, and we now wanted to follow up on those possibilities.

The purpose of our Biblical Education by Extension organization was "to create indigenous church-based training centers to establish growing and reproducing local churches." The "students" accepted for this training were those "approved by local church leaders and/or who are training for the purpose of being a church planter, church worker, elder/deacon, house church leader or pastor."

The curriculum at this time consisted of nineteen seminary level courses, with each course having a facilitator's guide, a student guide, a workbook, and typically, one or more textbooks. All in all, the plan involved printing two million seminary textbooks in Western Europe and then getting them into the hands of fifty thousand or so students in Communist Eastern Europe and the Soviet Union.

It turned out that the position they most would like Al to assume was Director of Distribution. That sounded like an innocuous enough responsibility, but it turned out to be a pretty intimidating challenge. Since this was all illegal in these countries, this meant being responsible for smuggling these books across the borders, arranging for safe storage, and then getting them distributed as needed to each of the groups in training, without anyone getting caught and thrown into prison in the process.

NAME: Al Baanna: Biblical Education by Extension
Distribution Dept. Manager

DATE: 5.10.83

I. **Purpose:** To coordinate and supervise the delivery of BEE World seminary materials to the anticipated 50,000 church leader students in Communist Eastern European countries and the Soviet Union.

II. **Responsibilities** (Condensed version)

1. Maintain warehouse and inventory of all BEE World materials.

2. Set up sub-distribution network in each country.

3. Ensure that all required books are delivered to each student before courses begin.

4. Develop relationships with, and recruit, couriers and others who can aid BEE World with delivery needs.

5. Develop new channels and forms of delivery.
6. Recruit and train personnel to assist Delivery Department.
7. Deliver medicines, manuscripts, and technical equipment to specific in-country contacts.
8. Maintain computer records of all finances, material inventories, and contacts.
9. Raise funds to help provide necessary funds for delivery needs.

After reading the job description, we were both pretty much taken aback. In addition to the dangers, the responsibilities were heavy, considering the importance of good training for the church leaders in these countries. It was also a position that included serious responsibilities for the safety of the Eastern Bloc nationals who would be working with us to receive and distribute the materials. They would face the threat of arrest and imprisonment if caught.

That evening, we were invited to dinner to meet some of the staff, so we'd have a chance to get to know them a bit better. They were all very lovely people, but the conversations centered on their stories of how they had accepted Christ at a young age, growing up in a church environment, seminary training, their experience in Christian training, etc. With our highly different backgrounds, I just felt I couldn't relate to any of this. I just wanted to go home! Al hadn't quite accepted the position yet, but I believed he would, and I had so much to work through. *Don't let me be a drag to Al, Father.*

Van Impounded

We needed to go downtown to the customs office and find out about the van registration problem that stopped us at the Austrian border a few days earlier.

They told us we must pay a $2,000.00 customs duty on the van before we could legally sell or register the van in Austria. The police came out and actually impounded the van, sealing it so we couldn't even get into it. Can you imagine? We felt like criminals with everyone around us staring at us while this was happening. We were told this was not uncommon, that the government here operated under the assumption that one was guilty until proven innocent! It seemed like such an unfair hassle to us; however, in months to come, we were reminded more than once of Romans 8:28, "And we know that God causes all things to work together for good for those who love God, to those who are called according to His purpose."

While this was a stressful experience at the time, it ended up providing safe and secure indoor garage storage for our van under police impound protection while we made a trip back to the USA for the winter. When we returned in the spring, they even cut our customs duty in half and returned the van to us.

Major Decision Made

Before leaving Austria, Al accepted the challenge of being this organization's Director of Distribution (hereafter referred to as Chief of Smuggling Operations). We realized all too well that we had a HUGE job ahead of us.

With most big issues in place, we planned a trip back to the States for a time of preparation and sharing with churches and individuals, in hopes of prayer and financial support for a longer, more extended time of service in Europe.

Flying Home to the USA

Our travel day arrived! It was a beautiful day, and I was so very excited about going home!

Family members were at the airport to meet us in Minneapolis, and oh, what a wonderful sight that was! However, things got rather discouraging after our initial homecoming. We wrongly expected everyone to be as excited about the possibility of serving the Lord

MAJOR DECISION MADE—SMUGGLING JOB ACCEPTED

One of Our Seminary Textbook Warehouses

in the Eastern Bloc as we were. However, that was far from what we encountered as we began to share in churches and with various individuals.

I found it so hard to hear people complain here in America when others were so desperately oppressed. It was hard not to be harsh in my responses when I would see grumblers in the mall unable to find just exactly what they were looking for. We have such infinite variety here and still we hear the dissatisfaction.

If only each one could spend even one day in Eastern Europe, where it was necessary to stand for hours just to get some bony, gristly piece of meat, which probably wasn't even consumable, maybe it would make a difference in their lives. But I'm sure I was the same way before encountering the things I experienced. I had to constantly remind myself of that fact and try not to be so judgmental.

All our moving around and the feelings of being so unsettled were beginning to cave in on me. It always takes time to adjust to jet lag after a trans-Atlantic flight, so we were expecting that. We were trying to set up a household where we could headquarter when in the States; however, the few things we had left were scattered around so it would take a lot of work and hauling to pull it together. After a few days of trying to get a temporary home set up, I was so weary, but we were seeing some progress, so that felt good.

While in the States, we decided to explore some possibilities for help with my back pain. Dr. C., who was well-known, with a good reputation, was a bit of a disappointment for us. He diagnosed me with a tumor on the lower back, but all he did was prescribe a few pills and send us on our way. For the upper back pain, he suggested some physical therapy and massage. Yes, it felt good to have that done, but I doubted it was doing any long-term healing.

In the meantime, Al was visiting with various individuals, small groups, and churches in the area. We were also interviewed by the local Christian radio station. I was so nervous, but it was a wonderful opportunity to gain some exposure for the work God had laid on our hearts. I wished Dr. C. could give me a pill to overcome my fear of sharing in front of groups!

Another visit with Dr. C. resulted in yet another diagnosis, a crack in the lower spine on both sides. The prescription for that was to wear a back corset. It did feel better, but again, I doubted it was an answer to the problem.

My feelings of not belonging seemed to increase as we moved from one setting to another. We'd gathered up enough items to furnish an apartment adequately for our times here in the States, but how did one furnish a home with a sense of belonging? The old hymn "This World Is Not My Home" coursed often through my brain as I felt more and more of a stranger in this world.

The back pain reached a critical point, so they admitted me to the hospital for a variety of scans and tests, as well as therapy. Dr. C. now said, "The problem is a ruptured disc, which has squirted off to the right side, therefore causing so much pain in a very localized area." He believed that surgery was NOT the answer, but wanted to check out some things via some traction, a Myelogram, and some steroid injections.

I was a bit nervous about all this, but I knew I couldn't go on this way. The doctors, nurses, and technicians were all very kind and understanding, but it was still a scary situation. My thoughts centered on whether this problem would eventually paralyze me. How would I be able to assist Al in what God had for us with this disability? They finally sent me home with little more in the way of help than when I was admitted.

God had other plans for me, however, like chiropractic treatments for this dreadful back pain. Our dear, dear friends, Dr. B. and his wife came to visit that night, and he told me how he felt God was leading him to help me with my back problem. He was a chiropractor, so although I didn't know much about this form of care, I was more than ready to have him do whatever he felt would be helpful. He did, indeed, end up treating me for years whenever I was in the States as part of how he served the Lord. I was convinced that I'd be in a wheelchair were it not for his expertise and kindness in doing this for us.

Thus, I began my journey into alternative care for my very puzzling and painful back problems.

Being ill and disabled plays not only on one physically, but also emotionally and psychologically in a very big way. I began to feel deeply depressed. I shut myself up, refused to go out, and saw nothing but that black hole, where there was no reason or meaning for all of this. The more I distanced myself, the more Al threw himself into the work. All I could see was that I was in the way, and that it would be much easier for Al to serve the Lord if I weren't such a drag.

But once again, the Lord provided help for me through His people. Our wonderful little house church group, with its dear, sweet friends, just wouldn't allow me to go on feeling sorry for myself! They literally forced me out of the house and got me involved once again. How good our Father is!

The difficult decision now was to determine whether or not we should continue with our plans to return to Europe or scratch those plans because of my health. Not only my health, but Al had one severe cold after another, and now a rash of boils was leaving him in much distress. Was all this illness coming from the evil one, or was God testing our faith and our commitment? Throughout all this pain we were held up beautifully by friends and, most especially, by our dear chiropractor friend, who was able to provide enough relief from the pain that I could consider returning to Europe for missionary service. He and his assistants tried their best to prepare me and make me fit for service overseas.

After much serious prayer, we came to the conclusion that it was God's plan for us to return to Austria, so I started sorting clothes in preparation for packing soon. We'd had so many wonderful times with dear saints who were truly encouraging us and wanted to learn how they might help the believers in the Eastern Bloc. Hopefully, we had been able to inform the churches here as to how they could be praying.

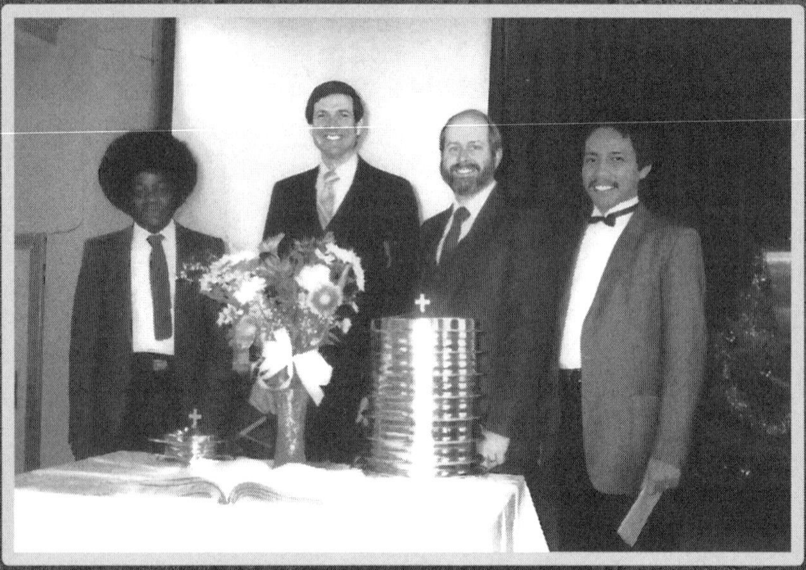

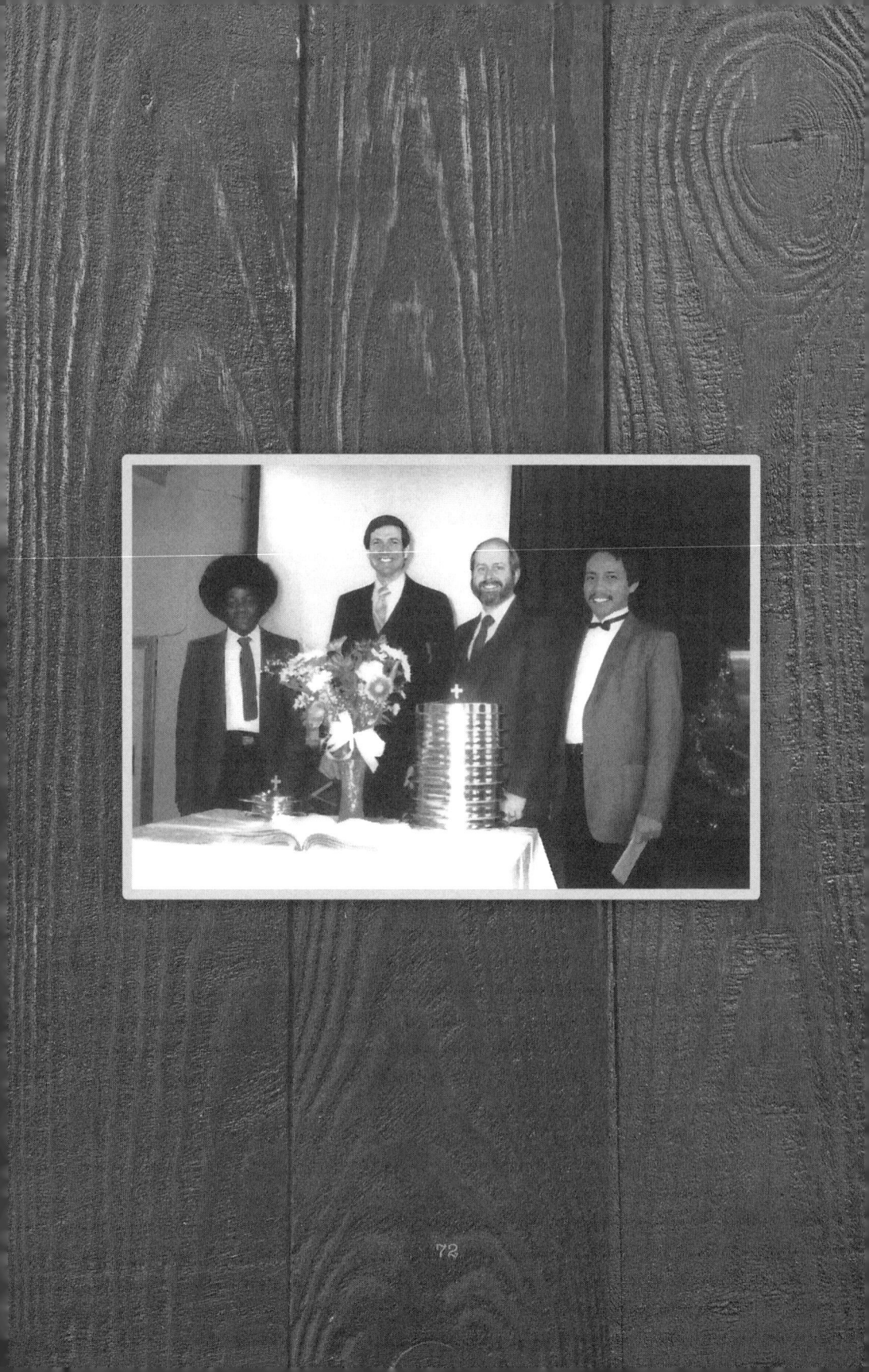

Part Two

Chapter 9

OUR DREAM BECOMES REALITY

Beginning in March 1984, dream became reality as we returned to Europe to begin our long-term involvement in the Lord's work among the four hundred million people living behind the Iron Curtain. During our initial six months in Europe, we had faced endless physical and financial difficulties and obstacles seemingly impossible to overcome. As our Lord faithfully led us through all these difficulties, we realized a much greater dependence on Him and a much closer walk with Him. For this, we praise Him!

Our six-month vision trip behind the Iron Curtain certainly had a very sobering impact on our lives! God's goodness was no longer measured so much by His contribution to our physical and material well-being, but by the loving gift of His only Son (the Christ child of the Christmas story) and His intense concern for our spiritual lives and well-being. Whether one was an American enjoying freedom and comfort or a Russian prisoner near death in a Siberian labor camp, one could share joyfully this Christmas season in God's great gift of a Savior.

Travelling behind the Iron Curtain from a base in Vienna, Austria, would help to bridge the present gap of fellowship between members of Christ's body, the Church, in Eastern Europe and those in America. There was much we could learn from the

Eastern European church and much we could do to encourage and strengthen them. We also had a tremendous opportunity to work with them in proclaiming the Word of Life to their countrymen. Millions of people in Eastern Europe had become disillusioned with the emptiness of atheism and secularism and other "-isms." In many areas, the fields were especially white for harvest (John 4:34), and the existing church needed our help in reaping the harvest.

We spent the last few days before our departure saying our good-byes to dear friends, with various opportunities for sharing. We also had to find places to store all our stateside belongings in homes of friends and relatives.

So, we began our travel back to Vienna to resume our Eastern European travels, now with a job to do. We knew this would take us to many different countries and to many different cultures and experiences.

The flight back to Austria seemed endless. We took a really inexpensive flight on Tarom, the Romanian airline, which was not known for luxury. Only six seats abreast with one very narrow aisle between them, and a cabin filled with the hazy smoke of the many smokers on board. The poor flight attendants were extremely patient, but it was certainly a stretch for them to provide service.

After arriving back in Vienna, we tried to get some sleep. Initially, we slept, but after a few hours, jet lag set in, and we were wide awake, even though we were still very tired. The eight-hour time change didn't help, but most of all, homesickness set in for me and the feelings of being so alone. I wondered more than once just what in the world we were doing here! The Lord had given us this task, so I was convinced He would also provide the strength and ability, but right then, it appeared hopeless.

In going out for a little walk, though, we found that we felt quite at home. It seemed so natural to be here; it was as though we'd never left. We were amused all over again by the many women with bottle-dyed red hair, the ubiquitous green wool outfits, the many dogs being walked by their masters, the quaint shops, the luscious-looking bakery displays, along with the marvelous smells of baking bread. Now our spirits were stilled, and the Lord had come to meet us, making us feel settled and exactly where we were supposed to be. I knew that there would again be those doubts, those feelings of homesickness, and those longings for family, but right now, God had salved our aching hearts.

Al focused on the job of getting large quantities of literature safely into the Communist Eastern Bloc. Knowing that this was terribly dangerous and that it could have serious implications for the believers there if he was caught weighed heavily on his shoulders. The work involved enlisting smuggling and distribution teams from seven countries in Western Europe—each with their specialties.

All I could see was that Al was off and running to various countries or working long hours at the office and meeting with organizations to discuss the work. I felt totally useless! I felt so worthless in the eyes of those around me too.

The days were long, but I liked cooking and enjoyed time to myself and with the Lord, so it was alright. It also helped greatly that we had an American couple living below us who had a little toddler, Donnie, who was such a delight. God placed us here for a reason. He knew full well that I'd need this friendship and the distraction of this wonderfully loving family.

Al spent a good part of his day planning, strategizing, and meeting with other believers who were also doing the same work. Al didn't share much with me. It was better that way. Should we be stopped while traveling in the East, it was safer that I didn't know much that could incriminate believers.

It was heartbreaking to hear of all the ways the Communist governments used to break the spirit (and often the body as well) of these dear brothers and sisters. *Oh God, give them the strength and courage to withstand the constant persecution they face! Help us here in the West to be more sensitive and burdened with our brothers' plight.*

The times of release from back pain were few and far between, but in the midst of my discouragement due to this disability, the

Lord came to me one night as clear as though He were sitting directly across as we spoke together. I'd had such a hard time determining why God would allow my back to continue being such a problem, but I believed I understood, in part, now.

My restrictions had kept me so isolated from BEE World work, and I struggled so hard with the feelings of uselessness and unimportance. But my dear Father showed me that only special people are chosen to spend much time with Him in prayer, and that sometimes He needs to force the issue. I'd asked for a long time already to have a closer and more intimate relationship with the Father and to learn how to develop a prayer life that was meaningful and precious, and now my heart "pants for Thee, O God" (Psalm 42:1-2) and was filled with gladness in this new dimension!

Many of Your people, Lord, have practical skills and gifts for carrying out your commission, but me, oh Lord, You have chosen to use as a soldier in the battle of spiritual darkness by teaching me how to pray and intercede on behalf of others and their work. What a privilege! How can I thank you, dear, sweet, Heavenly Father? No longer do I feel insignificant, but recognize completely that the practical working out of Your plan would be useless and futile if You were not in control. God, I'm so grateful for your faith in me and for this vitally needful and important role You have entrusted to me. I'll never be able to find the words to thank and praise You enough for revealing this precious insight to me, Lord.

Included in the work of living in a foreign land and culture was the language barrier. Al and I were just so eager to get on with what God had for us that we didn't really take the time we needed to become proficient in the language. However, God, in His infinite wisdom, had seen to it that I grew up in a German-speaking community back home in North Dakota; therefore, I had a working knowledge of the language when we arrived, which we often gave God praise for. We both watched children's programs on Austrian TV, which helped us with vocabulary.

Driver's License Challenge

One of the many challenges of living in a foreign culture is securing a local driver's license. We began the process of studying for the long and difficult exam, but the three thick manuals we needed to virtually memorize were very intimidating. At the beginning, it seemed absolutely hopeless, so I prayed for the Lord to give me His confidence and help me to be disciplined in doing what it takes. There were many steps to the whole procedure, including a physical exam and an eye exam, which made it a costly ordeal.

The good part, though, was that once a person was able to pass the exam and secure the license, it was for a lifetime—no need to ever repeat it, which encouraged us to put forth every effort. With the Lord's help, we would definitely prevail.

Finally, we finished our last-minute studies for our driver's license test and went into the magistrate's office to "face the gallows." I didn't know when I'd ever been so nervous! My whole being had been wrapped up in this for weeks now, and I was just weak with apprehension. The Austrian frau (woman) at the front desk had been waiting for us and went over a few last-minute questions we had. Then we were summoned in, me first! It all went so fast I hardly remember it now.

The magistrate was very pleasant and could obviously see how uptight I was, but was kind and gentle in spite of their usual response to someone who was less than confident. He asked me a number of questions, mainly having to do with the signs of the road and the priority pictures. To me, the pictures and signs looked as though I had never seen them before, even though I'd spent untold hours learning them. I became confused and responded incorrectly a number of times, so the magistrate had every reason to fail me. But God, in His graciousness, prompted him to pass me and grant me the driver's license! In a short time, Al also passed the test.

I couldn't believe the almost numbing relief I felt. We'd worked so hard for so long for this very moment, and now it was over. It was a strange feeling. I finally experienced the elation and significance of what had transpired once we left the building. I was more than ready to celebrate with a hot cup of lovely, strong Austrian coffee. Hallelujah!

The most difficult thing, though, was the separation from family and friends back in the States. Our families and friends were wonderful, always sending us letters, packages, photographs, and homemade tapes so we could hear their voices and learn about what they were doing on a daily basis, which were especially soothing.

They recorded things like Christmas programs at church, school activities, individual stories from people, and news items. All these things helped immensely, but oh, how my heart ached in not being able to be present at our daughter's wedding, at the birth of our son's twins, at the birth of our daughter's only child. These milestones will never be forgotten, but we couldn't go back and be present with loved ones during these precious times. We learned very quickly what the Scriptures meant when Christ spoke of counting the cost.

Chapter 10

CLOAK AND DAGGER DAYS 1983-1990

"Cloak and dagger" is a phrase that refers to secretive or clandestine activities. This describes our life as I (Al) served the Lord as Chief of Smuggling Operations. (My official business card identified me as Director of Distribution for an Austrian publishing company.)

In this role, I was responsible for planning and arranging the smuggling of two million seminary textbooks over a twenty-year period into the Soviet Union and Communist Eastern European countries. I also directed the underground distribution network within each country to hundreds of church leader study groups.

The Lord provided teams from seven countries in Western Europe to

Courtyard of Our Vienna Home—1985

accomplish this work. Most of these workers also used aliases, so to this day, I don't know their real names and would not be able to contact them.

As we worked with the people assigned to do the storage and distribution in these countries, Betty and I used the aliases Mike and Leah Hanson. Our work, of course, was illegal in the eyes of the atheistic Communist governments, which were trying to eliminate Christianity—or at least severely limit its influence.

Sometimes, Betty and I would do some of the in-country distribution ourselves. This next section describes our underground activities during these years. Most nights, we spent in campground bungalows as shown in this next photo, which also shows our personal distribution vehicle.

Campground Housing with Our Distribution Vehicle

The following notes are from one of Betty's journals telling of such a trip we made to Romania.

Monday, September 5
Had a rotten night. It's cold. The sleeping bag doesn't cover me. The bed has many uncomfortable lumps where it should have slumps.

The neighbors are noisy (some guy comes "home" at 1:30 a.m., but "Mona" won't let him in, so he roared off with his car).

There's no hot water to clean up, so we eat breakfast with yesterday's grime still on us. *Oh Lord Jesus, forgive me my childish and petty complaints. My brothers and sisters here have so little. They endure so much more. My little irritations dim so in comparison. Direct my eyes back to Yourself, precious Lord.*

I take a walk with Al to clear my head and see men and women with heavy burdens of kindling wood on their backs for their fight against the long winter ahead. Kids here in the camp are rustling thru our garbage and delighting in the "treasures" of Western food containers. My heart aches for them.

Begin preparations for our first literature pick up tonight. Need to reorganize our bags so we can use them for our distribution work. So now where do I put my things? Sure glad I included extra grocery bags in our packing.

Leave for town at 5:30 p.m. to "case" our contact point before dark, and then drive back out of town to a park place to wait and pray while the cover of darkness descends.

Interesting watching people as we wait. One little girl and her mom are "working" the park place we're in, going thru all the garbage cans to salvage what they can.

As dusk comes, we say a final prayer and head for town, trusting we've not been followed. We see the house now, but we also see a policeman not far away! Do we continue as planned? Do we abort our original hope of tonight's pickup? As we shuffle along in our dark coats and caps, we glance at one another and, with eye signal, decide to go ahead. The gate is unlocked. *(Thank You, Jesus!)* No dogs around to alert neighbors, so we walk up to the door, push the buzzer, and walk-in (again, we are grateful for the unlocked door), and noticed as we enter that the elderly neighbors in the adjacent building had been watching our every move!

But our initial greeting of "pacii" (peace in Romanian) with this dear family dispels any fear of being observed as we thrill in the joy and radiance mirrored in their faces upon our coming. Our brother and sister quickly assure us that their neighbors are merely curious and no real threat to God's work here in country.

After we show them our secret ID, they give God thanks for our coming and insist on preparing a meal for us as we wait for the pickup to be prepared. Our brother must now go to a different location—he takes his oldest son to help—and transport what we need back here for us to distribute to other strategic points in the country. The risk is not once considered except in the prudence he exhibits as he and his son leave the house unobtrusively. At 9:00 p.m., Al and I enjoy one of the few hot meals we'll have the entire time we're in Romania: delicious filled paprika in a soup-like sauce, fried eggs, bread, and a cake-like dessert.

After our meal, the younger son starts to prepare pillows and blankets for us to rest while we are waiting, but even though weary, we're too excited to lie down so we decline his offer. Our sister, upon seeing that we'd rather visit, tells us about her job at the hospital. She's a nurse from 8:00 a.m. to 7:00 p.m., six days a week. (My mind is marveling at how she had such a delicious meal prepared for us so quickly when she's been working all day.) I comment on her being tired, and she dispels it with confession of a slight headache from "all the crying babies" all day at the hospital.

Our brother returns at 10:00 p.m. He's completed our request—hopefully without being observed—and is now ready to make the transfer. His son waits with the car in a secluded spot nearby. But before we leave, he once again delights in each gift we brought, and then our sister presents us with five handmade crochet pieces as a token of their appreciation! My eyes fill with tears. I can hardly see the gifts now as I fumble for words that will convey our feelings. *Oh Lord Jesus, I have so much to learn in serving You. I give out of my abundance, but these dear children of Yours give out of their need!*

After prayer together, we say good-bye with kisses and hugs, our tears mingling as we part. The door is opened, furtive glances

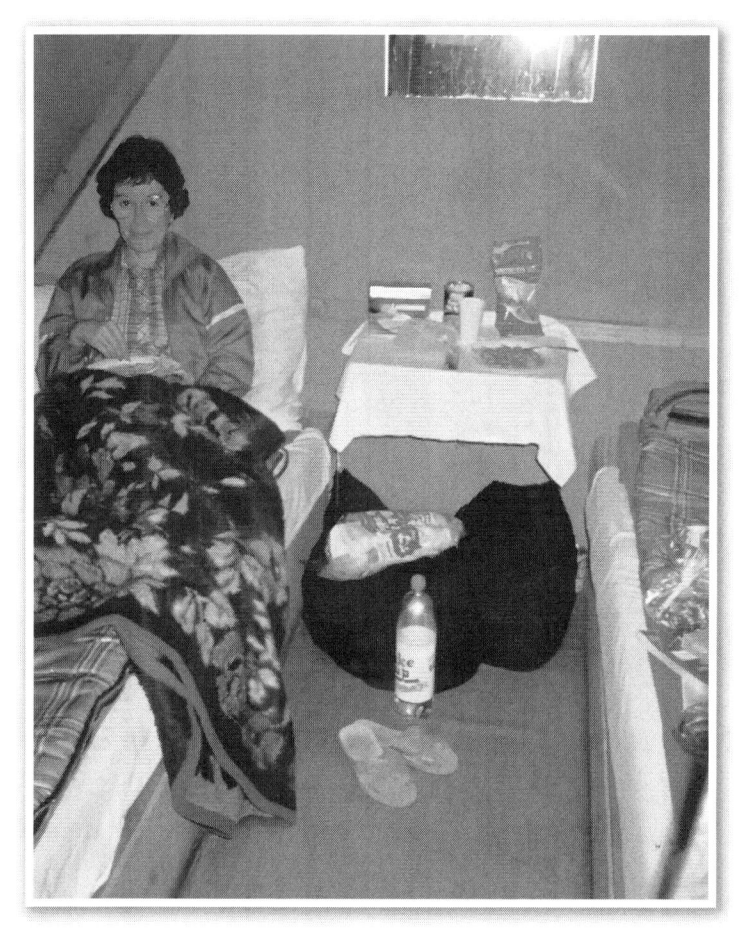

Romania Campground Bungalow

up and down the street to assure them it is safe for us to leave, and we step into the dark to go out to meet our brother at the pre-arranged spot to transfer the books to our vehicle.

Lying awake in our still cold, musty-smelling bungalow now, my heart soars with gratefulness for the privilege of "suffering" even just a little as I mull over our meeting tonight with those who risk and endure so much. *Oh God, teach me to love You with a burning urgency, and a servant attitude like the one so plainly demonstrated to me tonight. Wipe out my carnal and fleshly needs for comfort and help me see only You!*

Tuesday, September 6   Rain – Cool

Couldn't sleep—lay awake and reviewed previous eve. Feeling so unworthy. Leave Cluj at 10:00 a.m. Still raining. People standing in rain waiting in food line. Constant stream of bodies in dark, colorless dress with long, sad faces.

Feeling so rotten today—diarrhea, headache, nausea. Can't eat breakfast, so we drive on. We stop at a roadside cafe hoping to have tea, but the smells are so awful we return to our car and go on. We find a place to park and eat some crackers; kids surround our car, looking for gum/candy/perfume/pencils. Suddenly, a young girl appears with hand full of flowers. I give her sweets, but oh how my heart feels for her.

Eastern European Café — 1990

Go on to Oradea—feeling sicker all the time. Can't make it, so drive out to the country and take pills. Then back to town again. Risky going past the post control again. [Note: We must go through guard post at all entrances to towns.] Can't make our drop yet. Must wait till dark.

No rooms available at campground. Used toilet at camp—"slush" almost invaded my shoes and the smell was enough to make me even sicker.

Have been in car now since ten this morning—eleven hours. My back is miserable! Marking time while waiting for dark. Try to rest, but people are looking in the windows. Al eats, but I can't. We were able to make the drop with Dr. Dan and Dr. Nick. Try to make second drop, but still no answer there.

Wednesday, September 7   **Cool-Sunny**
Found hotel room for the night. Enjoy the breakfast here—tea, goat cheese, tomatoes, bread, jam, butter. It tastes good, even on the moldy tablecloth. Left Oradea at 11:30 a.m. Long monotonous drive to Arad. Still raining, but we see hundreds of soldiers in full military uniform out picking tomatoes!

Our next stop is Timisoara. No campground bungalows available, so I sit in the car and watch Gypsies "do business" while Al hunts for a room. He finally finds one in a downtown hotel. Not our preference, but nothing to do! No hot water, bathroom down the hall. (We refer to this one as the "Green Slime Motel" as the green walls were wet and slimy.)

[Note: We were to meet with Pastor Lazlo Tokes in Timisoara on this trip, but no one answered the door, even though we heard voices behind the door. He was a key figure in the revolution a year later, but was already having much pressure from the police and Securitate because of his rapidly growing church.]

We also learned that Pastor Tim has "disappeared." He has a wife and five children, and they are distressed beyond words. Pastor David knows he might be the next one to disappear. *Oh, God, our problems are so small by comparison. Comfort and sustain Timothy's wife, Lord.*

"Green Slime Motel" — Timisoara, Romania

Went shopping and found some post cards. Food stores are a real turn off. Have supper here in our room. So glad I brought lots of food along. *Thank You, Lord.* Still haven't found bread or water.

Thursday, September 8   Cloudy-Rain

Breakfast here at the hotel was the usual saw-dust-like bread, sheep cheese, tomatoes, and tea. The one exception today was lots of cold meat that looks like canned imports. I ate some, but stomach is still queasy. We made some coffee in our room and wrote postcards this morning. This is really not a pleasant place to hang around, but it's better than the camps. You should see these hallways—dark—I mean dark! There's no toilet paper, no hot water, everything stinks. And all this for just forty-three dollars!

Went out walking. Garbage really bad here—saw a woman picking up bones and putting them in her bag.

Spent time in the country this afternoon preparing for our contact tonight. It's dreary today—just like the whole atmosphere pervading this country.

Cornell and Marie weren't home when we arrived, but the grandma was so we were able to get inside and wait. After about forty-five minutes, Cornell arrived and then also Marie. She prepared a delicious veg soup for us, with eggs, cheese, tea, and bread. With their six children, I wonder if I'm eating their supper. We arranged the transfer of books for later in a secluded place. Marie asked us about smuggling a manuscript out for Dr. Tson, but we felt it better not to risk it.

We leave about 4:30 p.m. Check into campsite with a large cabin. It's good for re-arranging our "cargo," but it's a yukky place—toilet doesn't work, outlets don't work, it's freezing cold, no hot water, of course, and it reeks. Clouds of mosquitoes buzzing around us till after midnight.

Friday, September 9 — Sunny - Warm

Slept in till nearly 9:00 a.m. No reason to rush—can't make drop till after 5:00 p.m.

Drove to Lugoj and checked into hotel on main street. So noisy! Our room is on the fourth floor, and we had to totally empty our car—carrying all our boxes of heavy books up the four flights of stairs. The hotel clerk said it is a problem to leave anything in the car. Vandalism and theft are getting worse.

Enjoyed pork and beans and kiwi for supper in our room. Feel guilty even with these minor provisions. Will need to dispose of "evidence." Luxuriated in a wonderful hot bath tonight. Feels great to be clean!

Our room here is relatively nice, but even in this better hotel, windowpanes are broken out, the tile in the bathroom isn't finished, and the lamp doesn't work. The bed is just so-so. However, we strongly sensed God's presence in the darkness of our room as we viewed the bright, twinkling stars through a broken-out window.

Saturday, September 10 — Sunny - Mild

Woke up at 6:00 a.m. to the sound of horses' hooves on the rough cobblestone street outside our room. Church bells were ringing in the distance—probably calling workers to the fields. I hear voices now—people beginning their daily search thru the stores for much-needed food.

Get up and enjoy a warm shampoo—what a luxury to have hot water.

The dining room is empty as we go for breakfast. It took them ages to prepare our meal—the better to search our room. Finally, they brought bread, lukewarm tea with tons of sugar (yuk!), and grey-looking sausage that neither one of us could eat. I took one small bite and then quickly wrapped and "smuggled" the remainder into my purse to dispose of later. (I feel so bad leaving food when they have so little.)

Leave Lugoj at 10:00 a.m. Drive in the mountains is nice, but very slow-moving traffic. The villages look a bit better here, and the park places even have swings! We drive on to Simeria and check into a campground and have cold green beans for lunch. Policeman at camp is giving us "the eye."

Rested awhile this afternoon. Went into town at 5:30 to check things out and then drove out into the countryside until we came to a secluded spot where we could stall until "contact time." Al's uneasy tonight. Situation here in Simeria is not good. Cops galore and it's a small city. We're far too visible. With last-minute prayers, we head back into town, but now streets are dark—totally black.

I wait in the car with the books while Al goes on ahead on foot to make arrangements for transfer of the books. But "Teo" says, "Abort! Too risky tonight. We're being observed." When Al returns, I tell him I have been watched by police also the whole time! *Thank You, Father, that You are in control.*

We learned that in the past, they have successfully hidden books under their woodpile and even wrapped securely in plastic in a bucket full of dirty diapers, but tonight they were being watched.

After needing to abort tonight's planned drop, we return home to camp and see a policeman (the same one as earlier today) watching us again! No confrontation though.

So cold tonight. Piled on the covers and finally fell asleep. Maybe it's our diet that's keeping us awake—M&Ms, peanuts, cold green beans, crackers. No wonder we're losing weight!

Sunday, September 11   Sunny-Nice

Really froze during the night. Al got up and put one of his blankets on me and that helped, but my head gets chilled! Our food supply is dwindling now, and so are we! Al's using his last belt notch. We supplement our meals with home-grown items we can buy from those along the road. The tiny, tart, green apples are good for keeping us alert, and the sunflower seeds—even with the grime from the hands of the children selling them—still make a nice item to confront the boredom while driving these slow, rough roads. All the scrawny wild dogs we see are obviously on a less than opulent diet as well. In this country, even the animals suffer.

Left the camp about 10:30. Don't have far to go today so there's no hurry. It's always a challenge to find a toilet (i.e. tall enough cornfield) along the way, but today we've been fortunate. *Thank You, Lord.*

We arrive in Sibiu at 2:00 p.m. I stayed with the car while Al checked out our meeting point. We found Pastor Nick's wife at home, but she said not to come till seven tonight. So now what to do inconspicuously for five hours?! We decided the outdoor folk museum was as safe as any place. It's a gorgeous fall afternoon, and I'm so thankful it's warm. After four hours, we decide it's time to leave the park. We drive out into the country and have a snack.

At seven o'clock, we come back into town to make our drop. Things go well, and we think Pastor Nick understands our instructions. Later, I sit in the car and wait while Al checks us into the campground.

All of a sudden, Pastor Nick and a friend appear at our bungalow with questions! *Oh Father, the risks!*

The camp guard doesn't like our having company, but Pastor Nick convinces him he's our friend and with the help of a can of coffee (major form of currency in those days), he looks the other way. *Oh God, help Pastor Nick understand now, protect him and his friend, and bless their desire for teaching from You.*

Monday, September 12   Warm – Sunny

We leave Sibiu at 9:45 a.m. I put a few old-fashioned rollers in my hair. It's better than nothing!

The road is really rough today. The fog is quite heavy, so we stop for breakfast. Our food supply is dwindling. The pollution is getting to us. Our eyes are burning, but we arrive at Brasov at 1:00 p.m. We check things out and stand in line for bread and canned sardines.

We check into the camp—not bad—even has hot water! Have lunch of fish, bread, and wine. I'm reminded of the Lord's supper.

I give Al a haircut and then we go to take showers before it gets too cold. Feels wonderful! Take a little nap and then organize and re-group our remaining books and gifts for tomorrow.

The wild dogs are howling around the camp again. They look so thin and scrawny.

I'm thinking now of the group of Gummi kids who descended upon us today at the gas station. They nearly tore my arm off in their desperate attempts to get as much as possible. One boy grabbed the whole bag and then, after seeing my disappointed look, returned it again. Would I too resort to such savagery? Used my panties for a cap tonight—it helped!

Tuesday, September 13   Sunny – Warm

Got up at 8:30 a.m. It's so nice to have hot water and a toilet that works. Breakfast was tea and bread. It tasted good to have something hot. We arranged our books for drop-off and then left Brasov at 11:30.

Drive on to Bran and tour Dracula's Castle. It's pretty interesting, but we're merely marking time until we can make our drop tonight.

Left Bran at 2:15 and drove to a nice spot for lunch. We still have five more hours before dark. Used our mat for a little rest by the roadside. Saw a man vomiting—probably food poisoning—all too familiar to us from our personal experience.

Put on a skirt and go onto Ploiesti. See another person sick as we drive. Not feeling well ourselves—so much thick diesel fumes.

So much traffic on this stretch. Still have time to kill so stop a couple times and rest. The cornfields are getting dry so there's not much privacy for toilet duties.

Now it's almost dusk, and we decide to proceed to our drop-off point. So, after waiting many hours, we now discover our rear taillights aren't working! We quickly abort all plans for drop and drive hurriedly to a camp near Ploiesti. The cabin reeks of mold and strong paint—the worst yet. The wild dogs—seemingly hundreds of them—start in howling about 10:00 p.m.

Wednesday, September 14   Cool-Damp

We eat breakfast here in our cabin. Yuk! This place is so gross.

Al's working on the car lights. We must employ a different strategy now for our work. Also, we must consider reaching our Bucharest destination before dark.

Praise God! Al got the lights working! Just one tiny fuse had caused all these complications. Was it our negligence or was it providential?

I use the camp toilet (it's another one of those lovely hole-in-the-ground deals where everyone misses the hole) and then leave camp. It's now 10:40 a.m. as we go into Ploiesti.

I stay in the car and pray as Al goes to arrange delivery. Al has a good reception and leaves gifts with mother and daughter. And they, in turn, give Al a gift—a lovely red Romanian scarf. Can't arrange book drop till 3:00 p.m. so we drive out of town to a secluded spot and have our lunch.

At 3:00 p.m., we go back into town to arrange for our drop. Once again, I wait in the car with the books. As I wait, a funeral procession goes by on foot—the body of a young man laid out in the back of a truck, completely black from time and exposure. Procession is led by young adults carrying photographs of the deceased and flowers. No one crying, but all are somber.

Al had successful contact and arranged a meeting place for book transfer before we left Ploiesti.

The dollar shop is closed so guess we'll make do with what we have in food and drink. Once again, we have beans and fish. But now we're going first class—we have chairs to sit on while eating and a place to wash our hands.

Thursday, September 15   **Sunny–Mild**

It felt so good to stay in bed this morning. A bed that is relatively clean and comfortable and doesn't stink of mold and urine. There's no hot water today, but at least the toilet works.

Now we stop in a pastry shop and stand in line for some yukky, bland-tasting green drink and a pastry to hold us till we can get back to our car. The drink was awful, but the pastry reminded me of apple strudel.

Friday, September 16   **Cloudy**

Slept so fitfully last night—my mind was bombarded with every topic imaginable. Guess there's been an overload of intake lately. My legs and back are hurting a lot.

Got up at 7:00 a.m. and had a breakfast of cheese, salami, tomatoes, bread, and tea at a restaurant. The meat tasted awful, took a few bites, but felt yukky right away. Wanted a refill on tea, but the waiter ignored me.

Left Bucharest at 9:00 a.m. We're making good time today. Stopped once to mail postcards and had cake and whatever it is they call coffee. The cake was priced by weight—it was real good too. One can enjoy an occasional sweet if you don't think about the conditions it may have been made under!

At 5:00 p.m., we checked into another "lovely" campsite near Sighisoara. The bungalow doesn't even have a lock on it. We killed twenty-eight flies before we could go to sleep—they almost carried us off! Then there's this mangy dog that's adopted us—Joy! Thought we finally got away from the wild dogs. This one just lies by our door and howls every time he hears the slightest sound. My back is at its worst tonight. Hope it's better by morning.

Saturday, September 17   Foggy

Left campsite at 7:30 a.m.—couldn't wait to get out of this place. It's foggy here in the hills this morning, giving our surroundings an eerie look. Water here at the camp is orange/red! And the mattress smells like urine. Yuck!

At 8:00 a.m., we stop for breakfast. It's hard driving with the fog so maybe it will lift by the time we finish our bread and jam. Then we drive a couple hours over a minor highway, and it was so rough I thought I'd vomit from the pain.

Finally, we reach Cluj. We get out to buy gas coupons and walk around and do a little shopping. I bought some popcorn they were making over a wood fire. We found some dolls in national dress for our supporting Sunday schools. We drive on. At 1:30, we stop and eat our last can of beans, along with sardines.

My back is really raising a fuss now, so Al cleared out the back seat, and I was able to lie down for part of the day. That helped a lot.

Reached Oradea at 5:30. Al made arrangements for our last "drop," and by 7:00 p.m., we were finished! *Thank You, precious Lord, for Your grace and Your perfect protection in all the many situations where we could have found ourselves in deep trouble.*

Found a decent room with hot water at Baile Felix—feels great to be clean again! We had some fish and bread for supper. Tomorrow, we make the drive back to Austria and home!

Sunday, September 18

As we drive through Hungary on our way home, there is so much to think about. These past two weeks are one big panorama of God's suffering church. My own physical body is breaking out in hives as

I consider all that God has spared us from, and I have a hard time dealing with this outbreak for a good many days to follow.

Finally, we arrive home at 3:30 p.m., and at 5:00 p.m., a ministry team shows up at our door, needing meals and lodging. I don't feel like being hospitable and gracious! *Oh, Father, forgive me…I forget so fast these lessons and examples of service You've shown to us in the past two weeks.*

Monday, September 19

I'm still itching, unbearably, from this outbreak of hives, but today, I get to see a doctor. I learn that the "hives" are actually a reaction to some mites I picked up during our travels. The process for getting rid of this "debris" is long and tedious, but so worth it. My skin is raw from all the scratching, and I'm so tired of itching. Unfortunately, this was just one of the many experiences we had on our Eastern Bloc travels with severe itching caused by mites and spiders.

Some of our colleagues stopped by this morning to share some experiences from their recent trip. This time, the books they were carrying were discovered by the border guards. The searching and interrogations went on for many hours and finally ended with a steep fine and confiscation of the books, and of course, they were refused entry.

The team was able to remain "cool" and refused to tell who the books were for. *Oh God, we don't understand this "failure." We do know, however, that you can bring good even from this, so we trust you to do that.*

Chapter 11

AT HOME IN VIENNA 1983-1991

Historic City of Music and Art

People often ask, "Of all the places you've lived, which was your favorite?" Well, I (Al) have all kinds of enjoyable and meaningful memories of all of our homes, but in terms of being livable and enjoyable, I have to single out Vienna.

Settled by the Romans two thousand years ago, it was part of the Austro-Hungarian Empire, occupied by Nazi Germany during World War II, and by the USA, Great Britain, France, and the Soviet Union after the war until 1955. Only twenty-eight years later, in 1983, Betty and I arrived in Vienna, and it became our home until we moved to Latvia on a Soviet visa in 1991.

Of music and art, Austria has so much to offer, which we greatly appreciated while residing there. We especially appreciated the music of composer Johan Straus II, known for his beautiful waltzes. Back in 1975, Betty and I had met on a ballroom dance floor in Fargo, ND, when we danced a beautiful waltz together. We cherished the times we could dance to Straus waltzes while living in Vienna.

One especially appreciated aspect of Vienna life for us was the beauty of the historic city and the country of Austria as a whole.

During some of our weekends when we were not traveling, we took the opportunity to do a lot of walking through the Vienna woods.

Betty described it this way: "It's fall now, and the warm sun is shining through the trees; the warm wind is coaxing colored leaves to fall on a blanket of moss." It was a wonderful, refreshing place to go and be restored and prepared for the week ahead without having it cost us anything.

In my opinion, Vienna also had the best coffee and pastries of anywhere I've ever traveled. We had a very busy and demanding work life during our years in Vienna, so an occasional walk through our beautiful surroundings with a stop for coffee and pastry at a quiet, peaceful coffee shop made for a much-appreciated break. God provided so many good things for us during our eight-and-a-half years there.

Hospitality Becomes a Major Part of Betty's Ministry

Much of my (Betty's) personal time was taken up with providing hospitality. I enjoyed it and looked forward to each and every guest, but it was difficult for me, since my back was troubling me a lot. Our men's group from church met at our place each week, which meant providing substantial refreshments for them since most of these men came directly from work.

Our church experience in Vienna was sweet and joyful; however, it was extremely difficult to develop close relationships with other believers since we needed to be guarded about what we were doing here. We never knew whom we could trust, so to be safe, we didn't trust anyone and always had to have a ready answer to questions that were not always easy to answer.

Hospitality and Practical Helps for Mission Teams Traveling into Eastern Europe

Often, we would provide meals, a place to sleep, briefings, and help getting visas, and we would keep things for the mission teams that they couldn't take with them on their travels. Sometimes, we would have as many as fourteen team members for meals.

One such example was about a group returning from Poland. B.R. and the O.H. team returned to our place early one morning. They had difficulty finding places to camp, so they'd been sleeping in the ditch next to the highway for the last two nights of travel. They all looked pretty grubby and tired. They were all anxious to get their mail and pick up the luggage they had left at our place while traveling.

Everyday things, like doing laundry and shopping for food, were challenges that required a lot of time, as well as a lot of endurance. We did have a washing machine; however, drying clothes by stringing them up on homemade clotheslines was trying since the climate was so damp, and therefore, it took ages for things to dry. Often, I'd find myself washing things a second, and even third time, because the clothes would get to smelling musty before they'd had a chance to dry. Shopping for food was challenging since one needed to frequent many little specialty shops for the various things needed. I spent much time just searching for items that I learned later were not even available here.

Life Demands Our All

All in all, our life in Vienna was very demanding—physically and emotionally. For example, Betty wrote: "For Al to call me from the office and say that he'll be late is fast becoming a common occurrence. It's at these times that he meets with various contacts and makes arrangements for them to do smuggling and distribution work for us. Al is very discouraged tonight. The distribution in Romania is not going as planned, and there's so much pressure. Please, Lord, give him Your grace and Your patience. Help him lean heavily on Your abilities, since it's really out of our hands, anyway. Implant in him the plan that You have for getting this material into the country safely and to the right people on time."

A Balm for Weary Spirits

Physically and emotionally, our work kept us pretty weary most of the time. Betty wrote, "It's always so amazing to me how the Lord brings a balm to our weary spirits when it's especially needed. This time it was through an invitation from friends to accompany them to the traditional Vienna New Year's Concert. It's held in the Musikverein, one of the beautiful structures of Vienna. The magnificent floral arrangements hanging from the beautiful gold-gilded pipe organ and balconies were a sight that took your breath away.

New Year's Concert — Vienna, Austria

"We sat in awe through the entire performance, wondering just how marvelous heaven must be when even here on earth it can be so 'heavenly.' Our hearts are filled with never-ending praise for the privilege and honor of living and working our days out here on earth as children of the King. It was an experience we will long speak of and look back on as one of the highlights of our experience in Austria."

Celebrating Eight Years

Our ministry responsibilities made it difficult to make time for ourselves, but we did take breaks to celebrate special occasions, such as our anniversary on July 16, 1985. It was a beautiful, hot, sunny day, just as it was eight years prior when we were joined as man and wife back in Fargo, North Dakota. Al had to work, but before he left the house, he gave me two enamelware pendants.

One was a dainty dark blue design on a tiny heart, and the other was a larger one on a longer chain to go with my Austrian suit. *Thank You, Jesus, for one who cares enough to brighten my world like this.* We walked down to Figlmuller's for supper and enjoyed a long, leisurely meal of salad and Wiener schnitzel. The outdoor garden atmosphere was so relaxing and lovely; I could have stayed for hours.

Working Trip to Western Europe

From time to time, we made trips to Holland, Germany, and France to work out plans with partnering mission organizations and individuals for printing our seminary materials and to meet with teams from various countries who helped in smuggling and distribution. Along with our book warehouse in Vienna, we also had a lot of our materials stored in a warehouse in Holland and needed to see that they were properly organized for trips being planned.

On that day, July 19, 1985, I wished we could have visited longer with the team presently visiting us in Vienna, but our schedule made it imperative that we get on the road to Holland for meetings with some of our courier teams. Below are some of Betty's journals cataloguing our trip.

Friday, July 19, 1985　　　　　　　　Warm – Partly Cloudy

Now on our way to Holland, we traveled all day on very busy highways—a lot of the time on eight-lanes, where speeds of autos surely exceeded 100 mph! The pace in Germany is absolutely crazy! It was good to finally cross the border into Holland. This is the land of windmills, dairy farms, dikes, canals, and all with a very pleasant, serene, and peaceful atmosphere.

Saturday, July 20, 1985   Rain – Cold – Windy – Cloudy

Doing a little sight-seeing in Amsterdam, we explored the train station area and were greeted with the flavor of New Orleans Mardi Gras. Jazz bands all over, streets thick with hippie-looking punks, lots of blacks and Indonesians, obvious looseness with drugs and sex, and an overall flavor of a city filled with sin and corruption. Wonder if this is what Sodom and Gomorrah were like. How God must have grieved!

Sunday, July 21, 1985   Sunny – Windy

We're now out of the big city to meet with some of our coworkers elsewhere in this country. It's wonderful here in Holland, once out of the major city of Amsterdam—no traffic noise and only the rooster and the church bells to wake up to. I so appreciate this restful setting!

Wednesday, July 24, 1985   Sunny

With all of our scheduled meetings completed successfully, it's time to head back to Vienna. The roads are really lovely today, all overhung with green trees, as though we're driving thru a tunnel. Before leaving Holland, we stopped at a supermarket and picked up some maple syrup, pancake mix, peanut butter, and M&Ms! What a wonderful blessing. Can't get these things in Vienna.

On the trip back to Vienna I had plenty of time to meditate on all that's transpired in these recent days, as we met with these teams who risk everything to make church leader training materials available in countries where it's dangerous to be caught with them. We've been challenged, anew, to our commitment of serving Christ even unto death. Cooperation and unity is needed between all of God's people to get the job (the Great Commission) done. It seems to me that the reason so few "go" is because they're afraid they won't come back. The Bible clearly commands us to go, but it tells us nothing about coming back.

Traveling back to Vienna, we stopped for the night at Kitzingen, Germany. It's a US military base, so there are Americans all over! Al and I walked around looking for a place to eat and the whole atmosphere reminded us very much of the East, with lots of very old, rundown, grey, and drab tenement housing. Found a little Greek restaurant where we enjoyed a nice meal of gyros, Greek salad, and bean soup. Most enjoyable was the large group of three American families eating right next to us, and all speaking our language. It was so strange though, realizing we were sitting here in Germany, in a Greek restaurant, listening to Americans conversing in English.

We returned home to Austria in August. We got up early and prepared for our seminar at Tulbingen Kogel where Robert Coleman was speaking. Our first session began at 9:45 a.m. with Dr. Coleman going thru the various steps of Evangelism as a Lifestyle. His book on this topic was one we used in our Evangelism and Discipleship course in the Communist countries. Dr. Coleman looked and acted so much like Andy Griffith, it was hard not making comparisons while watching him. It was rather distracting.

Visits from Home Cheer Us Up

One of the things which encouraged us so while living in Vienna was the visits from friends and family from back home. The most precious of all was my (Betty's) almost seventy-seven-year-old mother! What a beautiful gift it was to have her with us for a few days in August. It was her first time flying internationally, so an extremely challenging step for her to take, but oh how worth it!

My brother and his wife flew in from their visit to Scotland also, so it was a sweet family reunion. I believe it was a great relief for my mom to see that we had comfortable living conditions, plenty to eat, and were getting along well in all the areas moms are concerned over. But I'm thankful she wasn't able to see us in our subsequent settings when we later lived in the former Soviet Union. Things were totally different for us there.

Chapter 12

VISITING GOD'S SERVANTS—POLAND AND HUNGARY

After a number of visitors from home (USA) this summer, we were now preparing to visit some of our contacts in Poland and Hungary. This time, it was simply to do some planning for seminary material needs for the upcoming seminar schedule. We decided to take the train to Poland and travel around to meet with our contacts there.

Monday, September 16   **Rain-Cool**

Finished packing for Poland and left home at 4:30 p.m. We've booked a sleeper compartment on this train, which is a lifesaver. Can't imagine having to sit for sixteen to seventeen hours. Our compartment isn't very nice, typical Eastern train, but we're thankful for it, nonetheless. Even has a porcelain potty! The "aroma" of dirt plus urine is almost overwhelming, but we're trying not to think about it!

Our border crossings were all without incident. Praise the Lord! Things already are notably different—dark, grey, and gloomy with a feeling of grim hopelessness in all of it. Buildings with paint peeling, dirt and ever-present guards watching for those "naughty" people trying to escape from this prison country. Border checks were around 11:00 p.m. and again from 3 to 5 so didn't get much sleep. The ride is too rough to get very comfortable anyway. I'm having some motion sickness from all the jostling.

As I look out at the cold, dark, grey foreboding atmosphere, I can almost imagine myself on the Siberian run and having no idea what labor camp I'll end up in. The trauma for those unfortunate victims must have been so terrible! One can only imagine what it must have been like.

Tuesday, September 17   **Wet-Cold**

Train was late getting into Warsaw. All one can see is grey cement; Warsaw was rebuilt after the war in the typical colorless style of the Eastern Bloc. It's very windy, wet, and cold here today. Walked with our bags to Forum Hotel. I'm still not feeling well—very fatigued and extremely unbalanced from the train ride. Took a short nap and then went out to see their four main department stores. Stores are big enough, but merchandise is the same in all of them. All very old, outdated, and lifeless—things that you would've seen forty or more years ago in America. Variety is very limited even here in Warsaw where it's supposed to be the best! Saw long lines for shoes again. The only fruit we saw was apples and some plums.

Wednesday, September 18   **Sunny-Windy-Cool**

Slept very well till nearly 4:00 a.m., then lay awake and had a good time with the Lord. Enjoyed a nice buffet breakfast. It was far more than I expected—food is poor quality, but they do have it here in this hotel, which caters to tourists. The dairy products aren't safe and the meat isn't good. The coffee is like imitation Postum, but the bread is edible, and the hot water for tea is not bad! Couldn't drink the mineral water—bottle was all rusty and chipped. Our lunch was bad—spaghetti sauce looked like barf and tasted the same!

This evening, we made our call to Pastor Adam and delivered the pens, aspirin, etc. to him. We so wish we had brought more, but we had no idea shortages were so severe here in Poland. Adam is pastor of a Methodist church here and also runs an English language school with five thousand students. We didn't stay long as Adam looked dreadfully tired. His wife was gone for rest—nervous tension and exhaustion. But in spite of the hopelessness expressed by the Polish people, he has such a sweet, pleasant, cheerful demeanor about him, which simply exudes the Lord's spirit in every breath.

Thursday, September 19   Sunny – Warm – Windy

Al stored one suitcase at the train station and then came back for me and our other bag. Bought a quick cup of coffee at a grody stand up bar but couldn't drink it. We went down to the platform to wait for our train. We stood for two and a half hours before learning we had missed our train! A Polish girl with broken German helped Al make arrangements for the next train at 4:20 p.m. *Thank You, Father, for this "angel" to help us on our way.* I'm so tired and still have four hours of sitting on the train, plus no place to go when we arrive!

Our fare is for second class coach so there are eight people packed in one compartment. No place to put my legs. *Lord, help me. Thank You for Your wonderful grace which has helped me endure this trip.* After boarding the train, we walked down to the "dining" car and found it to be a typical stand-up place with only a few small items for sale: soup, sausage, raw hamburger mixed with raw egg and onions, which seems to be a very popular item here. Yuk! I had a bowl of soup—turned out to be chicken but could have been almost anything since I couldn't speak the language. Al and I shared a bottle of tomato juice. Back in our compartment, I pulled out an orange I'd brought from Vienna and started eating it. I suddenly realized all eyes were upon me with longing, and oh, I wished I had been sensitive enough not to eat it here!

Arrived in Poznan at 8:30 p.m. Al went looking for a room while I stayed in the train station. Al finally found us a room on the fifth floor of a dirty old hotel, but how thankful we are for a place to sleep tonight. We rode a tram there since the taxi line is very long. Tram is an atrocity! Old, rusty, squeaky, bumpy, it's a wonder they stay on the tracks! Our room is right next to the old manually operated elevator (lots of noise), and the Lysol smell of the room is almost more than I can handle, but it's a roof over our heads and we're thankful!

We've had no lunch and no supper, but both of us were feeling really sick. This room with its peeling wallpaper, chipped paint, water-stained ceilings, tile that's been around for at least forty years, and grime over everything really doesn't do much for one's appetite. "All for Jesus" is what keeps me going, and it's He that gives me the strength and stamina to endure. We both fell asleep almost immediately—what a blessing! The grace of He who cares gives us refreshment and a renewed desire to keep going.

Friday, September 20   **Warm – Sunny**

After lunch we found the home of Pastor K. He told us there is much more freedom now in building, but fewer materials to do it. Oh the irony of it all! Their church was started three and a half years ago after another three-year wait prior to this for permission to build. They hope to be in it now this Christmas. K. shared that a great need now is good teachers and materials for teaching. There are so many new believers and no one to shepherd them and disciple them in their walk with the Lord.

So tired. But thinking of K.'s hard day makes ours seem easy.

Sunday, September 22   **Sunny – Mild – Windy**

Back in Warsaw, we bought some cheesecake and pop, but both are so grody and the surroundings so dirty we don't know if we can eat them.

Left Warsaw for the return trip to Vienna on the "Chopin Express" at 5:50 p.m. Got settled in our sleeper and then ate the cheesecake. Got sick from it and felt miserable the whole night.

With all the jostling and the smelly compartment and toilet, it was an ordeal to get thru the night. The border crossings were easy—no incidents and no searches.

Monday, September 23   Sunny – Beautiful

Our train trip back to Vienna was uneventful. The contrast from Poland back to Vienna stands out in the stark reality of the Viennese people dressed so nicely and in the colorful displays, the clean rest rooms, plentiful supplies. What a different world. How my heart bleeds for the people in the dire circumstances we've just come from. The grey, dismal existence with so few material comforts, but the hardest is the lack of spiritual freedoms. *Lord, I ask that you would uphold them in Your precious arms of mercy, for only Your power and love can get them through this hard life here on earth.*

Visiting Contacts in Hungary

Thursday, September 26

After a short time at home, today we're back on the road again via our Volvo wagon as we travel into Hungary. As "Western" as this part of the world seems, the roads bring one up short, and it wasn't long before we came onto a very serious automobile accident. This happens so frequently. Sometimes Al actually needs to park, get out, and walk long distances to learn where we are and how we might best navigate the distances. Those times are so frightening for me.

    What would I do in a strange country, with a strange language, and oftentimes not even having my passport on me, since Al usually carries them on his person for both of us?

    The market in Budapest today gave us a start with their dead rabbits in an open display case in the meat department. They were completely intact—open eyes staring up from the showcase and all! It's when I see things like this that I'm no longer under the illusion of being back home in North Dakota.

We need to play the tourist role, since we have some contacts to make later on, so we check into a local hotel. The food is awful. The eggs have been done in rancid grease and tasted as bad as they looked. Most eating places offer only the stand-up tables, where people simply stand there, eating their fare, and then move on again. Not exactly a very relaxed setting to our way of thinking.

There are no elevators here, so we had to carry our luggage up some eighty-six steps to the fourth floor, only to walk into a room that was stifling hot, and no way to regulate the heat. We survived by keeping the windows open and using the bathroom only when absolutely necessary for it reeked of sewer. It's hard getting used to these changes. We just need to accept things as they are and try to go on with the tasks God has assigned to us here.

Friday, September 27

The night was long in this hot room, so we were very much looking forward to breakfast, which goes along with the room rent. Well, never has either of us been turned off by tea before, but this was THE WORST! It was served in a large water pitcher, barely lukewarm, with a thick scum on top that turned both our stomachs. We did, however, enjoy the cold platter of various meats and cheeses. Bread is always plentiful, so one can get filled up, no matter how poor the rest of the meal might be.

Unfortunately, the bread isn't always fresh. Today was a case in point, when I actually broke my knife in two trying to cut my breakfast roll. They truly were "hard" rolls! What the meal lacks, the "entertainment" usually makes up for. Today, it was a little, pear-shaped peasant lady, dressed in black, coming through the restaurant with some hand-painted plates she was selling to help support her family. Of course, we didn't need the plates, but we purchased one, and she seemed encouraged by our smiles and compassionate looks.

Al went to make our contact this morning, while I stayed behind in our room. As always, we're not able to discuss anything important here—one can assume the rooms are "bugged," so we feel it's a better plan for just one of us to go on out and make the connection we need to accomplish. Even outdoors, we are always careful to check around us before speaking. English-speakers are always suspect, and we find ourselves being followed more often than not. Yes, it's scary, but the Lord is never farther away than our very breath. He provides the peace and security that nothing else can.

Saturday, September 28

With our short meeting agenda in Hungary completed, we're very ready to make the drive back to Vienna today.

Chapter 13

WORLD AND PERSONAL EVENTS CHALLENGE OUR SPIRITS

America Bombs Libya — 1986

As I (Betty) walked in the quiet of the woods this early morning, I could almost forget the tensions and tragedies of this past week. Yesterday, the US bombed Tripoli, and as a result, we Americans here in Europe were feeling the hateful antagonism of not only the outside forces, but also the locals here in Vienna who saw us as a very real threat to their peace and security. The American embassy had been informed of planned terrorist attacks on Americans here and was taking what precautions they could. They were evacuating all government compounds in our district and cancelling all activities and organized gatherings by Americans.

We'd been warned to stay off the streets as much as possible and, particularly, to refrain from using English when we were out in public. These were things I'd only read about in other missionary stories, so it seemed really bizarre that we were now actually living it. In the midst of all this upheaval, hate, hostility, and revenge, I thanked God for being who He is—a Rock that is unchanging and an Anchor that holds and never wavers.

Chernobyl — 1986

Among other things that kept us unsettled was the nuclear scare from the Chernobyl nuclear plant explosion in Russia. The fallout was a big concern. Parents were advised to keep their children indoors and to avoid milk and other dairy products, which carried the most dangerous levels of radiation. We, ourselves, tried to stay away from fresh produce and dairy products, but we learned later that we had been seriously affected by this disaster.

Regina in Bulgarian Prison — September 1986

Back in Vienna, we learned some disturbing news. One of our Austrian colleagues who did some in-country distribution work for us was being held in Bulgaria. It was hard not being anxious when we knew that the prisons there are about the worst in the Eastern Bloc. This served as a reminder that we were not playing games. Sometimes, I felt our attempts at security were far too lax. Only God, Himself, was able to keep Regina safe, so we continued to pray for His peace to surround her in every way possible.

Released from Prison

God worked through the Austrian government to get her freed after about four months. Her arrest and imprisonment were not for her work with us, but because she got caught trying to help a Bulgarian Christian family escape from the country.

After her release, we spent an evening with her to learn about her experience, and she told us the story of what it was like: When she was first arrested, she was questioned for five hours, then put into a cell, made to undress, and given her two sheets, a blouse, and a bucket for toilet duties. Twice daily, she was given just a few minutes to wash, clean her bucket, etc. Every three weeks, she was allowed to take a shower and was issued a clean blouse at that time. She had no socks and said she was cold all the time. Her meals were a breakfast of bread and jam or cheese, while lunch and dinner were usually soup with virtually no substance.

The time was endless. She saw very little daylight, so lost track of time. She was occasionally permitted to sit and read her Bible in an area where the sun shone for short periods of time. She had a cellmate at two different times, but most of her time, she was alone in her cell.

We found it astounding to hear her say she looked forward to the interrogations because it was a break in the endless hours of just sitting in her cell (lying down during the day was not permitted). She got by with singing a little when she did it very discreetly.

After the first eight weeks, she was allowed to receive mail from the outside; however, no parcels were allowed, and she needed socks so badly.

Regina shared how the Lord used this time to bring her face to face with herself and her true motives for serving Him. As is true of so many of us, we think of ourselves as the "elite" level of Christians because we work in dangerous circumstances, but God pulled away the coverings of purely selfish reasons for serving. So now she was spending time sorting out her thoughts, adjusting and re-evaluating what the Lord would have her do with the remainder of her life from a different perspective.

Back Treatments

My (Betty's) treatments for back pain continued at the Austrian clinic. My treatment today was so rough that it made me terribly sick with a headache and gave me such pain that I began to wonder if this was what it was like to have a stroke or a heart attack. I was so-o-o sick, but after about an hour, the worst intensity of it was past.

Betty's Thorn in the Flesh

Yet you do not know what your life will be like tomorrow. For you are just a vapor that appears for a little while, and then vanishes away. –JAMES 4:14

In spite of the long, beautiful, warm summer months we'd had that year, I was keenly reminded that this too was coming to an end.

The leaves were falling; the flowers no longer held their fresh and vivid appeal; the chestnuts were ready to roast; the temperatures were dropping; and we were finding it necessary to put on more and more layers of blankets at night. All things have their season, and I was impressed once again with the urgency of using each day for that which holds eternal value. Whether we had a mere twenty to thirty years or were blessed with the full expectancy of seventy plus years, it was all just a trickle of time in the Lord's plan for us.

The Lord had taught me some things about time these past few years as I'd struggled with what many of you know as my "thorn in the flesh" (severe, unending back pain), and I saw how I could not possibly have learned them any other way. Not always had I been so willing to submit to His will. Many times, I expressed my anger, my frustrations, and my impatience in my refusal to accept limitations and pain, but the Lord truly revealed how insignificant our short while here on earth is—whether filled with the blessings of good health, or with restrictions and enforced limitations that keep us from what we see as being important. Often, I sought His face for true understanding. Because of my zeal to serve, I felt He was making a big mistake in not allowing me good health. Little did I realize how much I yet needed to learn how to be submissive to His will no matter what!

It had been a long time coming, but I was finally making some progress in learning that wherever we are—in whatever He allows—if we are willing to make ourselves available for His instruction and His leading, He will give us countless opportunities to learn, grow, and give witness to His glory. To see things from His perspective is my prayer for me and for you.

In recent months, we'd seen many unsettling things: the terrorist attacks in Vienna and elsewhere, with such senseless destruction of many innocent lives; the Chernobyl incident and the masses that would be affected; Regina's imprisonment in Bulgaria; the poisonous gas catastrophe, which took so many lives and caused so much heartache; and most recently, the earthquake in the east. I was sure

God had many and varied messages for us through these obvious attention-getters, but to me, they served to reinforce our helpless insignificance and His powerful and mighty control over the entire universe.

When I look at the big things surrounding us, the little thorns we struggled with faded quickly in comparison, and I was humbled and repentant and willing to live each day for Him, with my weaknesses, and not waste precious moments trying so hard to understand why. My problems were big to me, but I prayed that I was learning what He wanted me to learn. I praised Him for using each one of us where we were and in spite of what seemed like handicaps to our effectiveness.

When I study the people of Scripture, I am encouraged at how many struggled with what they too saw as infirmities, but how the Lord used them anyway. It seems God is not so much interested in perfect vessels, but in willingness and obedience to His leading.

As I look back on these thoughts I've shared with you, I can only pray that the Lord will continue to reveal to me, and to all of us, that His ways are best, that He will see fit to use us regardless of our weaknesses. I praise Him for allowing us, His creatures, to have a part in the whole plan of redeeming mankind, bringing us into true understanding of what's really important.

Chapter 14

EVERYDAY LIFE IN VIENNA NOVEMBER 1986 TO FEBRUARY 1987

While we needed to travel a lot for our work, we did spend time at home in Vienna. Betty's daily journal entries described our everyday life in Vienna. You'll see that two things affected us greatly. First, Betty suffered much pain from her back issues, and second, most of our days included stressful situations and were pretty demanding of our time and energy.

Monday, November 17, 1986   Mist – Cold – Dreary
Went out for an early walk and weather was real yukky. I went downtown and had my glasses adjusted. This time he didn't holler at me. I walked in with my leather coat and high boots and acted as though I were going to demand service. He smiled so nice and asked me what he could do for me! I'm learning what it takes to get respect here.

Tuesday, November 18, 1986   Cloudy – Rain
It's been a very dreary, dark, wet day. Good for writing, reading, etc. Al gave me a long neck and back rub tonight. Think it helped

a lot. He worked out some of the knots. My whole head, arm, and neck hurt and tingled as he did the massage. *Thank You, Lord, for a husband who cares.*

Tuesday, November 25, 1986   Cold-Dreary

Rode along with Al this morning and bought some veggies for Thanksgiving. My shoulders and neck muscles ache so from carrying even just a few things. I get so tired of always feeling miserable. Lord, help me to be more patient and less complaining.

Friday, November 28, 1986   Weather Still Pretty Nice – No Snow Yet

Al's forty-second birthday. Al and I went to Regina Hotel for breakfast. It was nice, fairly quiet and peaceful. Had a quiet afternoon. I prepared chicken, etc. for guests tomorrow.

Saturday, November 29, 1986   Sunny-Nice

Took a walk with Al this morning. Then prepared food for lunch with Lewey (from Sierra Leone) and Jay (from Sri Lanka). They're so sweet—both brought flowers. Had a good meal—they enjoyed the chicken and rice, etc. I also prepared chicken soup for several of our colleagues. Seems all I do is cook and bake lately. No wonder my back is hurting so much!

Al tried to approach Jay about the gospel, but Jay wasn't interested in pursuing it. I think we need to be more pointed in our questions; we're making it too comfortable for Jay.

Tuesday, December 2, 1986   Cloudy-Cold

Al has a church meeting tonight. He's worn out. *Lord, give him Your strength and the wisdom to know when to say "no."*

Wednesday, December 3, 1986   Cloudy-Cold

Al has meeting again this morning at church. Went to Pam Pam and spent over a hundred dollars for groceries and only have meat for one meal!

Saturday, December 6, 1986 — Cold

Al and I went to Donau Center to do a little shopping. I bought a scarf and gloves. The gloves had a flaw, but I was able to deal with the clerk—all auf Deutsch. Made me feel good to get a reduction; they rarely do that here. You either take it or leave it!

Sunday, December 7, 1986 — Cold-Windy

Doesn't feel like Sunday. Couldn't go to church because Al had to stay home to receive books from Dutch couriers coming through.

Thursday, December 11, 1986 — Mild-Dreary-Drizzly

Received a huge box from a North Dakota Sunday School today with just all kinds of food products. One class included pictures they had drawn. What a joy and a thrill to receive all these things. I couldn't stop crying for several hours after opening it, and even now when I talk about it, the tears start flowing. God is so good, and His riches and blessings never cease. "The Lord's acts of mercy indeed do not end, For His compassions do not fail. They are new every morning; Great is Your faithfulness" (Lamentations 3:22-23).

Friday, December 12, 1986 — Mild-Windy

We're thinking about moving from our apartment to the rental house in Wiener Neudorf being vacated by one of our colleagues. *What is wise? Lord, should we pursue this even though it's so far away from the office? Please show us your will, Lord.*

Thursday, December 18, 1986

Stopped at Bernie's (living in the house we're looking to rent when they leave for England). Visited a long time (Al and Bernie did!) about their upcoming work in London to prepare for ministry in the Soviet Union. I feel so sorry for them, pioneering in such a difficult ministry as the Soviet Union. Even the language is such a hard one.

Both Al and I are very favorably impressed with the house. Not that there's anything beautiful at all about it. It just feels so comfortable. We believe this is what the Lord has for us. Al and I couldn't sleep last night. We're excited about moving, having a yard, privacy, more room—all these things. I rearranged our furniture twenty times in the house before I finally fell asleep! Feel so nauseous too—really yukky!

Friday, December 19, 1986   Cold-Strong Winds-Rain
Tonight, we told Bernie we want to rent the house. *Oh God, if this is wrong, then please close the door for us, or show us clearly that we should not take it.*

Monday, December 22, 1986   Snowy a.m.
Mom called. We talked a long time. *I praise You, God, for allowing her to live so long and giving me such security and love.* She said Julie (our daughter) had called her and the baby may come around Christmas time! *Oh God, please keep Julie from being resentful and angry over my absence. I know how easy and how tempting that would be. You know how much I want to be with her, Lord. And now this house deal, Lord, I feel so uncomfortable and scared over this. All these additional costs and responsibilities that came out in our visit are making me have all kinds of second thoughts. Please, Lord, give us wisdom in this decision. What is Your will in our moving?*

Wednesday, December 24, 1986   Snow
Al and I walked downtown this morning and got a few groceries. Then for lunch we had hot dogs, chips and dip, and Christmas cookies. Tasted good, but not exactly as it would have been roasting hot dogs over our wood fireplace back in Fargo, North Dakota, with all the kids around.

Our Christmas Eve was lovely! Al and I had chili by candlelight and then some goodies while we exchanged gifts. Al gave me a beautiful card with the parliament pictured on front and such a sweet letter. He gave me a lovely brown tone pendant and a photo album and then the darlingest little crystal koala bear. It's so precious! *I praise You, Lord, for giving me such a caring and loving husband. You have blessed me "exceedingly abundantly" thru him.*

Thursday, December 25, 1986 — Sunny–Lovely

It's a beautiful Christmas day! Al and I had a nice, leisurely breakfast, with a good visit about the house and the move, and I feel a lot better about it all now. *Father, I praise You for Al's "solidness" and confidence as he follows Your leading. I'm always so unsure, and he helps me put things back into perspective.*

Sunday, December 28, 1986 — Windy–Mild

Loving Lord, I thank You for giving Julie and Harve a healthy baby girl. I praise You for bringing both Julie and the baby thru safely, and I trust You now to watch over them while I can't be there. Help me, Father, to leave this, too, in Your hands.

Monday, December 29, 1986 — Strong Wind–Rain

Terribly stormy today—winds up to 135 kilometers per hour doing a lot of damage. Huge trees being uprooted. Tram burned because of electrical wires catching on fire. Trees falling on cars. Pieces of roofing, etc. torn away by the wind. Haven't even gone outdoors today. Al went to see new landlord tonight to sign the contract. *Precious Jesus, may this be Your will, and may we see Your hand revealed as things unfold so we can be sure this was Your choice for us.*

Sunday, January 4, 1987 — Sunny–Mild

Attended the prayer time before church with Anne and Frieda. Talked about God's peace and how to enjoy that peace on an everyday basis, not allowing little irritations to rob us of God's presence.

Saturday, January 10, 1987   Cold–Snow–Wind

Al has an all-day planning retreat today at the pastor's house. I prepared snacks to send along, but just can't handle sitting all day.

Wednesday, January 14, 1987   Very Cold–Snow

Spent time preparing meal for "courier team" from Holland. They arrived at 6:15 p.m. They were hungry and enjoyed the pork chops, rice, beans, and cranberry salad.

Thursday January 15, 1987   Cold–More Snow!

Had long leisurely breakfast with time of prayer and meditation on God's Word with the Dutch team. Ben and Peter are good to be around, and it's been a pleasure having them. They're so fun-loving and also so very committed.

Sunday, January 18, 1987   Quite Mild

Al has a church meeting tonight. I didn't go. *I ask, Lord, that You will encourage Al to eliminate some of these meetings. It's getting to be far too much, neglecting other, more important, tasks.*

Monday, January 19, 1987   Fairly Mild

Got a letter from Julie and our first photos of Cassandra. She's a doll! Oh, I ache so to hold her and to help Julie care for her. She's dark like Harve and has the cutest little round face. Precious!

Wednesday January 21, 1987   Typical Winter

Went to Pam Pam for groceries this morning. Had a treat when I came home—*Little House on the Prairie* movie was on TV—a whole one and a half hours in beautiful color. What a blessing.

Al went downtown to get some money. Our salary just doesn't reach to the end of the month anymore. *Lord Jesus, this is such a heavy issue. The dollar is down to 12.50 now—almost exactly half of what it was when we came. We seek Your face and mind in this, Lord, and stand ready to obey Your will.*

Monday, January 26, 1987 — Sleet-Snow-Wind

A yukky day—streets and sidewalks are extremely slippery. I slipped and twisted my back and neck and now am really hurting. Went to bed early—feel so sick.

Monday, February 2, 1987 — Very Cold

It hasn't been a good day—had to get off the tram at the Nussdorfer tram stop and walk home because the tram wasn't going any farther. I think it was because of snow removal this time, but this has been typical this winter. Never know where the tram will stop and all passengers are told, "Bitte, alle aussteigen!"

Saturday, February 7, 1987 — Rain-Mild

Went to bed early. Al gave me a back rub, and I took a relaxant so slept quite well. Al had a terrible night—so many things on his mind. *Oh God, please help Al to trust you with our financial problems. It's hard not to worry, but help us put our energies into good planning instead.*

Saturday, February 14, 1987 — Dreary-Rain

Al and I had a nice breakfast at the Regina. I ate far too much. It was so good! Al gave me a Valentine with a lovely note, and I gave him a Valentine with fourteen reasons for my love, a cassette of Beethoven's Ninth, and some M&Ms. Did some packing, writing, etc. this afternoon.

Saturday, February 21, 1987 — Sunny-Mild

Took a car load of things down to the house and met the landlord there to get the keys. Spent the morning planning our redecorating. All of it has good potential except the bathroom.

Feeling so awful today. Al did dishes and gave me a long back rub. He's always so kind to me. *Thank You, Lord, for such a loving husband.*

Tuesday, February 24, 1987   Sunny – Cool

Al loaded up the car and then we went to Huma to shop for wallpaper, paint, refrigerator, carpet, etc. By noon, my back was so knotted up, it felt like it was on fire! *Oh God, give me the strength to go on with Al.* He must get so sick of hearing me complain and always having to consider how I feel when he makes plans.

Friday, February 27, 1987

Al—tired as he was tonight—set up our bed on the little couch and even rigged up my heating blanket. So sweet. Slept quite well.

Saturday, February 28, 1987   Rain – Snow

I'm so thankful we got the major move completed before the rain and snow. *Thank You, Lord!*

Then at 3:00 p.m., we met with our landlords to make our initial payments. We didn't have quite enough, but with my one thousand Austrian schilling emergency fund, we made it and satisfied them for the first month. *We're trusting You, Father. This is Your house! Help us be wise and prudent in caring for it.*

Our House in Wiener Neudorf — 1987–1991

Chapter 15

SPRINGTIME IN THE VILLAGE OF WIENER NEUDORF

We were getting settled into our new home in the small village of Wiener Neudorf, just south of Vienna. We were thankful for this quieter and more pleasant situation compared to our apartment in the bustling big city of Vienna with all its noisy traffic.

Sunday, March 1, 1987   **Snow–Slush**

Big, fluffy, wet snowflakes coming down today. *It's a beautiful wintry day to worship You, Lord.*

Paul had an excellent sermon from Romans 7 this morning. *Thank You for that message of love for God being our motivation. Oh God, I asked for a deeper, more committed love to You. Help me not notice the inconvenience of "walking that extra mile." Help me love You more.*

Worked all afternoon here at the house. Al got our new refrigerator going, and I cleaned and unpacked some. Can't get organized till Al gets kitchen painted, papered, and carpeted.

Went to bed about 9:00 p.m. Feels so good! Very little noise here in this little village—feels like we're in the country. Wonderful!

Tuesday, March 3, 1987 — Cold–Sunny

Took a walk this morning and discovered a discount grocery store nearby. It seems so strange to walk up town here. People will greet you on the street; smiles appear on their faces; all businesses are on this one main street, so much like my little hometown of Medina back in North Dakota.

Thursday, March 5, 1987 — Cold–Sunny

It's a lovely, sunny, cold day for my birthday! Our days are so hectic right now, so there will be no celebrating, but Al brought me a lovely card (with daisies), and we plan to do something special later on. Al had to go to the office, and I stayed home and worked all day scrubbing cupboards, doing laundry, unpacking, and organizing.

I'm absolutely beat tonight—feel at least twice my age of fifty-one! *I do thank You and praise You, Father, for giving me another year of life. Life is precious, and I have so much to learn yet! I ask, dear Father, for more opportunities of growth and a deeper desire to become holy as You are holy. Help me be accepting of Your methods of teaching, knowing You are all wise and loving.*

Friday, March 6, 1987 — Bitter Cold–Blustery

Al met with Ron and Tricia from Holland this morning to discuss their smuggling trip. I served coffee.

We received a wonderful package from the folks. They sent me a little picture album with Al's picture on the cover when he was young, and then also one of themselves on their twenty-fifth anniversary back in 1962. So neat! I can hardly wait to fill it up with old pics of Al and me.

Saturday, March 7, 1987 — Snow–Cold–Blustery

Al and I went to Carrefour for a leisurely breakfast (my belated birthday outing) and then did a little shopping. We finally finished wallpapering the kitchen! Now Al's going to lay the carpet.

Tuesday, March 10, 1987 — Cold–Snow

Meeting with our men working in the East was discouraging. The teaching materials are not getting in, and those that do sometimes disappear before our facilitators get in to teach! *Use these resources the way You would have them used, Father. Don't let our plans get in Your way; help us to hear Your voice and be willing to follow Your direction.*

Sunday, March 15, 1987 — Sunny–Windy

Diane called early this morning and said Mom's in the hospital with what they believe to be a heart attack. *Oh God, give us wisdom in making clear and wise decisions about this situation. Keep Mom in the shelter of Your loving arms. Lord Jesus, I commit her to You, trusting Your perfect will and plan for her.*

Wednesday, March 18, 1987 — Snow–Beautiful!

Diane called. They did an angiogram on Mom and found one vessel 99 percent blocked and two others partially blocked. They tried the balloon procedure, but it didn't work so now she's scheduled for a bypass. *Oh, precious Lord, would You please help her thru all this pain and distress.* All day long, Al and I have been praying for Mom, watching the clock, and walking thru the various stages of surgery.

Thursday, March 19, 1987 — Lots of Snow! – Beautiful!

Thank You, dear Lord! Diane called to let us know Mom's surgery was successful. It took four hours. *I praise You, Father, for bringing her thru this ordeal.*

Saturday, March 21, 1987 — Sunny–Bright

Spent all day at the church retreat. It was held at the Schloss Neuwaldegg. A beautiful old castle-like building that has been restored and is very nice.

Pastor Adam, from Poland, spoke all day and told of his experiences in the Russian army and as a prisoner in a labor camp.

Then he experienced the struggles of being a committed pastor in an Eastern Bloc country. Constant harassment to resign and always the restrictions of what a pastor can actually do in his capacity.

Adam was very tired, and his fatigue left little in the way of enthusiasm during his sharing. Somehow this aura of exhaustion actually enhanced his sharing as we, as soft Americans, were touched even more than had he been real dynamic. Once again, Romans 8:28!

Wednesday, March 25, 1987   Beautiful! – Sunny – Warm
Al had an early morning church meeting, and I've been on the go since before six. Really getting tired! Al came home really beat and feeling more and more the pressure of fighting a battle on a number of different fronts: work on the house, work deadlines, church commitments, and family crises.

Thursday, March 26, 1987   Cloudy – Warm
Lord God, please show me how I can help Al handle the pressures just now—give me ideas that will help him relax and be a comfort to him.

Respite in the Alps

Sometimes, it seemed that our work and the challenges of personal and family life began to leave us feeling weary and discouraged. But just when it seemed the hardest, and Satan put ideas of quitting into my head, was when our precious Lord provided such sweet and blessed relief. This time through dear friends from America who were also living and working here. They invited us to a few days' holiday with them in a little village in the foothills of the Alps.

The first morning in this setting, I woke up to the beautiful sounds of singing birds. In the city, it was far too noisy to hear these things, but here in this little mountain village, it was so quiet and peaceful. The scene from our room was incredibly beautiful.

It looked exactly like a winter alpine village scene you'd see on a postcard—complete with the little church nestled in the center of the village, surrounded with the lovely Austrian Alps. The snow all around was undisturbed as it melted slowly during the mild temperatures of early spring. Watching the sleds pulled through the village by docile horses with bells on their harnesses brought back so many memories of my childhood school days, when my brother and I would ride to our little one-room country school back in North Dakota with our beloved Sissy pulling our sleigh.

The mountains, glistening white with snow, reached skyward in majestic form. Everything was just so impressive, and I could only thank my wonderful God for allowing us this special little break.

God Encourages Via a Lost Glove

While our respite in the Alps was a wonderful lift to our spirits, every now and again, the Lord allowed for special, simple encouragements to keep our spirits uplifted. One such incident occurred when I had lost my good leather glove, a gift sent to me for Christmas. I felt so badly about this loss. The worst part was that I was wearing two pair, so now two pairs of gloves were ruined, and good ones were so costly. For days, I retraced my steps through the parks and my route to the stores, but no sign of the gloves.

Then one day, as I was walking and praying, the thought of "church" came to me. There was a large, castle-like church near our place, and I would often stop there to warm up and spend time with our Lord. The moment that thought came to mind I just KNEW I'd find my gloves there. What a thrill to see my gloves lying on the ledge in front of the church, just waiting for me to come and retrieve them. What a boost to my morale, as well as my faith, in once again seeing the Lord's love and concern for us, even for the little things in life.

This was important to our Lord because it was important to me. How beautiful to see this kind of love demonstrated through this experience! These were things that stuck with us and increased our faith on a daily basis when the enemy would attempt to discourage us. We had so much to learn in our walk with Christ.

Becoming a believer is in many ways like moving to a new culture. We found that many times the things we'd be searching for would indeed be available, but we just didn't know where to look. And so, it is with Christ. So much is available for us, but we fail to appropriate all that we have and so we struggle on our own, perhaps even giving up, because it's too hard for us. Of course it is! Only Christ's power within us makes it possible to live and respond, supernaturally, to life and its varied situations.

Thursday, April 16, 1987   Cool–Cloudy

Spent all day at the office today with Al for the prayer meeting. Al fixed supper and washed dishes. *Thank You so much, Lord, for a compassionate, understanding husband. You have blessed me so!*

Saturday, April 18, 1987   Windy–Warm–Sunny

Worked all day baking, cooking, cleaning, etc. Al did work around the house and yard. It feels so good to get out in the yard and feel the warm sun on our backs. *Thank You, Father, for Your provision of this house! Help us to maintain it and use it to Your honor and glory.*

Sunday, April 19, 1987   Gorgeous–Sunny Day

It looks like Easter, but it doesn't feel like Easter. Miss family and friends. Should have made plans to have someone over. It's lonely on holidays.

The contrast between easy and hard life made me think again of our "family" in the East. We have so much here, not because we deserve it, but merely because we were born outside of the Iron Curtain. *Oh God, be with those who face such tremendous hardships. Give them Your hope and Your power to endure.*

Wednesday, April 22, 1987 — Cloudy–Rainy

This has been such a "loose-ends" day. Don't know if it's homesickness or what, but I'm feeling terribly alone and disorientated. *How I thank You, Lord, that You are my solid Rock, the one who never changes, and that You hold me close as I cling to You.* Al came home really beat. He hasn't slept well lately.

Sunday, April 26, 1987 — Cloudy–Windy–Cool

Al picked flowers from the backyard and brought them into the house. *Lord, help me show him I appreciate these little acts of thoughtfulness and love.*

Thursday, April 30, 1987 — Warm–Sunny

Busy day, so we were both really tired tonight, so we went to bed early. No more than got to sleep when the fireworks started. Literally! May 1 is a very important holiday here—kinda like our Labor Day, New Year's Day, and Fourth of July all wrapped up in one. The fireworks display was held in a sports arena near our place, so we had a perfect view of all the beautiful, sparkly demonstrations. They were really impressive! I couldn't help but wonder as I watch the brilliance of these fireworks how much more beautiful and awesome it will be when the Lord returns in the sky with angels and heralding bands of trumpets. What a day that will be!

Monday, May 11, 1987 — Partly Cloudy–Mild

It's been a lonely, discouraging day, and I feel so worthless! I guess that's exactly what Satan likes—to get us thinking we aren't capable, and we're not contributing. So help me see Your face today, Lord. Let me hear Your loving promises and give me strength to do Your will.

Wednesday, May 13, 1987 — Rain–All Day

I've been trying to pull some thoughts together for speaking Monday evening at our women's meeting, but I'm not having much success.

Just when I decide on what I'll use and become familiar with it, then other things enter in and I get all "undone" again. *Lord, I ask that You would bind Satan in this. Keep him from trying to distract me, and then just, thru Your Holy Spirit, make it plain to me what I should share and help me put it together. Thank You, Jesus.*

Friday, May 15, 1987   Sunny-Fair-Wind

Al and I watched the Billy Graham video film on Romania. It was shocking to see the Romania film—things look so good! Couldn't believe we'd actually seen those same cities—they look so good on the film! Couldn't see the dirt, grime, rundown buildings, long lines waiting for food, gas, empty store shelves, etc. Even the commentary was grossly inaccurate in that what was said was so incomplete. And the terminology! They made it sound so reasonable and tolerable! *Oh God, help us all in giving a clear picture to the West.*

Sunday, May 17, 1987   Sunny-Beautiful

Al helped me a little tonight in preparing my sharing for the women's meeting tomorrow night. *Oh God, work thru me to encourage and teach Your ways.*

Monday, May 18, 1987   Sunny-Wind

Spent most of the day praying and preparing to speak for the meeting tonight. I can't believe how anxious I get! *Lord God, help me to get things into perspective and to take my eyes off myself and focus on You.*

Chapter 16

BETTY'S SOLO TRIP TO USA

The following entries from Betty's journal describe how we learned that Betty's mom was back in the hospital again only a short time after having major heart surgery for blocked arteries. After some days of agonizing over whether to go back or not, we decided that Betty needed to go back for a time to help with her mom's care.

Tuesday, June 2, 1987　　　　　　　　**Mostly Sunny – Windy**

Diane called this afternoon saying Mom's back in the hospital again. The new vessel is 80 percent closed! *Oh God, this must be so discouraging for Mom.* I feel I should go back and be there with Mom, so Len and Diane don't have to do it all. *Lord Jesus, I know we don't have the money, and I know I'm needed here, so what should I do? Father, I ask that You show me clearly! So clearly that even Al will know it's from You.*

Thursday, June 4, 1987　　　　　　　　　　　　**Sunny**

Al and I went to Donau Center for his meeting while I shopped. We met at noon, had a bite to eat, and went on downtown to check airlines and flights back to the States. I got real tired so decided to go home on the train; Al would come later. It was pouring rain when I got to Wiener Neudorf, and I then realized I didn't have my house keys! What to do? I bought some aerogramms, went to a café, and wrote. I was so tired, but had to wait till Al got home. What a day.

Friday, June 5, 1987 — Cold-Rain-Dark

Got up at 4:00 a.m. Still no word from Diane. Al worked in the basement all morning. The drain had overflowed, and now we have a soggy mess—wet books, boxes, etc.

Diane called at 2:30. Mom is better now and will be released from the hospital on Saturday. The pain is better, but the vessel is still 80 percent restricted. Now we need to decide if I should go back if she needs another surgery.

Saturday, June 6, 1987 — Lovely-Sunny-Warm

Al worked on his sermon all morning. I did cleaning, cooking, shopping, etc.

In the afternoon, we drove down to Baden; we just walked all over town, enjoyed a concert in the park, had coffee near the town square, and then realized we had locked the keys in the car! We took the train back home, broke a window to get into the house, got the keys, and Al took the train back to Baden for the car. Ein schlechter tag!

Sunday, June 7, 1987 — Very Warm-Windy

Had lunch on the patio, did a few tasks, and then watched the *Heidi* movie. I'm feeling so sick today! Al's been so sweet and understanding. I can't even imagine being without him for five to six weeks. *Thank You, Lord, for his love for me. But help me be strong if I need to be. I depend on You and Your strength, Lord, to get me thru these coming months and make me a blessing to those I'm around.*

Monday, June 8, 1987   Sunny – Windy – Cool in p.m.

It's been such a beautiful day. Al worked in the garden. I did laundry. We ate on our deck and took a rest under the apricot tree. *We're so grateful, Father, for Your goodness to us in giving us this comfortable home.* I love being able to just walk outdoors into a private yard, pick flowers, pull weeds, hang up clothes. It's wonderful! We had our first radish today! It was pretty strong, but we loved it!

Saturday, June 13, 1987   Sunny – Warm

Did a lot of walking today. Al's at the office working on his sermon for tomorrow. Won't get home till late tonight.

These Saturdays without Al are yukky, but thank You, Lord, for his commitment to You and his obedience in accepting the challenge of preaching when he has so many other things to do.

Sunday, June 14, 1987   Sunny – Warm (Actually Hot!)

It was a good worship service, and church was nearly full. Al did well in delivering his message. I'm always so filled with love, respect, and yes, pride when I see him up there behind the pulpit. *What a work You have done in his life, Lord! I just praise You and thank You for Your beautiful way of teaching and maturing us.*

Friday, June 19, 1987   Cloudy – Rain

Al and I went downtown and reserved a flight back to North Dakota for me on Sunday. I'm so scared! Don't think Al really understands how difficult these long trips are for me.

Saturday, June 20, 1987

Called Diane yesterday to say I'd be there on Sunday.

Sunday, June 21, 1987

Coming back to the US proves to be quite stressful. It's wonderful to be with family; however, hearing people complain about what is or is not available here just blows my mind! There are so many products available, and yet I hear this disgruntling attitude. *Thanks, Lord, for the opportunities I've already had to witness to people.* Virtual strangers are awed by what I share, but are willing to listen and to try to be more grateful for what they have.

Mom's Second Surgery

Mom had her second major heart bypass surgery on the twenty-eighth of July. I'd had time to relieve Diane of Mom's care for a while and to help Mom visit a lot of her friends and relatives prior to her surgery. Having already gone through this horrendous trauma before, she knew what was coming. Although she tried to be brave, she was understandably anxious and afraid of what lay ahead.

During the surgery, there were complications, such as bleeding that couldn't be stopped for many hours, so the day was filled with tension and anxiety. We were ever so grateful for her survival, though, and prayed that she would recover and enjoy the freedom from pain once healed. She was in so much pain she would say, "It's so much worse than last time." My heart broke each time I was permitted to visit her in intensive care.

In the midst of all this uncertainty, the Lord brought a wonderful gift to me in the form of our daughter, Julie, and her family, who lived in Colorado. It was my first introduction to our granddaughter. Oh what joy to see this little bundle with lots of dark hair, olive complexion, and dimpled chin. Of course, she was the most lovable baby ever.

Then it was time for me to return to Vienna. It was awfully good to be reunited with Al after being in the USA for about a month's time. We got caught up on a lot of things the first few days after I returned; however, soon, he was working late a lot of nights, and so I didn't see much of him. He took trips to distribute literature and coordinate the drop-offs in the East.

Chapter 17

GRACE CHURCH— VIENNA

Prayer Letter Sent by Al—April 1989

Grace Church is an evangelical, interdenominational, English-speaking church that we started in early 1988 with a group of a dozen or so. By the time we left to move to the Soviet Union in 1991, Betty counted 265 people attending on a particular Sunday, with over twenty countries represented from around the globe. (Church potluck dinners were very interesting!) We also had started a small German-speaking congregation.

> There is one body and one Spirit, just as you also
> were called in one hope of your calling; one Lord,
> one faith, one baptism, one God and Father of all,
> who is over all and through all and in all.
> —EPHESIANS 4:4-6

Where will you find a Conservative Baptist from the USA, a Pentecostal from Nigeria, an American Presbyterian, and a Filipino from the Assembly of God denomination all working very closely as a ministry team? The answer is at Grace Church in Vienna, Austria, where these four men (including myself) are the elders. [We didn't have a paid pastor; rather, the four of us elders took turns preaching.]

Grace Church Vienna Elders — Al is Second from Right

While our main purpose for being here is to help train pastors and other church leaders in Eastern Europe, the Lord has also given us a leadership role in this newly established church in Vienna. In both situations, the Lord is working in a powerful way that is totally beyond our comprehension.

In spite of incredible diversity of backgrounds, there has been unity and love for one another demonstrated in a way that God has used to bring many new people into His family. We've seen a real enthusiasm for evangelism among the congregation, and this has resulted in rapid growth of the church.

Each week people bring co-workers from their jobs, a neighbor from their apartment building, or often even people they met on a bus or tram. One lady was on her way to church and invited a young nurse from the Philippines who was on the same train that morning. She agreed to come along to our worship service—and over two hours later, after the worship service and fellowship time, we learned that the package she was holding all this time contained fresh fish that she had been taking to her sister across town. We've experienced the joy of seeing many of these people come to trust in Christ for salvation and now they're growing in faith and in service and sharing the Good News of Christ Jesus with others.

Working with Grace Church has been a very rich experience and helpful in relating to those with whom we work in Eastern Europe.

In both cases we work with an incredible diversity of people in every way; culture, language, education, denominational backgrounds, and the gifts that God has given to individuals.

Teaching Sunday School

One of the special joys God brought into Betty's life while living in Vienna was the privilege of teaching Sunday School to a very diverse class of children from Ghana, Nigeria, Canada, USA, and other countries. Reaching across these cultural boundaries with the gospel was indeed a challenge, but oh what a foretaste of heaven, as well. We never fully got over the incredible confidence God placed in us, to allow us this lovely, if difficult at times, experience.

Betty's Sunday School Class — Vienna, Austria

Chapter 18

EASTERN EUROPEAN TRAVELS CONTINUE— 1980s

Eastern Europe Travel Challenges

Throughout the 1980s, we, and our smuggling and distribution teams, made many trips into the Iron Curtain countries of Eastern Europe, where life was very different from our life in Austria. Because we would carry various quantities of our seminary training materials, we traveled via our personal vehicles. Just a few of the most common difficulties we experienced were:

- **Language difficulties:** While most of the individuals we worked with spoke at least a little English or German, all other languages made clear, accurate communication difficult.

- **Being followed to a believer's home or reported to the secret police by neighborhood informers—of which there are many**: Providing Christian leaders with training materials and biblical teaching was highly illegal and strongly opposed by the government. If we were seen visiting Christian leaders, they could be questioned and possibly arrested, tortured, and imprisoned.

- **Finding gasoline**: As visitors from the West, we were allowed to buy gas coupons, but there were very few gas stations, which were often closed because they had no gasoline or no electricity for pumping gas. It required some serious strategizing to keep gas in the tank.

- **Car breakdowns:** The extremely rough roads were hard on our car. Repair parts for our Western cars were not available. Mechanic services, if available, were generally very primitive. Generally, if your car broke down, you needed to have it towed back to Western Europe (an expensive two- or three-day project).

- **Finding safe food:** A lot of our meals were taken in our car. We brought cans of sardines, some canned beans, and similar goods and then would pick up fresh bread as we traveled. Food or polluted drinking water purchased while traveling often caused sickness.

- **Eye and breathing problems from air pollution:** The heavy diesel fumes on the highway and other air pollution, such as from factories spewing out thick black smoke, caused eye and breathing problems.

- **Difficulty keeping clean:** Often, there was no water, or due to various circumstances, we went a long time without washing, brushing out teeth, or changing clothes. One colleague reported going seventeen days without being able to take a shower or bath. Phew!

- **Traffic trials:** Accidents were a common occurrence on these roads. For example, when we arrived back in Vienna from one of our trips to the East, we learned that one of our dear friends in Yugoslavia and his family had been in a tragic mishap that took the life of their small infant and left our friend in critical condition.

- **Places to sleep:** Tourist hotels were expensive and closely watched, with cameras and microphones typically found in the rooms, in the restaurants, and in the parking areas. When we stayed in a hotel, we were often followed whenever we left the hotel. Therefore, we used hotel rooms only when necessary or after we'd completed all our contact visits. We typically stayed in campgrounds or sometimes slept in our car. One colleague commented on one place where he stayed, saying, "It wasn't too bad, except for the torture device they called a bed." With the back problems that Betty had, the lack of good beds was a concern for us.

Train Travel Stories

While Betty and I—and our smuggling and distribution teams—needed to always travel by vehicle in order to transport our cargo, our teaching teams typically traveled by train. Several of my teammates (names withheld) told some of their train travel experiences:

A Change in Perspective

It was a bad overnight trip on the train. I nearly froze to death even though I tried to sleep with all my clothes on. Every time the train hit a rough stretch of track, the window would pop open, fully exposing me to a blast of cold arctic air. I had to get up each time to close it, so I got no sleep. I did get my miserable head cold to go down and become a full-fledged chest cold.

Our training group met in one apartment, and I stayed in another. They bundled me up in a local style coat and scarf for the walk in between. I set my alarm for 4:45 a.m., and my driver got me to the train station in time for me to freeze out in the cold for a half hour waiting for the train.

I'll never forget the crowded train—standing room only! Being pressed together in a standing position for four and a half hours does not do wonders for my temperament! Just as I was really feeling sorry for myself, a group of five or six people at the other end of the car began to sing. As I listened, I realized that they were singing Christian songs! My anger and self-pity began to wane as the sweet spirit of these young Christians flowed through their singing. This gift from God brought my temporary inconveniences into better perspective.

Barefoot in Bucharest

[Another teammate experienced a frustrating theft while traveling by train to Bucharest for training church leaders.]

At the border entering Romania, the guards asked the usual questions.

About 2:00 a.m., the guards did a thorough search of my luggage. At 2:30 a.m., the guard came by again and seemed very interested in certain items in my bag. Finally, I dozed off about 3:00 a.m. for the usual thirty-minute snooze.

I was surprised to wake up at 6:15 a.m. since I never slept more than an hour on the train. I was astonished to find no shoes to put my feet into! I was petrified to find that my entire luggage had been stolen. I was greatly relieved to find my passport and money still in the pocket of my jacket, which was hanging in the opposite corner of the compartment—and miraculously missed by the thieves.

After dealing with the reality that I had been robbed, and prayerfully working through the feelings of having no shoes for walking around, I located the porter and reported the theft. The porter thankfully searched for some shoes once we debarked in Bucharest and brought them to me.

After attracting all this attention, I decided to leave the city immediately rather than lead the police to my contact. The train was very crowded, with people literally fighting for seats—especially the group of Poles who were totally drunk and fighting with the people in my compartment. Finally, after crossing safely back into Hungary, I was told by train personnel that thieves would inject a gas into a compartment, inducing a deep sleep in everyone in the compartment, and then with a special key would enter the compartment and steal everything they wanted.

The Howling Mob

After completing a long day of meetings in city "A," I tried to catch my train to city "B," leaving shortly after midnight. The train appeared to be overbooked by at least a thousand persons, and there was no one there to supervise the boarding process. It was a mob scene, with people climbing in windows, plus a solid body jam of around fifty people trying to force their way in at every train door, even though every car was already jammed full.

I tried to get on my car and got one foot on the first step and my right hand on the pull-up rail, when a young fellow put his arm across my throat from the left and choked me as he gripped the rail below my hand. The crowd behind was pushing hard, and I became faint, lost my grip, and was pushed back out into the howling mob. I retained my grip on my one piece of luggage, but as the train pulled out without me, I realized my passport case was missing. It contained my American passport, almost $500.00 in US currency, $500.00 in American traveler's checks, my return ticket to Vienna, and my hotel coupons.

Al and Betty Return to Romania

We found it necessary to stay in a hotel tonight. There was one small light bulb on the high ceiling, so there'd be no reading that night. The blankets and sheets had not seen soap and water for a very long time, but we tried not to think about what bugs we might take home with us from here. The faucet was broken off in the bathroom, so no water. The paint was peeling, and the drapes were a sorry sight to behold. I (Betty) couldn't even begin to describe the smell in this room. Sleep would be limited tonight.

Nevertheless, we did get some sleep in spite of the shortcomings of the room. We ate some snacks in our room in the morning and then headed out to make our next contact. The fog hung heavily over the city, giving everything a dark, eerie sense of foreboding.

Perhaps God would use this cover to protect us as we made contact. We entered the home safely, and it seemed as though we were back in the time of Paul and Timothy. Our friends were sitting in this simple dark room with a dim light focused on the Bible open on the table. Their faces were aglow with the strength and love of their commitment to God, drawing from Him, and from each

Slow Highway Traffic Romania — 1980s

other. It was beautiful. They treasured these times of fellowship with brothers and sisters in Christ from the West. They were most grateful for the bananas we brought from Vienna, which were not available in their country.

As we visited with them, they shared how badly they needed Bibles for their people. They readily agreed that food and medicine would be nice, but Bibles were what they MUST have.

Back in our hotel room, we had some hours to pass before attempting our next contact. We spent time praying silently about this challenge, and I gave Al a Scripture verse I had written on a piece of scrap paper. As soon as he had memorized it, I destroyed the paper.

We left our room and saw a nearby policeman really giving us "the eye." As we waited for our tram, we saw him discreetly talking to a man nearby. This man suddenly started acting very drunk and quickly got on the tram with us, keeping up the pretense. For a "drunk," his eyes were completely clear and focused directly on us, so we strongly suspected he was assigned by the policeman to tail us.

Sure enough, he got off the tram exactly where we were planning to get off to visit our contact. So instead, we stayed on the tram and went on to a further stop. This could have had dire consequences if we had gotten off as intended and gone to our contact. *Thank you, Father, for alerting us!*

We were on our way out of the city now. There were more horse- and oxen-drawn wagons and diesel trucks on the road than cars. The sun was shining as we pulled over alongside the road, found a tree for shade, and had lunch and considered all we'd just experienced.

Information Gathered by Us from Our In-Country Contacts

One of our contacts that we did visit informed us that another member of his church leader training group had been questioned and drugged by the police with "truth serum" and consequently spilled much information about the group and their studies. Praise the Lord that we had been unsuccessful in meeting this intended contact when we were being followed. We were thankful he knew us only as Mike and Leah Hanson.

Pastor J., a member of one of our study groups, had a close call with death just before Christmas when he noticed something charred black near a downspout on his house. While examining it, he touched the downspout. He said the shock he got probably would have killed him had he not been standing on three inches of ice, which caused him to slip and fall free from the metal downspout.

The electrician he called to disconnect the live wire from the downspout said it had to be a deliberate attempt to kill or injure anyone who touched it. All three of the "live" downspouts were in areas where his children and their friends often played. In a subsequent mandatory visit to the secret police headquarters, Pastor J. said their prior knowledge of the incident almost certainly implicated them in this.

Another group member reported that government authorities had bulldozed their church building and another nearby because they were accused of meeting illegally for prayer.

On a more positive note, one pastor told one of our teammates of their encouragement as they saw God working. He stated, "What we see here is only the tip of the iceberg. We are facing a spiritual explosion. The Spirit of God is at work, and no one can stop Him! We expect a great breakthrough of the Spirit. I feel it in the air. I see it coming. Pray for us."

We were scheduled to visit this pastor very soon. Hundreds in his city had recently turned to Christ. His excitement and enthusiasm over what God was doing explained why we and our teammates were so willing to experience the discomforts and hassles of traveling to meet with him and other similar servants of God in his country, one of the most difficult countries for Christian workers. God was doing great things there, and it was a great blessing to have the privilege of bringing material gifts, spiritual teaching, and encouragement and to be personally involved and see it all firsthand.

One of the stories we heard from our Romanian study groups had to do with a chart on the wall at one of the government offices. They said teachers in the Romanian school system were required to come down to this office periodically to view this chart, which showed the steady decline of Christianity in their country. Apparently, they used this chart to make the point that, eventually, there would be no Christians in Romania. More recently, they said this chart showed Christianity actually growing. The chart disappeared, and teachers were no longer made to come down to this office to view the chart.

It was the positive stories we heard and the optimism of the spiritual leaders in Romania that provided so much encouragement for us to keep on keeping on in our work with them.

Albania was one Communist country where we did not have any church groups studying with us. The Albanian Communist dictator, Enver Hoxha, boasted that there were no longer any churches in Albania. Christianity had been eliminated, and Albania was declared the world's first atheist state.

Nevertheless, I (Al) did have the privilege of having a very small role in getting a manuscript of the Bible translated by Albanian Christians into modern Albanian smuggled out of the country to me in Austria. From there, it was sent to England to be published. A few years later, these Bibles were brought into Albania by the thousands, and Enver Hoxha was no longer in power.

Chapter 19

FEAR AND STRONG CHRISTIANS

They band themselves together against the life of the righteous and condemn the innocent to death. But the LORD has been my refuge, and my God the rock of my refuge. –PSALM 94:21-22

Sometimes, we took for granted the ability of the spiritual leaders with whom we worked in Eastern Europe to stand firm and without fear against all opposition. It was important that we recognized how determined and how intensely hateful the opposition could be when God's people chose to honor and serve Him regardless of the cost to themselves.

We also needed to acknowledge that these people were also weak human beings who often experienced great fear and stress over what might happen to them. In fact, victory over fear was recently mentioned by one group of believers as being one of the greatest needs among Christians in their country.

We often heard that fear was a problem even among the youngest Christian school children. Teachers in the atheistic school systems sometimes put unbelievable pressure on children to renounce Christ and to inform on their parents. The daughter of one key Christian leader suffered a nervous breakdown as a result of such pressure. Many others told us of their children being interrogated and threatened, not only by teachers, but by the police!

Possibly even more difficult than personal fears for themselves was the fear that parents have for their children, and the children's fear for what might happen to their parents. A couple months prior, the police beat someone we worked with into unconsciousness for having Christian books from the West. Afterwards, the police sat outside this family's house watching all their activities, probably eavesdropping electronically on everything that was said in the house. Could you imagine the stress this would put on you and your family?

Their answer to combat the fears they faced every day was to constantly turn to the Lord in prayer for His reassurance and encouragement that He was with them. Their dependence on the Lord in prayer is addressed by Rodica Maianu in our April 1986 newsletter that follows below.

Rodica is a relative of Dr. Alex Maianu, founder of our Emmanuel Ministry organization in Fargo. She came to the USA as a Romanian immigrant and served with our office staff. She wrote the following article about serving God in the USA versus serving God behind the Iron Curtain.

Strong Christians — Communist Eastern Europe vs. USA

Many people here in the USA see the Christians behind the Iron Curtain as brave, strong Christians—more faithful to their God than those here. I was attributed with such qualities myself many times, and I was tempted to accept them as support for a "legitimate" pride. But I couldn't do this without looking a little deeper inside life here in America as compared to there. Here is what I found out:

Being persecuted as a Christian in Romania means to be mocked, ridiculed, threatened with loss of your job, and often followed by the police. These are hardships that many Christians here think they wouldn't be able to endure. Living in a Communist country where faith in God is a crime, you need to depend on God not only every day, but every hour of every day. How can you forget to pray when your prayer is a cry for strength and wisdom for the day ahead? How can you miss your devotion time when you are in such a need for a word from God? Every day is a matter of life and death.

Prayer is a state of mind, an almost permanent conversation with Him, your Friend and Counselor. Does this mean that these people are strong? They are actually very weak, unable to face the circumstances they are in—unless they rely completely on God.

Under persecution, the difficulties force you to depend on God, while here in the USA, where life is easy and free, it's much harder to keep a close walk with Him. We feel able to manage all things and situations alone, and thus we are easily caught in the trap of trying to live our Christian life on our own strength.

Living in the USA, the temptations are not evident; they are hidden under the veil of a life free of fear and persecution. Traps exist on both sides of the world, even though they are very different. To live a genuine life in Christ is not an easy task, no matter where you live. We need His strength and guidance here as well as there. Only the struggle may be different.

Trip Back to the States

It was time to make a trip back to the States to report to our mission leaders, to those who supported us with prayer and finances, and of course, to see our family.

Family members had been truly remarkable in how they supported and encouraged us. I (Betty) knew they didn't understand our calling and the why of it all. But that didn't stop them from being there when we needed them. We were so blessed in many and untold ways too numerous to state. How I needed them. Our schedule of speaking and sharing with churches, small groups, and individuals turned out to be rather grueling. We had very few meals by ourselves, so maintaining our relationship with each other became a real challenge.

Among the more practical things we needed to take care of during our time in the USA was to shop for clothes that would help us blend in as we traveled and worked in Eastern Europe. However, finding things that looked like they came from the forties was truly difficult. To "fit in" and appear as though we were part of the society in Eastern Europe, we needed to dress like they did. So, we attempted to find things that would allow us to be in country without getting the attention of the authorities.

Beginning our long-delayed doctor appointments, one of the first things that came to light was that I was diagnosed with Reynaud's syndrome. It's when the blood vessels become compressed by cold and restrict to the point of not being able to transport the much-needed life force that keeps us alive. This is an uncomfortable and incurable condition. The only treatment is to work up a sweat each day and live in a warm climate. Unfortunately, we live in a cold climate in Europe. We often have long waits in the cold for public transportation, and we're often in homes or hotel rooms with little or no heat. It was often a challenge for me to keep the blood flowing normally.

There were much more serious diagnoses later on, but first, let me share about our return to Vienna.

We were so excited about being back in Vienna and couldn't wait to set foot in our home. Unfortunately, we had people staying in our house while we were gone and didn't expect to see such filth and disarray upon our return. The dirt, the grease-caked kitchen, the filth, and the dead plants had me praying nonstop as I unpacked, asking God to help me cope with this disappointment. I remembered how the Lord suggested food and rest for Elijah in his depression.

So, I sat down, ate an orange, and went directly to bed. The Lord permitted me to sleep, and when I awakened, the situation was still the same; the filth had not changed, but I had.

Still, the adjustment to life in Europe seemed harder this time. We struggled with loneliness, lack of English resources, limited variety of familiar goods available to us in the stores, and traveling long distances for shopping each day. Making it even more difficult was our need to go to different stores for almost every individual item on our shopping list. The public transportation was good, but oh how cold it was to stand out in the open, waiting for the buses or trams. *Help us, Lord, to be thankful for all the good things we have and not to focus on the things we wish we had.*

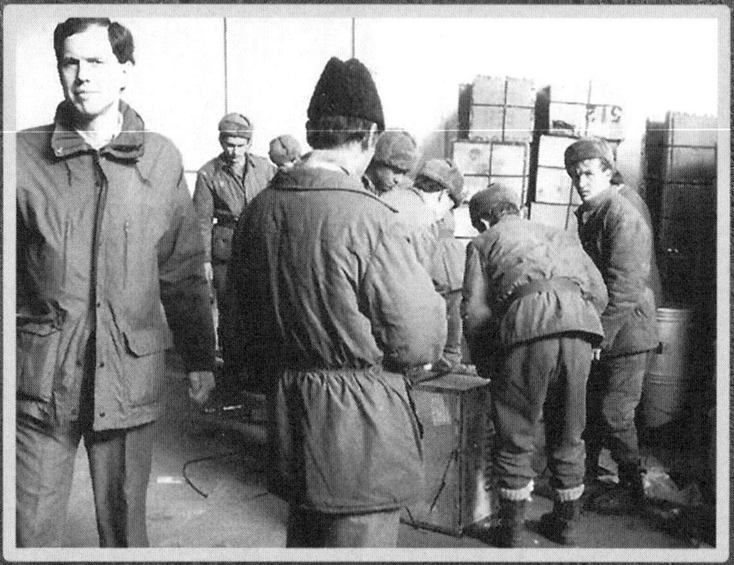

Part Three

Chapter 20

EASTERN EUROPEAN REVOLUTIONS BREWING

Al and Betty's Letter from Europe — Fall 1989

A young East German couple and their six-year-old son cautiously approached a remote spot along the Austro-Hungarian border. They were one family among the many trying to escape across this section of the Iron Curtain, where some of the barriers had been dismantled and surveillance had been reduced. Freedom was within reach. Suddenly, gunshots rang out, and the young father was dead. In their search for freedom, they came so close, but their hopes and dreams of a better life were ended by the act of one border guard.

Changes in the Soviet Union — 1989

While it was still dangerous to attempt to escape from the Communist countries of Eastern Europe and the Soviet Union, present church leaders in the Soviet Union believed they had more openness and pleaded with us to show them how to use the new opportunities they had. They said they'd been invited to minister in the prisons, but they didn't know how to do open Christian ministry now that they were legally allowed. They'd been invited to minister in the hospitals, but they didn't know how to do that openly either.

We prayed that God would work through our ministry and others to train leaders for existing churches, new house churches, prison and hospital ministries, street evangelism, and on and on.

At the same time, our coworkers returning from there reported that there were now thousands and thousands of disillusioned people who were searching for "real freedom"—the freedom of the Spirit that can be known only through Jesus Christ as Savior. The spiritual hunger and openness to the gospel was awesome! They said that almost everyone in almost every situation was interested in talking about God—waitresses, taxi drivers, university professors, public officials, tour guides, and people on the street that recognized them as Westerners.

We felt a deep urgency to help reach these people with the Good News of eternal life through faith in Jesus Christ. We wanted to see them brought safely "over the border" into the Kingdom of God.

Here at our home in Austria this September, we experienced an incredible crop of apricots from the tree in our backyard. Betty made apricot jam, breads, pies, and cobblers. She even prepared apricots to store in our freezer for use later. We also gave away as much as we could, but in the end, there was still far more than we could harvest and save. Much of it was simply lost.

We viewed the spiritual harvest in the Soviet Union in 1989 in much the same way. From our location in Austria, the Soviet Union was virtually in our backyard. We could "see" the bountiful potential spiritual harvest, but the task seemed overwhelming. What could we do with our limited resources in this land of over 270 million people with over one hundred languages spread out over six thousand miles from east to west? Adding to the sense of urgency, almost everyone we talked to believed that the present opportunity would only last for a few years. Of course, only God could accomplish this task, but we had the privilege of serving Him in this task at this time.

Jesus told His disciples, "Do you not say, 'There are still four months, and then comes the harvest'? Behold, I tell you, raise your eyes and observe the fields, that they are white for harvest. Already the one who reaps is receiving wages and is gathering fruit for eternal life, so that the one who sows and the one who reaps may rejoice together" (John 4:35–36).

As we extended our ministry into the vast new areas opening up to us, we faced the immense task of providing solid, positive teaching in the face of so many negative influences. In the Soviet Union especially, we heard the same request, again and again, from the true spiritual leadership (i.e. those not subject to the Communist government), "We need Bibles, and we need solid teaching." For decades, both had been largely unavailable.

Here are a few of the main problems caused by these shortages:

- **Shallow Teaching:** Teaching was all too often very shallow and represented the speaker's opinions more than solid Biblical teaching. This was due to several reasons. Most pastors worked long hours at secular jobs and had no time to prepare for teaching or preaching. Most had very little, if any, training and virtually no resources. Many had only a New Testament, with others having only portions of that.

- **Emphasis on Works:** There is all too often an emphasis on "works" rather than on God's grace. Outward appearance (dress, behavior, etc.) was given more importance than faith in Christ's sacrifice as the means of salvation. Because of this, many had no assurance of salvation.

- **Limited Discernment:** People in the church had so little teaching that they were ready to absorb everything that came their way—good or bad.

- **Focus on Materialism:** With the new possibilities for acquiring material things, even many pastors and lay leaders were being pulled away from their ministry by money-making opportunities. Many saw Westerners simply as a source of material benefits.

- **Christian Infighting:** Perhaps the most discouraging of all were the many instances of Christians fighting with each other, instead of demonstrating love and unity among the brethren. Such instances were all too often an effective negative witness in the eyes of nonbelievers.

- **Weak Evangelistic Efforts:** With a weak foundation in the Bible, the attraction of materialism, and a preoccupation with legalism and traditionalism, there was often little effort directed towards evangelism even though there was an unprecedented interest among nonbelievers in spiritual things. The harvest was riper and richer than most of the national churches realized or were prepared to deal with.

As we faced these great needs in the newly opened areas, perhaps the thing that encouraged us the most was that we could clearly see the growth that had taken place in the ministry of the men we'd been training for several years or more. One of our students who pastored several churches made this comment: "People in the churches are noticing the difference in the men who are receiving Biblical Education by Extension training. These men are much more effective in their preaching. There is content and application. Many laymen in our area have become pastors, with new churches being started because of the training."

We praised God for these encouraging signs that He was indeed using BEE World in His work. Even though there now were definitely greater possibilities to do Christian work in this area, there were still many in positions of authority who were committed to opposing all that God was doing.

"How are they to believe in Him whom they have not heard? And how are they to hear without a preacher? But how are they to preach unless they are sent? Just as it is written: 'How beautiful are the feet of those who bring good news of good things!'" (Romans 10:14–15).

News Time by Al — December 1989

"News time" had come to be a time that almost everyone looked forward to here in Vienna. Even in our office building, radios were switched on when it was time for the latest news broadcast.

The Egyptian and Turkish newspaper vendors on the street corners of Vienna did a brisk business as they ran up and down between the cars when the lights turned red, tossing their newspapers with the latest news into the cars and quickly collecting their seven schillings from the drivers before the light turned green.

At home, we'd started recording the evening news broadcasts as nearly every day history making changes took place all around us. It began in Poland this past summer, followed by the Hungarians as they did away with Marxism-Leninism. They then tore down part of the Iron Curtain between Austria and Hungary and scheduled free elections.

Then it was the East Germans' turn. First, thousands traveled across Czechoslovakia into Hungary and out to the West through the newly opened "holes" in the Iron Curtain on the Hungarian border. We watched them come through Vienna by the tens of thousands on their way to West Germany in special trains and buses and in long columns of their tiny little two-cycle Trabant cars. Then, suddenly, their hardline Communist government resigned, the borders were opened, and they poured into West Germany by the millions, only now just to visit.

Next, it was the turn of the Czechs and Slovaks. On December 12, newspaper headlines proclaimed boldly, "Czechoslovakia Celebrates Democracy with Bells and Sirens!" The story went on to tell how all the church bells in the country were ringing, all factory sirens were blowing, and all car horns were blaring in a great countrywide "noise concert." Two hundred thousand people poured across the border into Austria on foot just to celebrate their new freedom to do so. We witnessed the hundreds of thousands that came the thirty miles into Vienna in a hodgepodge of buses, cars, motorcycles, bicycles, and whatever vehicles were available, causing traffic chaos.

Few had any money, but they brought flowers and handmade gifts to give to Austrians they hoped to meet. Austrians met them with food and hot drinks, offers of overnight lodging, and gifts of cash so they could buy something to take home with them.

Many of the Czechoslovaks were proudly wearing their red, white, and blue "freedom ribbons" that had been hastily made out of whatever material they could find. I asked one Czech visitor if he would sell me his ribbon. He kept shaking his head "no" until I explained that I was an American and that I would love to have it as a souvenir of the historic changes in his country. Then he unpinned it from his jacket and gave it to me, refusing to take any payment for it.

In the midst of these exciting happenings, we made a trip to Budapest, Hungary, for a few days of rest. Our host gave us a ride to the police station, where we needed to register our presence. Along the way, in his very fragmented German, he commented very emotionally on the historical changes taking place in his country. As we drove past a huge statue surrounded by scaffolding, he explained that it was a statue of Lenin that was about to disappear.

As we continued down this wide boulevard, he described with a sweeping motion of his arm how in 1956, Russian soldiers had mowed down large numbers of the Hungarian people with machine guns on this same street. Now, with another wave of his arm, he proclaimed, "Russkies' weg! Russkies' weg!" After decades of imposing their destructive will on the country, the Russians were going away, leaving the Hungarian people to solve the great economic, political, and moral problems resulting from more than forty years under Communist rule.

All these incredible changes kept us looking forward to the next newscast to see what would happen next. In some of these Eastern European countries, the successful revolutions led to a very vocal, exuberant euphoria.

However, many expressed much pessimism and even whispers of war soon to come. There were great problems yet to be solved in each of these countries, and virtually everyone agreed that many things would get much worse before they got better. The biggest single question hanging over everyone was, "What will happen with Gorbachev and the Soviet Union?"

By mid-December, the newspaper headlines were not so encouraging. They read, "Now Romania Is Caught Up in Revolt, But There the Blood Is Flowing!" The Romanian borders were sealed. No one knew how much blood would be shed and what would come from it. The big question concerning Romania and its people under their Communist dictator, Nicolae Ceausescu, was: How will it end? At this point, only God knew.

How All These Changes Affected Us

We saw the incredible historic changes of 1989 as an answer to prayer. For decades, thousands of God's people had prayed for just such changes to take place, providing a greater opportunity to make Him known to the 400 million people in the Iron Curtain countries. We expected we could now travel more openly, more often, and work in vast areas that were previously closed to Westerners.

There was an even greater need to train pastors, teachers, church planters, and evangelists, as the millions who had never had access to the truth of the gospel were now being exposed to it and were generally very responsive. Thirty thousand people came forward in response to the invitation given by Billy Graham at one meeting in Budapest just prior to the Hungarian revolution in the fall of 1989. This was only one illustration of how God was working in Eastern Europe and how great a need there was to train leadership.

In early 1990, there was a sense of urgency that the Lord wanted us to use the great opportunities He had prepared through the overthrow of the Communist Eastern European governments and the greater openness for Christian witness in the Soviet Union.

There was considerable concern that we had only a limited time before there would be a reversal in the present situation, especially in the Soviet Union. There was also great concern that Western materialism and non-Christian cults would quickly fill the present vacuum unless people were reached with the true gospel first.

Chapter 21

NEW ROLE FOR US

Back in May 1989, we were asked to move to a different role—to serve as USSR Administrator for BEE World. In that role, we would concentrate solely on the Soviet Union, helping to administer the Biblical Education by Extension ministry of training thousands of pastors, house church leaders, and other lay leaders.

We viewed this as an incredible opportunity, but we were concerned about the limitations imposed by our various health problems. We also needed considerably more financial support, and we realized that our own training was much less than we would like it to be.

Delay in Job Change

However, before we were able to fully assume our new role of serving as BEE World administrator for the Soviet Union, the developing revolutions in the Communist Eastern European countries put things somewhat in limbo for a time.

While the other Eastern European Communist countries succeeded in overthrowing their governments without bloodshed, this was not the case in Romania. There, many people were killed in the revolt before the Communist dictator, Nicolae Ceausescu, and his wife, Elena, were executed by the Romanian military on December 25, 1989, after a brief military trial.

Shortly thereafter, we were asked by our organization in Vienna to visit Romania to learn how we might best provide badly needed aid of all types. In fact, during our visit (January 12–15), there was still some shooting going on as those who had been loyal to Ceausescu were still holding out in the mountains.

Al and Betty's Call to Emmanuel Office in Fargo

The message was short. Al reported to our Fargo office, "We are spending two thousand dollars of our expense account in order to immediately take much needed items (food, clothes, medicine, and specially required goods) into Romania in a van and to learn more first-hand what the greatest needs are."

Paulo M., a Brazilian who had recently joined our BEE World team in Vienna, accompanied us as he was planning to join the Romanian BEE World ministry. He had a van, so we loaded it with all kinds of gifts and items we knew were badly needed.

Betty's journal entries from January 12 through 15 described our 1990 visit to Romania at the tail-end of the revolution.

Thursday, January 11, 1990   Very Cold

On our way to Romania, we stop at a coffee shop in Hungary. The coffee shop with its Eastern European clientele was really a sight. Toothless old men gabbing away; little pear-shaped women in their babushkas; everyone wearing their coats and hats as it's far too cold to take them off. There was a flea market there, and Al finds a black fur hat for ten dollars. Good deal! He looks like Omar Sharif in the Dr. Zhivago movie.

Al's Dr. Zhivago Look with Fur Hat Purchased at Hungarian Flea Market

Friday, January 12, 1990　　　　　　　　Very Cold – Fog –
　　　　　　　　　　　　　　　　　　　Ice Crystals in the Air

As we cross the border into Romania this time, the atmosphere is completely different from last month, before the revolution. Everyone now greets us with the victory sign! There are smiles on everyone's faces. The guards were all wearing the freedom arm band—signs of allegiance to the Romanian people. No questions were asked; no search of us, or our vehicle.

As we head for Zalau in northern Romania, the road is horrible. It's narrow, with hairpin curves. There's lots of frost, with some ice crystals coming down. The mountains are lovely, the trees thick with a fresh, white covering of frost. My back is taking an incredible amount of abuse today, and toilet stops come no more than a couple times all day. We pass by a large herd of sheep and a shepherd with long wool cloak and staff.

We reach Zalau about 4:00 p.m. In our search for Levi's church, we stop and are deluged with Gypsies. Pastor Levi tells us the Gypsies now hang around the church because they know relief supplies are coming from the West.

Levi tells us some factors which precipitated the revolution, and factors which made it such a united effort and so successful.

1. **The TV station in Bucharest was extremely courageous and extremely instrumental.** The staff at the station directed the efforts of the revolt across the air waves and encouraged the military to join the people against the Securitate. There was a crisis one time when armed Securitate men broke into the station, but the army (now on the side of the people) "destroyed them," and the TV station remained on the air to continue directing the Romanian people in how to respond to each development.

2. **Another factor—a miracle of God—was the mild, springlike weather.** Never had Romania had such fair weather in late December. It allowed the people to remain on the streets day and night to maintain their front.

3. **"The cup was full."** The people could not take even one more drop of Ceausescu's tyranny. Pastor Lazlo Tokes's arrest in Timisoara was the "drop" that overflowed the cup and fueled the revolt.

[**NOTE**: Pastor Lazlo Tokes was one of the church leaders we'd been working with in the Western city of Timisoara. His church had grown from a few hundred to around five thousand as he preached powerfully from the Bible. As a result, the Romanian government determined to remove him to a small village where he would not have such an impact. When they sent men to remove him, the members of his church—and many others—all surrounded him and prevented them from taking him away. Orders were given to open fire on the crowd, and the revolution exploded from there.]

We travel on to Cluj and find a hotel for the night and watch the very moving scenes of the revolution being shown live on TV.

The beds here are like a deep soup bowl. Doesn't do much for my back. I tried sleeping on the floor until I remembered the mites. That changed my mind in a hurry.

Saturday, January 13, 1990

The atmosphere is so incredibly different now. No police around, very few soldiers, people talking openly and expressing themselves without fear.

In the bookstore, the staff was removing all Marxist/Communist books from the shelves. No books of Lenin or Ceausescu remain.

Many Romanian flags flying, though all with the Communist emblem cut out, and each flag with a black streamer to signify mourning.

Downtown Cluj has many places with memorials where candles are burning and floral wreaths and pictures of those who died in the revolution are displayed. Many people were standing around and reading the names of those who had been killed. It's a sobering scene—such a high price for freedom.

Books on Communism Being Removed from Bookstore Shelves

At 11:15, we head on over to Vasile's house [one of our students]. This was a new and exciting change—to be able to pull right up to our contact's house in broad daylight. We see Sven's van parked out front. [Sven was from Sweden and one of our smuggling and distribution team members.]

We visit with Sven and with Vasile's son until Vasile comes home. The son was in downtown Cluj during the shooting—seeing bodies fall all around him—but as far as we know, none of the people we know from our groups were killed or even injured.

Vasile expresses fear of being abandoned by us and other Western Christians and expresses a great need for our help now. They pray that we will not lose their vision, because we gave them hope. Because they felt our support, they were very brave and were very eager to risk much. Vasile asserts that even if we desert them, God will not. Vasile also shares with us that he has been approached to become the mayor of Cluj.

Al tries to reassure them that we are only beginning. We will help them, and we will support them. The vacuum needs to be filled quickly. The time is now to fully develop our training centers.

Before we left, we had an incredible prayer time together in Swedish, Brazilian Portuguese, English, and Romanian. *What a privilege to come to your throne together, Father, with these brothers.*

Portugese, Swedish, Romanian, and American Brothers in Christ

Our next stop was to see Dr. Dan, another of our study group leaders. His daughter, Christine, responded to our question as to what their greatest need now is. She said, "First of all, we need prayer to be effective and equipped as witnesses to non-Christians and for wisdom as to how to live in this newly received freedom."

Material needs:
- Equipment for printing
- Video teaching materials for Christian life

She feels food needs are not so great now as Romania will not now be exporting all their food. However, there is a critical need for medicines.

The Romanian people express their fear of Russia interfering in their newfound freedom. The Orthodox Church also is seen as a danger as they have declared war against the "new Protestants."

We watch TV tonight. People being interviewed are expressing their views on what they want to see in their new government. People really don't even know how to react to their new freedom, except to say they can now express themselves. There's a lot of confusion, and it may take years before some semblance of normalcy can be realized.

Sunday, January 14, 1990 Looks Like Snow – Dreary – Bleak
We're on our way to attend worship service at Second Baptist Church in Oradea. We're met at the church door by some of the staff who usher us in to the middle of the very front row. We can barely squeeze in through the packed hallway. I've never seen so many people trying to get into this church that normally holds about nine hundred. I'd guess today there are about two thousand people, with children and old people alike now finding a place to stand in the crushing crowd. Right now, there is no more standing room. What a thrill to see a church so packed and people so eager to worship. To God be the glory!!

After some hearty singing, there is a time for foreign visitors to give a greeting. We agree that Paulo will give the greeting for us. He is very well received, and his greeting is very appropriate, using the illustration of the church at Philippi—faithful in persecution and faithful in freedom.

As I look around, I see children listening attentively even after standing here in the crowd for several hours during this service. What a joy to see such a demonstration of reverence and discipline.

After the service, Bibles were made available for those who wanted them for as long as they lasted. We were caught right in the thick of it and couldn't even move out of our pew. With hundreds of hands reaching over and around us, we were unable to move for at least a half an hour until the Bibles were gone. What a thrill to see people so eager and hungry for the Scriptures! Even the children were eager to receive them.

After the crowd thinned out enough for us to move, I was able to visit with a couple girls who spoke English, and I was able to give them some English tracts and also a *Good Housekeeping* magazine. You would have thought I'd given them a rare jewel. They were beside themselves with excitement and gratitude.

Al asked a young fellow about obtaining some Romanian flags with the Communist seal cut out of the middle. He said we could go home with him, and he would give us his. The Romanian people demonstrate a servant attitude and loving, generous spirits.

While we were waiting for this fellow, a young girl joined him and insisted we all come to her place, and she would also gift us with a flag. Well, when we arrived at Camelia's home, she insisted that we come in with her, and we soon had an invitation to stay for dinner.

Here we were, three strangers, and she graciously invites us for dinner. Not only that, but she gives us her flag, postcard pictures of Romania, precious editions of their new free-press newspapers with stories and pictures of the revolution, and then photos of herself. It's all too much!

After a scrumptious meal, we exchange addresses and get ready to leave. It's hard now to leave these dear friends who were total strangers just a few short hours ago. Will we see them again? Only the Lord knows, but I do want to start correspondence with them real soon.

Monday, January 15, 1990   Misting – Grey Day

The room was very hot again last night. I left my pillows at the hotel in Cluj, so I was pretty uncomfortable all night. We crossed the border into Hungary with no problems. Traffic was heavy, and driving is slow. We come onto a very serious accident as we drive. A big semi has pretty well crushed a little Eastern European car. It appears there are no survivors. It's a sobering sight. We crossed the border into Austria with no problems and arrived at our house in Wiener Neudorf at 4:20 p.m.

Chapter 22

IMPRESSIONS FROM JANUARY VISIT TO ROMANIA

Our January Visit

The lights were on again in the cities of Romania! After years of being blacked out at night, we now saw many streetlights lighting up our way. Along with the darkness of the streets, the darkness of oppression was also gone. After forty years of living in fear of the dreaded Securitate, Romanians were joining the other countries of Eastern Europe in proclaiming, "The fear is gone! The fear is gone!"

As we drove through villages and towns and cities, it seemed like every building was flying a Romanian flag with the Communist seal cut out of the center. We were honored to be presented with two of these flags as a gift. The large round gaping hole in the center of every flag seemed so representative of the huge spiritual vacuum in this country. The twenty-three million people of Romania had lived for forty years under a system that denied the very existence of God, and the absurdity of this was very clear to them. With what would they fill this vacuum?

We were told everywhere we went of the great hunger for the Word of God. Christians and non-Christians alike all seemed to give the credit for their new freedom to God and His powerful and personal intervention in their country. They described how all the many factors miraculously worked together in their favor, saying, "It could not have been just a coincidence; only God could have done this!"

God miraculously protected all of our friends. Many of them were at the top of the Securitate hit lists, yet to our knowledge, not a single one was killed in spite of the fact that during the fighting, many of them publicly spoke to and prayed with the large crowds on the streets.

The country was an economic basket case, and it was difficult to imagine how it could ever recover.

The response by Christian groups, governments around the world, and multitudes of individuals to the need for food, clothing, and medicine was overwhelming. One Christian group alone had already gathered an enormous amount of medicine and clothing, asking us to take it to Romania and distribute it to churches in areas where it was most needed. This is just one example out of many.

It was now the middle of January. Because BEE World had become acquainted with church leaders through our BEE World ministry, the Romanian government provided warehouse space so we could help coordinate the receipt and distribution of aid pouring into the country.

Also, after years of doing everything possible to avoid contact with anti-Christian government police and military, I (Al) was now given a room in Romania's best hotel and was assisted by the Romanian army in the process of receiving and distributing aid shipments.

Can you imagine the excitement I experienced in being able to meet such desperate needs that had gone unmet for so long? At the same time, I experienced concern and fatigue. Concern because we worked openly with the post-revolutionary government now, but

Romanian Soldiers Help Distribute Aid from North Dakota

there was no assurance how long this grace period would last after the election in April. A new government might very possibly revert to the old ways of the Communist dictatorship. The suddenness and enormity of such workloads and so few workers was exhausting.

We deeply needed prayers for strength, wisdom, and endurance in these extraordinary circumstances.

Romanian Aid Project — April 1990

Our mission office in Fargo had for some time wanted to help the Romanian people by sending material assistance geared to their current need. Serious plans for a shipment started in April 1990 when several people met at our mission office in Fargo. They discussed how they could get a shipment off before the Romanian elections were held and while the shipments would still be duty free.

Then discouragement set in. It didn't seem possible to accomplish such a task in so little time. Despite the odds, they started buying a few things at garage sales, people brought them things, and items seemed to multiply. A local church offered us a couple of their rooms to assemble, sort, and pack. This large space was invaluable as people kept bringing in items. Cardboard cartons were donated. Each person had different abilities that fit together. For example, one person took responsibility for medicines that came in due to a local radio station airing our need. God's hand was evident at every stage.

Good Works to Romania — By Radu C. from Our Fargo Mission Office

Like cold water to a weary soul, so is good news from a distant land. –PROVERBS 25:25

From Christians in Romania, I am in charge to transmit a brotherly Thank You to everyone who participated in preparing and sending our large shipment of Romanian aid.

As we all know, the political and social changes in Eastern Europe in the last few months have a huge impact in every country's economy, and further in every person's life. There is a shortage of practically everything. Children are suffering without understanding why. They have no warm clothes, no heat, and no possibility to have them soon. The nonprescription medicine (aspirin, Tylenol, cold medicine, etc.) is a luxury. The taste of beef or chicken soup has been forgotten.

The Christians in our Fargo/Moorhead community wanted to do something to help. Under our organization's coordination, people and businesses from the area gathered an aid of 1,712 lb. in goods (winter clothes–1,150 lb.; medicine–162 lb.; canned meat, concentrated soup, and chocolate–400 lb.) to be sent from Minneapolis with PanAm direct to Bucharest, Romania.

The telephone communications with Romania are still deficient. Only a few lines are available for international calls. This makes the contacts delayed for two months sometimes.

Here are the facts received from the last conversation I [Radu] had with the church leader in Bucharest who led the processing of the aid shipment from our mission in Fargo:

- A group of seven people had been formed to be in charge with sorting and distribution.
- An itemized inventory had been made to have precise figures about the aid's kind, quantity, and condition.
- The clothes had been arranged on sizes, kinds (children, women, men), winter coats, sweaters, etc. The items that needed ironing were set aside for this purpose.
- The canned food, chocolate, candies, etc. had been checked. Everything was in perfect shape.
- A special attention had been given to the medicine box, which was in perfect shape in spite of the fact it was the heaviest—over 162 lb. The church leader in Romania is in daily life an open heart surgeon. He will be in charge of distributing the medicines.
- The distribution committee had been chosen from among those who know well the Christian families from churches in countryside and mountain areas. They know the families' needs, the children's age, gender, etc.
- The aid will be distributed by geographic areas in smaller packages specific for each family, and the Christians will deliver them directly.
- There is an estimation that over one hundred families and individuals from over ten churches did, or will, benefit

from this aid shipment. I believe the most part of the candies or chocolates will be given to children on Christmas in a celebration atmosphere.

- People here had been so generous in donating the items or the money to buy specific canned ham or chocolate. One family came from two hundred miles with two children, each one with a bottle of Tylenol in his hand taken from their medicine cabinet.

We have been amazed at how smoothly everything went, in spite of our worries and our impatience. We praise God for His blessing and thank you for your contribution.

Prayer Letter from Al and Betty in Europe—February 1990

What follows is a report on Al's return trip to Romania in February to learn the greatest needs for aid:

"You've left the most critical needs off your list!" our Romanian doctor friend told me. I was back in Bucharest, Romania, at the request of a number of Christian aid organizations to research the medical/health situation in Romania. They were seeking to provide basic medical equipment and supplies for the country by working through Christian doctors and through churches.

All of us knew that the medical/health situation in the country was appalling, but frankly, none of us were prepared for what we found. What we anticipated as basic needs turned out to be "luxuries" for them. One doctor friend explained to me that many medical personnel in Romania lacked even the means to disinfect their hands and medical instruments. Often, they didn't even have ordinary soap for washing their hands. The same syringes and needles have been used for many years with no means of sterilizing them. When giving shots with the ancient needles, they use diesel oil as a lubricant! Needless to say, we added soap and disinfectants to the proposed aid package.

Other basic medical equipment and supplies to be included in the proposal are new syringes, stethoscopes, sterilizers, blood pressure cuffs, antibiotics, medicine for the common problem of intestinal worms, etc. It's necessary to channel such aid through honest Christian medical workers; otherwise, it's likely to end up on the black market, available only to those who can afford to pay high prices for it.

While there is cause for great concern over the future of Romania, there is also much good news to report. Evangelistic opportunities abound and most churches are very actively pursuing those opportunities. Perhaps one of the most incredible things to happen is the planned showing of the evangelistic film *Jesus of Nazareth,* on Romanian national TV on Good Friday!!

For us at Biblical Education by Extension, there is an even greater call to train pastors and Christian workers to meet the spiritual needs of the people of Romania. It's an exciting time, and we praise God for what He is doing.

Chapter 23

BUGS STILL THRIVING— FIRST USSR TRIP

Al and Betty's Prayer Letter — March 1990

Dear Friends,

Can you identify this bug? I'll give you several clues. 1. It cannot fly. 2. It's made of plastic and metal. 3. It lives in lamps, ashtrays, flower vases, and telephones. 4. Its purpose is to spy on those who are suspected of having views contrary to the official Communist Party line. This particular "bug" was found in the telephone of a friend of ours in Romania. We've learned that "bugging" homes and hotel rooms has not stopped in Romania, nor in the Soviet Union, in spite of all the publicity given to "Glasnost" and "Perestroika." While many things in these two countries have changed, for some things, it's business as usual. While we still expect to have greater freedom to work in the Soviet Union than we did several years ago, we hear many reports that concern us.

The spiritual vacuum that exists in Eastern Europe and the USSR is being filled to a great extent by Eastern religions, black magic, drug use, and all kinds of cults and false teaching. A Polish pastor said the Jehovah's Witnesses are growing at

Sample "Bug" Found in Romanian Telephones

a rate twelve times faster than his Christian denomination. Another group experiencing success is the Christian Unity Church, which mixes some elements of Christianity with belief in reincarnation. All this is to say that the spiritual battle is INTENSE!! We see more and more evidence of the direct involvement of the spiritual forces of darkness. Please be praying that God will restrain all of these forces, and that He will prepare and protect and strengthen all those who are working to bring the gospel of Jesus Christ to this part of the world. Please pray specifically for us as we minister in the Soviet Union, Lord willing, April 19–May 10.

Our First Personal Trip to the Soviet Union— April 19–May 10, 1990

Travel Route: Budapest — Warsaw — Leningrad — Tallinn — Riga — Brest

While I'd been briefing and debriefing other staff for ministry in the Soviet Union for several months now, Betty and I had our first chance to personally set foot in the Soviet Union when we landed in Leningrad on April 19, 1990. What follows are her journal notes from that time.

Thursday, April 19, 1990   Rain

From the plane, we're transported to the terminal in an old, dirty, rundown bus, loaded down with lots of young Russians, mostly wearing black. Once inside the terminal, we're lined up in rows, like cattle, to wait passport control. People here are used to waiting—long expressionless faces stand in resigned acceptance of this illogical system.

There are lots of military and police running around here at the airport—all looking somewhat purposeless. We went through customs without problems, except that Al's Swiss Army knife and the chocolate we were bringing as gifts all disappeared in the process.

Now comes the experience that was the highlight of the entire day—our taxi ride to the hotel. I have never had a ride like this before! It was something like an amusement park tilt-a-whirl and roller coaster ride all in one. The driver—stone-faced with big dark circles under his eyes—placed himself behind the wheel, and we were off! I thought speeds and maneuvers like these were reserved only for racetracks. The acrobatics and screeching in and out of traffic, through spaces that didn't seem big enough even for a bicycle.

Wherever there was the slightest bit of light, he went for it. And all the while, I'm sitting in the back seat sucking up pure gas fumes from his open window. My brain is affected, my stomach is barfy, my eyes burn, my head hurts, my throat and nose are sore, but the driver doesn't seem aware of anything unusual at all. While driving, he just continues on in a most persistent way to "do business" with us, wanting to change money with us and to take us to our next destination four miles away. I think I'd rather walk!

We reached our hotel and checked in, only to find out our scheduled flight for tomorrow to Tallinn is full. We stand around and look dumb until they finally agree to put us on another flight tomorrow. Everything here is such an ordeal. The restaurant is full, and we can't get in without reservations, but Al finds some imported Western snacks in the hotel gift shop, so we have "supper" in our room.

After a nice warm bath in the yukky yellow-brown water, I gratefully crawl into bed, and I'm so thankful for a quiet room.

Friday, April 20, 1990   Sunny-Warm

At 8:00 a.m., we head down to the dining room for breakfast. What a surprise! The buffet spread is very elaborate and very good, all except the syrupy drink they call juice. There is everything from salads—all made with potatoes and cabbage—to hot cereals, baked tofu, sausages, susse kraut (just like what I grew up on back in North Dakota), potato patties, rolls with raisins, plum jam, breads, tea, and coffee.

We leave Leningrad for Tallinn at 2:45 on Aeroflot. These Russian planes are really yukky. The urine smell is enough to make one feel like declining any food offered. The whole plane is really tacky, so I just pray a lot.

In one of the first groups we'll be with, three former Russian army officers sat in on the last seminar. All had become believers while in the army and consequently served one year prison sentences for their "religious activities." They were then released from the army as "undesirables."

Now in Tallinn, we meet our contact at a set time discretely in the park near our hotel by the statue of the famous Estonian poet, Anton Tammsaare. No eye contact. No words exchanged. We recognize our contact from instructions given by our previous traveler, and as he strolls past us, we casually follow him at a reasonable distance to a waiting car to be whisked off to the scheduled seminar.

The ten men present are all young (25–28 years old) with the exception of Stefan, but all are very zealous to learn.

Before beginning the seminar on evangelism and discipleship, we pray for peace in the Baltic States, opportunity to combat evil forces of cults and astrology, etc. After the meeting, we head back to the hotel [it was still illegal to stay in peoples' homes at that time], manage to get served a late dinner in the restaurant, and drop into bed and are asleep in minutes. Al is somewhat discouraged tonight in being so ill-equipped for this tremendous challenge of teaching, but God is so patient with us in giving us much encouragement in the next day's seminars.

Saturday, April 21, 1990　　　　　　　　　　Warm – Sunny

Our alarm goes off at 6:15, and even though we had only a few hours of sleep, we jump out of bed and prepare for a full day of seminars.

While waiting for the first of the two seminars scheduled for today to begin, one of the men told about the history of the Russian oppression of the Estonian people. He told of one seventy-three-year-old pastor and his faithful housekeeper whose funerals were held today. They were "accidently" killed by the KGB.

They also shared much encouraging news about their ministry. For example, they had over one hundred baptisms recently, and new believers are coming in droves as a result of the church's new freedoms to evangelize. They shared the tremendous need to disciple these new converts before they fall into the clutches of the various cults now becoming active in their city.

April 22 – May 1, 1990

From Tallinn, Estonia, we traveled to Riga, Latvia, and on to Minsk and Brest in Belarus. All in all, on this trip, we met with thirteen groups and did a four-hour seminar with each group.

As we moved from city to city through our circuit, the last group was in a city that is not experiencing the greater openness and freedoms of Glasnost and Perestroika. Our previous traveler to this city traveled by car. He said they had to drive their car over a pit for a thorough inspection of the car, then a thorough inspection of all belongings, then endless questions, and confiscation of all "religious materials" found in their car (which were later returned to them).

Our contact instructions this time were as follows, "You'll meet your contacts at 1300 hours in the small parking lot behind the hotel. They'll be in a green Lada with license #_____ and with a Galatians/Romans workbook on the dash of the car. Neither man speaks English, so brush up on your Russian."

At this seminar, Al and I shared our backgrounds and gave our testimony as to how we came to know Christ as our Lord and Savior. Once again, my ancestral background of grandparents being from Ukraine strikes a bond between us, and once again, I see how the Lord has prepared every detail of my life to be used by Him. This was our experience in city after city as we traveled through the Soviet Union.

Thursday, May 2, 1990   Sunny – Warm

We're safely back home in Wiener Neudorf, and my mind and body are rather numb tonight. So much has happened these past two weeks. We've been exposed to an endless array of experiences. My heart is filled with thanksgiving as I think of God's careful protection for the many hours on rail, in the air, in taxis driven by crazy drivers, in our long walks around strange cities, our border crossings, all the different foods we ate, and the icy cold rooms we sat in for hours on end. Then there were the full-on-the-mouth kisses from so many dear brothers and sisters in Christ, and the supernatural tolerance I was given for my back problems. So much could have gone wrong and given us untold problems. But it didn't. God is so good, and I do not take all the prayers of His saints back in North Dakota for granted. He hears and He answers.

So, tonight, we drop into our own beds again, feeling very grateful for all that's happened and even more grateful for all the bad things that could have happened but didn't.

June 1990 Prayer Notes

Prayer items shared by groups we met with on this trip:

Pray for skills and ability to mobilize a new army of converts. One church had more than one hundred baptisms in December, and new believers are coming in droves as a result of the new freedom to evangelize. There is a tremendous need to disciple them before they fall into the clutches of the various cults now becoming active in the Baltic republics.

Two months ago, a group of high school students came to Pastor U., showing up at his front door to ask if he would please come and speak at the high school. They pled, "No one there knows what to believe, so we all decided to come to you and ask you to come and tell us what the Bible says."

Pastor U. now teaches a two-hour high school class each week on the Bible and contemporary issues. A few short months ago, only atheism could be taught in the public schools. Now both teachers and students alike are searching for truth in the Bible.

There are many, many, many situations like this now. Please pray that God would make His truth known through these opportunities. Pray that God will give strength to each person who has been given such opportunities, as all of them are already carrying a heavy workload. Only as God prepares and enables can they take on more.

In Riga, and other stops along the way in Belarus, we heard the same story. There is a new openness to Christianity and huge responses. One friend in Riga told us of one example where a Norwegian evangelist held a short evangelistic drama in a park and 250 people came forward to make a commitment to Christ. She said she almost panicked at the thought of discipling them all! People are thirsty for truth and ready to respond, but there is no one well-equipped to nurture and disciple them afterwards.

There are increasing tensions of all types all across the Soviet Union. There is the drive for independence in the Baltics, in Moldova and other republics, great ethnic tensions in Soviet Central Asia, economic problems, ecological disasters, and on and on. Even as I (Al) brief people each week on their way to the Soviet Union, we don't know whether they will be allowed to go to their planned destinations or not. Lithuania is already closed to us, and some have been refused entry to other republics because of the problems there.

- Please pray that the doors will remain open for us to travel in every area.
- Pray that the uncertainties and the tensions will lead people to turn to Christ.
- Pray that the problems will be resolved without bloodshed and war.

With so much turmoil in the Soviet Union and in Eastern Europe, many don't know where to turn.

Al's Letter to Supporters Back in America

In July, I made a trip to the Soviet Union with a pastor friend to do Bible conferences on church leadership in each city we visited. It was interesting to be the first Westerners to visit a group of believers in a city, which was still officially closed to Westerners. Somehow, the guards at the guard post at the entrance to the city neglected to check the papers of my American colleague and me.

As we saw earlier in our April–May trip, I again observed the absolute control that the Communist Party has had over the people for so many decades was rapidly evaporating. Certainly, they remained a powerful force, but they were being openly challenged on every front.

The many empty shelves and boarded up stores made me think of a country in the closing days of a national going-out-of-business sale. Most of the goods available now were rationed. I observed policemen handing out numbered ration coupons to people who would then be allowed into the store to purchase whatever was available. To make a purchase, each citizen was required to show their passport and produce the necessary ration coupons.

We saw people standing in long lines for many things, but now the longest line was the one waiting to get into the new McDonald's restaurant in Moscow. For the privilege of enjoying a "capitalist" hamburger, people were willing to stand in the rain for one and a half hours.

Not too long ago, the only references to Christianity allowed in the media were those condemning or ridiculing any belief in the supernatural. Imagine my response on our last night in the Soviet Union when we walked into the Intourist hotel lobby and the staff was watching a group on TV singing (in English) a popular song in America by Hank Williams, "Praise the Lord, I saw the light." I thought for a moment that I was having a strange dream!

For Prayer:

- Pray for safety of N., our translator in one city. He was a highly trained KGB agent for seven years before becoming a Christian. Now he cannot get a job to support his wife and two-year-old daughter, and the KGB is threatening to kill him.

- One of my agenda items for this trip was to deliver official invitations for a special conference with R.C. Sproul to be held in Vienna this summer. I was able to extend formal invitations to key leaders from each of our groups that we met with on this trip in Estonia, Latvia, and Belarus.

Chapter 24

BETTY'S CANCER BATTLE BEGINS

Cancer Battle Begins — Fall 1990

Now back from my July trip to the Soviet Union, I was working at home putting together to-do lists for our upcoming trip to the States in September. Over the next week, I'll complete the task of turning my responsibilities for the Soviet Union over to others for the next few months. In other words, we were about to shift gears for a time and focus on the Stateside part of our ministry.

Our first task when we arrived in the States was to find a car to use and a temporary home for a few months. Then, because we were really burned out, we felt a great need to take a little time off to recuperate. We'd simply tried to do too much for too long! In eight years, we'd taken very little time for rest and relaxation and now realized how essential that is for all of us.

While in the States, we needed to consider several possibilities concerning our future ministry in the Soviet Union. For example, we felt a need for further schooling. We'd had this on hold for eight years now because of the great need for staff in Europe. We were also concerned about our need for a much higher level of financial support as the US dollar had dropped to its lowest value in Europe since World War II!

We saw the possibility of living in the Soviet Union as becoming more and more realistic in the not-too-distant future.

While in the States, we needed to visit churches and individuals to report on our ministry before returning to Europe. This, in itself, took a huge toll on our strength. We also hoped to visit family in Colorado and Louisiana.

Cancer Surgery—October 1990

Before we ever responded to Christ's call on our lives to serve Him in foreign missions, we were warned by a number of well-meaning saints who said they were fearful for us in our relationship as man and wife. We'd always been close, and felt this was surely an unnecessary concern. But as the stresses grew greater, and the obvious needs in Eastern Europe became so clear, it was hard not to become totally absorbed in the work and neglect the areas of family relationships. Al became completely enthralled and preoccupied with the work to the point where it became his deep desire to do what was humanly possible for him to get Christian literature and good teaching to our brothers and sisters behind the Iron Curtain.

I was "left in the dust" as they say and felt the void very deeply. Al came home most days too weary to even think of discussing my concerns, and so it was that we drifted farther and farther apart until the day when we were brought face to face with my mortality, which then turned things back to where they should have been all along. Isn't it interesting how God works in our lives? If He can't get our attention in the traditional ways, He always finds ways that are unique and oftentimes not so pleasant to bring us face to face with needed change.

We were well into our visit to the States when I began another series of doctor appointments to seek help for my various health issues. One of them was to check out the lump in my breast.

Wednesday, October 17, 1990   Fargo, ND

This day seems like some terrible scary nightmare that is happening to someone else. Al and I went to see Dr. J., and he did an aspirate biopsy of my breast lump right away, and it is positive. I guess I'm not fully comprehending all of it yet. My stomach is churning, but it still feels unreal. Al said he felt so sorry for me during the biopsy. My whole body was almost shaking off the table. I do that when I'm faced with medical procedures—must be nerves. The biopsy was pretty uncomfortable. The first withdrawal wasn't bad at all, but the second one, he just dug and dug and dug. Al said he thought he'd never quit! I'm very tender and sore now, but guess it's nothing compared to what's coming.

After the biopsy, there was a long consultation with doctors and nurses, setting up appointments, watching a video on breast cancer, etc. We didn't get out of the clinic till almost 6:00 p.m. We're exhausted. It isn't every day that one hears one has cancer.

Al's been so supportive. How awful it would be to have to go thru this alone, or even worse, with a husband who can't relate or is not very compassionate. We've been doing a lot of reading, trying to learn as much as possible about how to make a wise decision. There are possible treatment options to consider—Lumpectomy or Modified Radical—hardly seems any different. With the lumpectomy, one needs more aftercare, and with the Modified Radical, one has a larger surgery and cost of prosthetics, etc.

We went to bed about 10:00 p.m., but we are both pretty hyper (numb?) about all that's happened today. So we lay and talked a long time. Al has been so good about talking thru my questions and concerns with me. But I'm still terribly confused and feeling almost disorientated. Or maybe "fragmented" is a better term. I feel like I'm being chewed apart—bit by bit—by the ugly enemy. But God is greater! Hallelujah!

Mary called. We talked and prayed a long time. *Father, I thank You so much for her friendship. Thank You for Your care thru her loving spirit.*

I did sense some pressure, though, from one church in response to my possibly not being available to share with them as scheduled. They were so disappointed and pointed out quickly that their

Sunday school kids had sent us packages, money, cards, letters, etc. Made me feel quite guilty. *But Lord, how am I ever going to be strong enough so soon?! And even if I were, how would I ever have time to prepare for these kids?!*

Thursday, October 18, 1990

I called Mom this morning about my surgery, and she called Diane and Len. So Diane called me tonight, and we talked about an hour. It was good, and she's a support to me.

Len also called me, reassuring me of his prayers and also that he had gotten me on the prayer chain of his church, Missionary Alliance.

About 10:20, I finally went to bed. I did the laundry today—a bunch of skirts and blouses for Eastern Europe too—so I was really tired. I didn't even take a relaxant or anything, and the Lord just helped me go to sleep almost immediately. How kind of Him! *Thank You, Father, for Your compassion and Your everlasting goodness.*

Friday, October 19, 1990   Cold – Windy

This morning has been good. Al went to the Emmanuel office to work, and I went browsing in the thrift stores. It took my mind off the cancer, at least for a little while.

Then when I went to pick up Al, Arne and Gordon [EMI board members] were there, and we told them about my cancer, so we prayed together. It was very comforting. *Father, I praise You for all the people You have brought already to hold us up and to strengthen us.*

After lunch, we came home and spent some time resting and loving one another. It seems the physical expression of our love for each other has a way of releasing tensions. I can't help wondering how much time we'll have together. As rotten and unfair as life is sometimes, I still desire very much to live and can't help feeling sad about the idea of dying.

Maggie C. came to see me this afternoon. She's had a mastectomy and is a volunteer for the Cancer Society. What a joy and encouragement it was to visit with her. *Thank You once again, precious Father, for Your care and personal concern in bringing Maggie into my life to share my grief.* And it is grief. It is a loss I'm facing, and the terribly hard part is not knowing whether there is cancer in other parts of my body too.

Al called Mike to let him and Steve know about my cancer and upcoming surgery. I hated to alarm everyone, but I know how I feel when people don't let me know what's going on.

Tonight, we did our first ministry presentation at one of our local churches. Al did well. It's hard the first time thru, but God gave him the words and also guided in the time element (can't see the time in the dark).

Monday, October 22, 1990   Sunny-Fair-60°

Had breakfast here at home and then I took Al to the Emmanuel office while I went to the clinic for pre-op exams. Had EKG, chest x-ray, etc. Visited with Dr. M. about decision on surgery. She's also going to do the endometrial biopsy while I'm under, so I'm thankful for that.

Tuesday, October 23, 1990   Sunny-Windy

This has been a hard, exhausting day, and yet a very encouraging day. Our visits with Doctors J. and H. went well, and we just both saw the Lord leading. We felt His presence in such a clear way. Dr. J. is a Christian, and he assured us that the lumpectomy with radiation was equally as safe as a mastectomy. When we were all done talking, he took our hands and prayed with us. What a comfort and encouragement that was! *Thank You, dear Father, for walking thru this with us.*

Al fixed a nice supper for us while I napped. C. stopped by while we were eating supper. People have been so kind and caring.

Julie called tonight. She's been going thru a hard time since the news of my cancer, but has come thru now and is handling it well. *Forgive me, Lord, for neglecting to pray for her. This affects her as well as me.* She was all ready to come up and be with me during surgery. I assured her it wasn't necessary. So, she and Cassie are thinking about coming up for Thanksgiving.

Father, I pray You will direct her, so she doesn't make this trip unnecessarily. Julie said many people are praying for me—her church, her school, her friends. *Thank You, Father, for what You are going to do in the lives of my kids thru all of this.*

Wednesday, October 24, 1990   Sunny-Mild

Loving Lord, I thank You for the hard things in life. For it is the hard things that draw (push?) us to Yourself. It is wonderful to feel Your nearness during difficulties. Don't allow the Enemy, even for a moment, to come between us, but may my trust in You cause Satan to flee quickly. You are trustworthy Father, and I praise You for permitting—desiring—me to draw strength from Your strength and faith from Your precious hand.

I thank You, too, for keeping me strong emotionally, in trying circumstances, so I am better able to display Your peace and loving care.

Dr. J. called today to learn of my surgery decision. We talked about finances (he brought it up), and he offered to waive his fees if our Austrian insurance didn't cover the medical bills. *Father, it is awesome to see Your hand going before us—even before we ask.*

Sunday, October 28, 1990   Windy-Cool-Sunny-50s

We got up early, had coffee and fruit for breakfast, and prepared for church service. Al was very nervous about preaching today, but his message on godliness and persecution was good, and I believe people were challenged. Sunday school hour went well with Al showing the slides. People were overwhelmed with the changes and the potential for God's work in the Soviet Union.

Monday, October 29, 1990

I got a call from Dakota Hospital saying my surgery has been re-scheduled for 11:30 a.m. tomorrow instead of 1:00 p.m. So now I need to shower and wash my hair. My hair is a mess because I can't use hairspray (too flammable for surgery). I finish up with my hair, etc. and with my last snack and drink about 12:20 a.m. Nothing now till after it's all over. I feel like I'm facing my executioner and there's no turning back. *How thankful I'm not alone, but that you, dear Father, have promised never to leave me. "Never will I leave you; never will I forsake you."*

Tuesday, October 30, 1990   Mild – Sunny

For God has not given us a spirit of timidity,
but of power and love and discipline.
–2 TIMOTHY 1:7

I'm feeling quite calm this morning. We get ready, then pray before we go to the hospital. We arrive there at 9:20, and I'm admitted at 9:30. No matter how much faith, one still experiences "butterflies" about the unknown.

Al goes down for lunch. They've given me my pre-op meds now—morphine and Valium—so I'm pretty zonked. We continue to wait and wait and wait. Finally, at 3:40 p.m., they come for me. It's been a horribly long day. Mom, Diane, Al, and others are all in the hallway by the elevator, so we say our good-byes. It's neat to have them here. Al's up by my head so I can't see him. *Bring him closer, Lord. It's him I want to see last.*

Karen somebody was with me in the surgery room. She gives me a warm blanket and prepares me for anesthesia. The anesthesiologist comes now and puts in an IV catheter, and now I'm off to oblivion. I wake up as they bring me back to my room—nearly five hours later. Thru the haze of my anesthesia, I see Mom, Diane, and Al, but am not able to respond to them.

Wednesday, October 31, 1990 — Beautiful – Mid-70s

This morning has been a rough one. I got up to go to the bathroom for the first time, and the room started spinning. I felt nauseous and had dry heaves. Oh how weak and sick I feel. But it wasn't long before nurses were scurrying quickly as my blood pressure dropped dangerously low. I've had too many medications. My body can't handle it all. The charge nurse quickly orders a narcon that reverses all meds and puts it in my vein. I felt myself slipping into the pit. It felt as though she were pouring ice water thru my veins as I was submitted to the horrible feeling of having all meds withdrawn from my system.

Never do I wish to experience that again! But fortunately, it did the trick, and it wasn't long before my blood pressure came back up some. It vacillated from low to high several times before stabilizing. So now I feel all the pain after surgery, but they don't dare give me anything for it. Al and others stop by. *It's neat to see Your care, Lord, through loving people.*

Thursday, November 1, 1990 — Gorgeous! – In the 70s!

Today is not a very comfortable day for me. I started out feeling rather depressed—guess my expectations are too unrealistic. *Heavenly Father, give me the grace and strength to deal with the bad as well as being joyful and filled with gratitude during the good times. Oh God, never let me forget how fortunate I am in having a loving, caring, compassionate family—especially Al!* Al came by this morning and then again this afternoon. I've been down to PT and OT twice today, so the time goes quite quickly. I tried watching TV or reading, but the pain is too distracting. Lunch was a yucky veal steak with some tasteless mashed potatoes. The only good thing was the Rice Krispies bar.

Dr. J. came by and said I could go home today! It's not even been forty-eight hours since surgery! It's exciting to think about going home, but also a bit scary. I pray about it, think about it, and talk it over with Al, and then decide to go home. We leave the hospital about 5:00 p.m. My nurse assures me of her prayers. *Lord, I'm feeling absolutely and totally miserable. But I'm thankful to be home.* Al fixes supper for us. He makes some phone calls to the kids, etc. And then we go to bed early. I take a pain pill at 8:00 p.m. Al insists on sleeping on the couch so as not to disturb me.

Friday, November 2, 1990   Mild – Sunny

Feeling just a smidge better today, but still really sore and hurting. It's so good to be home though! The home health care nurse came to see me, checked blood pressure, wound site, etc. She is really nice, and it's so comforting and reassuring to know someone is available if we should need it. We visited a long time about our work in the Soviet Union. She seemed genuinely interested. Al fixed mac and cheese, etc. for lunch. He takes such good care of me. *Thank You, Father.* Al read to me a bit tonight. He's sleeping on the couch again. I hope he can sleep in bed with me soon. His neck is really stiff and sore from the couch. Phone calls from two churches that want to provide meals for us for a time. *Thank You, precious Father, for these dear saints.*

Saturday, November 3, 1990

Al slept in bed with me tonight. Neither one of us could get to sleep very easily—so much on our minds. I keep thinking about all the treatment ahead. *Oh dear Father, please help me take only one day at a time.*

Wednesday, November 7, 1990   Sunny – Windy

My appointment with Dr. J. went well. He removed the drain! It feels so much better now! Except now I'm "draining" all over my clothes. It's a small price to pay though. Dr. J. is a gift from God.

Saturday, November 10, 1990 — Sunny – Cold – A Bit of Snow

This afternoon, I've been trying to prepare for my speaking to the S.S. kids at Page. I'm scared, but really feel I need to do that. Al's helping me prepare. We took another long walk this afternoon. I'm getting stronger, but still not much endurance.

Sunday, November 11, 1990

We got up at 6:00 a.m. and prepared for sharing our ministry at a church out in North Dakota. What a marathon! Since the pastor here serves three churches and all at a distance to drive, it's a mad rush to get thru them all in the time allotted. Al only had about twenty minutes to preach at Page, but it went pretty well. Then Al and Pastor S. went on to the next stop, and I went downstairs to talk to the kids. When I got downstairs, the kids all sang, "Jesus Loves Me" to me, and then Karen sang, "Oh How He Loves You and Me." I was so touched, couldn't control the flow of tears. They are such a neat bunch of kids. Always hugging and kissing. So sweet! It was a special privilege to be with them. Then Al showed the slides of our ministry, and at 2:00 p.m., we left for Fargo. Boy, am I beat and sore! I've been draining a lot too. What a mess. But I'm so thankful for the strength I had to come and be a part of this neat day.

Tuesday, November 13, 1990 — Sunny – Windy

Had my appointment with Dr. J. this morning. They had me in radiation over an hour, measuring, making a mold, taking photos and x-rays. All in prep for my thirty-three days of radiation. It's scary, but Dr. J. says there's a 50 percent chance of the cancer returning without this treatment. So I'm grateful for this opportunity of care. I'm so thankful too that we live only a few minutes from the clinic and it will not be a hardship to get there.

My arm hurts a lot—wonder if it will ever get better. Couldn't sleep tonight. Keep thinking about the recurrence of breast cancer. How could I ever handle it! *Oh Father, help me take just one day at a time.* "'So do not worry about tomorrow; for tomorrow will worry about itself. Each day has enough trouble of its own'" (Matthew 6:34).

Monday, November 19, 1990   Sunny – Mild – 50s

It's a lovely day again, but I'm feeling so apprehensive about radiation treatments. I had my first one today. It was really a weird feeling lying on this sterile, cold, steel table with all this equipment pointed at me. Then all the technicians leave the room while they "turn on the juice." Never have I felt so alone and vulnerable. And it seems forever (actually about two minutes) that they have this radiation going into my body.

Sunday, December 2, 1990   Cold – Sunny

Speaking today at the church we had pastored in northern Minnesota. It was so neat seeing all those folks again! I really miss them. They're so genuine and so caring. And so appreciative of our sharing. Thank You, Father. I can hardly hold on. I'm so tired from visiting. I'm hurting so much from all the hugs, but yet I'm terribly exhilarated by seeing everyone. We left about 2:45 p.m. Whew!! It was a very intense and emotion-filled weekend, but a very splendid one too. We got back to Fargo about 5:30. I'm hurting a lot.

Monday, December 3, 1990   Sunny – Mild

Saw Dr. J. today. He seems pleased with my condition. Al talked to Bill T. in Vienna on the phone today. Three cities Bill suggested we live in are Moscow, Kiev, or Tallinn. I think I preferred Tallinn, but Moscow has McDonald's! *Where do You want us to live, Lord?*

Monday, December 24, 1990   Very Cold – Snow

The weather is perfectly ideal for Christmas Eve.

    Got to Al's parents' home in Fergus Falls about 10:30 a.m. Alice is all prepared for dinner—turkey in the oven, table set, tree decorated. We had a fun time around the table for dinner. Then Al and I made Austrian-style Melange coffee to go with our dessert. It was fun and everyone seemed to enjoy this German cultural touch. How thankful I am that my kids consider Palmer and Alice to be their grandparents.

Got back to Fargo about 6:00 p.m. Al and I are both so weary, so we take a rest till 7:00 p.m. Then we have some snacks, refreshing drinks, and open our presents: Al give me a gold chain, a North Dakota cookbook, and several other books including a German-Russian one which is so good! *Thank You, Father for a husband who loves me enough to make my Christmas celebrations ones with precious memories and personal gifts.*

Wednesday, December 26, 1990   Very Cold!

The Lord has been so faithful in seeing us through the difficult times this past year, including our return to the US with no direction for the future, but a move being imminent, and then cancer. God is a God of compassion and mercy and has given me strength for all of this. How thankful I am to be His!

As I look ahead to this new year of 1991—a year beginning with so much dreaded uncertainty—I am ever thankful for the steadfastness of our Lord.

The Storm (Betty's account of her cancer experience)

A raging storm has come my way, the rain is pouring down. The clouds have hidden the light of day, there's darkness all around.

My soul is tossed with fear and doubt, Lord, why must this storm be? I've tried to live my life for You, and serve You faithfully.

A gentle hand reached out to me and took me in his arms. Child, I will guide you through the storm and shelter you from harm.

There is a special purpose for this storm that's in your life. Just trust in Me, I know what's best—my child you can survive.

You can survive the storm that's come your way. You can survive the heartache and the pain.

Though your eyes be filled with tears, My Word will calm your fears. I will stay close by your side; you can survive!

Lord, I'll trust You with my life, to lead each step I take. May I bring glory to Your name, in all I do and say.

Your precious Word will strengthen me; Your love will comfort bring. I'll keep my eyes upon Your face, and from that joy I'll sing.

I will survive though the storm has come my way; I will survive through the heartache and the pain.

Though my eyes be filled with tears, the Word will calm my fears. I will stay close by Your side.

Jesus, stay close by my side. I will survive.

202

Part Four

Chapter 25

BEGINNING A NEW YEAR

The year 1990 was filled with incredible ministry experiences in Romania and serving in the Soviet Union. The last three months of the year, we experienced the cancer diagnosis and surgery for Betty. As we began 1991, we didn't know if God would enable us to return to our ministry in the Soviet Union. What follows are Betty's journal entries.

Tuesday, January 1, 1991   **Cold - Windy - 15° Below**

Well, here we are in 1991—still haven't gotten used to writing it. As I look ahead to this new year—a year beginning with so much dreaded uncertainty—I am ever grateful for the steadiness of my Lord. Oh He is so wonderful! *Father, I place myself in Your able hands, and just ask You to continue to increase my faith that I might rest confidently in all Your plans for my life.*

Tuesday, January 8, 1991   **Sunny - Cold - Windy**

Today is my last treatment! Al went with me to watch the therapy and then to talk to Dr. J. with me. I won't have much follow-up care until we return here next summer. To "celebrate" my life, we had lunch at the Olive Garden—nice place and delicious food.

Friday, Jan. 18, 1991   Mild – Beautiful!

Earlier this month, we had decided to make a trip to Colorado. Today is the day I get to see Julie, Harve, and Cassie, Lord willing. It's a gorgeous, sunny day.

    How wonderful to see Julie and her family! They all look so great, which always does a mother's/grandmother's heart good.

Thursday, January 24, 1991   Sunny

On to Louisiana—Harve got us into the airport and checked into United for our flight to visit Mikel and Steve.

Sunday, January 27, 1991   Rain – Cool

Up at 6:00 a.m. to get ready for church. Mike came at 9:30 to pick us up for church. Our time at Grace Harbor Community Church was so, so special. Al shared our ministry with our dear brothers and sisters here at Grace Harbor. People were genuinely interested and blessed by what God is doing in the Soviet Union. Pastor Glynn stimulated people to take advantage of the openness now in the Soviet Union and to invest in eternity. When Al finished sharing, Brother Glynn had us up front where we were "commissioned" once again thru prayer and the blessing of people here at Grace Harbor.

Friday, February 8, 1991   Mild – Warm

Back in Minnesota now, we've decided to return to our ministry in Europe, so we have a long talk with Dr. J. discussing my aftercare, etc. He will take extra precautions; normally not doing this much while a patient is still doing so well. But he is concerned about my not having access to ready medical care should something surface quite suddenly.

Wednesday, February 13, 1991   Snow – Blustery

Lots of last-minute things to do today before leaving tomorrow. I did the fridge and stove, but Al's doing windows, bathroom, etc. It's quite a job to leave a place again. We're both tired tonight and also excited about flying tomorrow. I slept very little.

Thursday, February 14, 1991 Snow – Windy – Blustery!
My alarm was set wrong, so I got up an hour too late and had to do things a bit faster. Al—in the midst of moving and flying today—still remembered to give me a Valentine. I gave Al a heart-shaped cookie, which we ate en route.

Our return trip to Europe didn't go as smoothly as we would have liked. Due to bad weather, we spent many extra hours on airplanes, waiting to take off and circling airports waiting to land. We arrive in Frankfurt about eight hours later than scheduled. There's a lot of chaos going on, guards all over the place. Because of the war in Iraq, they're pulling all the Arabs aside and searching them, questioning them. There is a nice welcoming group in Vienna to see us back "home" again. We missed two of our scheduled flights and finally arrived safely in Vienna, but no luggage!

We walked into our house to find that the water heater in our bathroom was kaput, and water had been spraying all over and was soaking through the floor into the basement. In the basement, we learned that the furnace (hot water type) was also kaput, and water from it was flowing over the floor and soaking the carpets.

The one good thing about arriving home is that we're safe. But the furnace doesn't work, so the house is icy cold, and the hot water heater isn't working either. We use space heaters to get us thru the night.

The house is dirty, and the plants are dead, and a few things are broken or missing, and there are spots on the carpet, but generally things are in pretty good order. To sum it up, our first few days back in Vienna were not the time of rest that we had in mind!!! A good sense of humor was very helpful!

Saturday, February 16, 1991 Snow – Heavy
Huge flakes drifting down and piling up on trees, etc.

It's a gorgeous sight of winter-wonderland outdoors. Young moms pushing baby carriages and most adults wearing big, furry hats. Now if only we had heat! Al finally gets the furnace working. Next is the water heater. We're still just as stinky as when we arrived home!

Sunday, February 17, 1991   Cold – Sunny

Didn't get up till 8:30 this morning. The sun is shining brilliantly on the new-fallen snow. It's so pretty! This jet lag is the pits. And then with the furnace not working, it doesn't make for much sleep.

We walked over to Sudstadt and enjoyed a wonderful Melange. That's one thing I'm really going to miss once we move to the Soviet Union—just relaxing in these quaint, old-world Coffee Konditerie's, having coffee, reading the paper, and visiting. Al and I were up till about 2:30 a.m. tonight. Al can't relax because the furnace keeps going out. So we read, we ate, we talked, etc.

Monday, February 18, 1991   Sunny – Calm

Poor Al has been getting up every few hours during the nights to check on the furnace and add water to keep it going. So he hasn't gotten much sleep.

Our landlord sent the water heater people out today, but they need to order a new one, so we won't get it till tomorrow. I finally did heat enough water to shampoo my hair and take a bath. I almost even got wet! What a blessing it is to have hot water—don't realize it till it's gone.

Tuesday, February 19, 1991   Partly Sunny – Fair

They finally brought the new water heater and installed it this afternoon. No furnace help yet though. A bummer!

Al rubbed my back a long time tonight and then he read to me. *Thank You, Father, for such loving care.*

Wednesday, February 20, 1991   Partly Sunny - Mild - 30s

Al read to me again tonight. It's kinda neat not having TV. We do other more meaningful things.

Thursday, February 21, 1991   Cloudy - 30s

Al went into the office today to meet with Bill. Bill thinks our moving to Moscow in the fall would be great. So I guess that means the end of our little comfortable haven here in Wiener Neudorf. Lord, You have been so good to us to allow us this privilege for four years. Thank You!

Saturday, February 23, 1991   Very Mild - 50s

Tonight, we spent some time lying on the living room floor just listening to classical music. It was so enjoyable to have this quiet time together. We need to do this more often.

We're beginning to take steps to leave this area now and find a new home in the Soviet Union. I'm going to miss this little village of Wiener Neudorf. I feel so at home here, and the local people are beginning to view me as one of them. Al had his last elder's meeting tonight and didn't get home till 1:00 a.m.

We're excited about the privilege God has given us of living and ministering in the Soviet Union. We're also more than a little apprehensive about many of the things we'll face. Please continue to pray that we will experience God's strength and direction as we make this move.

Chapter 26

THE TOWER CALLING— MARCH 1991

In March, I (Al) made a teaching trip to the BEE World Baltic Circuit (Estonia, Latvia, and Belarus). At this time, we anticipated moving to Moscow later in 1991. The following is a prayer letter we sent to our supporters in the States.

MOCKBA, USSR

That's Moscow in the Soviet Union. Lord willing, this would soon be our new home. While there are numerous concerns and questions remaining to be worked out, we anticipate having an apartment in Moscow by late summer.

Precise ministry responsibilities are not yet finalized, but most likely, they will be to administer the BEE World program for the Baltic republics of Estonia, Latvia, Lithuania (presently closed to us), and the republic of Byelorussia.

As we work towards this major change, we ask you to join us before the Lord in PRAISE and PETITION:

- Praise for the precious privilege God has given us as we begin another year of serving Him in this difficult but extremely needful and rewarding ministry.

- If it is His will for us to live in Moscow, pray for His provision of an apartment that will meet our needs and for people to help us in the challenging task of finding food and other necessities.
- Continue to pray for necessary health and stamina as we contemplate leaving our home in Austria and moving into another very different culture, where material comforts are few and health care minimal.
- Pray that the political situation in the Soviet Union will stabilize and improve; and that the doors that are presently open for the Lord's work will not be closed. (The KGB is still making very explicit threats about a return to past methods.)
- Pray that God will clearly guide us as we seek His will in another major anticipated move.

> For our citizenship is in heaven, from which we also eagerly wait for a Savior, the Lord Jesus Christ; who will transform the body of our lowly condition into conformity with His glorious body, by the exertion of the power that He has even to subject all things to Himself.
> –Philippians 3:20–21

The Tower Calling — Change in Plans — March 1991

High above the city of Riga, in the Soviet republic of Latvia, the four of us climbed through a small trapdoor into a tiny tower, no more than five feet across. From the tower, we could look out over the rooftops of the city, now turning white in a heavy snowfall. Away to the west was a seemingly endless convoy of Soviet troops that had just passed through the center of the city. (We had been told by locals that there were now a quarter of a million Soviet troops in this tiny republic of two and a half million people.) Below us was a huge four-story building run by the government as a sports hall.

In our passage through the building, we had seen basketball courts, rooms for table tennis, large rooms for gymnastics, and

Salvation Temple with Prayer Tower (Top Right)

rooms for many other activities. Our purpose this morning, however, was not to enjoy a basketball game or to work out in one of the gyms. Instead, we were here in this little tower to talk to the Lord about the future use of the building below us.

Our host, a Russian pastor, explained to us that before World War II, this building and a neighboring building had housed a church, a seminary, and a mission organization. Various congregations speaking Latvian, Russian, German, and possibly others had gathered for worship in this huge building known then as the Salvation Temple. Then, when the Russian army occupied Latvia, the Soviet government appropriated the building, allowing the believers to keep only a large picture of the baptism of Christ, which had hung on the back wall of the largest auditorium.

As we stood cramped together in this little tower looking out over the city, my great fear of heights made my legs a little shaky. However, as we bowed for prayer, I forgot my fear in the emotion of praising God for returning this building to His people in Riga. Lord willing, it would once again be used as a church, mission center, and training center for pastors and other Christian workers.

Under Communism, something like 80 percent of the churches had been closed and converted to other uses by the government. Now a number of these were being returned. Like others, this building was in a sad state of disrepair and needed a new roof and a lot of other work before it could be fully used. This little tower atop the building was the first space in the building returned for use by the church, and it had already been lovingly repaired.

Now we prayed that the rest of the building would be returned without any hitches, and that God would provide the means for all necessary repairs. We prayed that it would again be a place where voices would lift their praises to God in many languages. We prayed that here God's laborers would be equipped to go out into the city to reap a rich spiritual harvest, which we believed He had already prepared. We prayed that this would be a place where all that happened would bring honor and glory to His name.

Our Russian pastor friend had already designated a portion of this building for our use as offices and classrooms. He was committed to helping us get visas to live in Riga. All of this happened so quickly in a situation where many people had not been granted visas to enter, even just to visit, much less to live here.

Nevertheless, we saw many indications that God had prepared a place for us to work here and contacts who could arrange for a visa. We expressed to the Lord our willingness to go if this was His will for us.

The following are prayer requests we sent to supporters:

- Pray that He will clearly guide us each step of the way in the path that He wants us to take; and should this be His will for us.

- Pray that visas to live in Riga will be granted before we return to the States in June for Betty's medical follow-up.

- Pray for His provision of a home that will be appropriate for our needs.

- Pray for decisions concerning what possessions and supplies to take with us as very little of anything is available there.
- Pray that our working relationships with all the various churches and denominations in these republics will be honoring to God.
- Praise Him for the encouraging trip I made through these republics in March. In nine days, I conducted seminars with twelve different groups in three different courses: Galatians/Romans, Evangelism/Discipleship, and New Testament Survey. The enthusiasm I saw and the testimonials I heard from these students made this one of the most encouraging times I've ever experienced. The Lord was clearly with us!
- Pray for the preparations for our next trip (May 15–26) to again conduct seminars with all of these twelve groups. Once again, I need to do these by myself, as my hoped-for partner was not granted a visa to make this trip. Pray that God will grant Betty the ability to participate in this trip with me, and that she will be as encouraged as I was in March.

We continued to see the love and power of God at work as He answered prayers concerning our lives and ministry. We appreciated more than we can say your faithfulness in standing with us.

Chapter 27

TRIP TO SOVIET UNION – MAY 14-26, 1991

I (Al) had made a solo trip in March to teach our BEE World church leader groups in Tallinn (Estonia), Riga (Latvia), and Minsk and Brest (Belarus). This time, Betty went with me as we sought to further explore possibilities for living in Riga, Latvia, instead of Moscow. At this time, it was still necessary to fly first to Moscow before traveling on to the Baltic republics. Betty's journal entries catalogue our experience on this trip (May 14-26, 1991).

Tuesday, May 14, 1991   Sunny-Warm

This is the day! Yes! This is the day which the Lord has made, but it's also the day we're flying to Moscow. I'm so excited, and yet in some ways it hardly seems real.

Once again, we're on our way to the Soviet Union. Memories of past trips flashed on the screen of my closed eyelids. The vast grey, desolate lands making up these republics stretching across eleven time zones. Lands so immense it's impossible to picture in one sitting. But the people of the Baltics are the ones that have captured my heart. I love the soft, elegant ways of the Latvians, the passionate personality of the Russians, and the quiet, composed demeanor of the Estonians.

Each one so different, and yet each one with very similar experiences in life under the Communist government of the Soviet Union. Sufferings and hardships beyond compare. Under the oppressive rule of Mother Russia, these dear people have seen untold numbers of friends and loved ones fall under Stalin's crazed madness. The torture of those directly affected reached well beyond the walls of dark prison cells.

Jeff comes at 10:00 a.m. to take us to the airport. We have two big bags and two carry-ons. Our bags are so, so heavy again. Al's books weigh a ton as we're testing the possibilities for openly bringing in our seminary training materials. And, as always, we're bringing lots of gifts too.

We board Aeroflot at 12:30. It smells just like I remembered it. The plane looks pretty decent at first glance, but as I sit here, I see how old everything is. Paint worn off the chairs, holes in the carpets, seats ready to "adjust" by themselves at the most inconvenient moments. Oh how "fun" it is to be in this system! If our family and friends could only see us now, they wouldn't view our life as so glamorous and exciting.

The plane squeaks and squeals as we take off, sounds ready to fall apart, but it gets us off the ground in a hurry, and we soon reach our cruise altitude.

Once we're up in the air, we are served cold drinks, and following that, a meal of meat (anybody's guess what kind), potatoes, carrots, bread roll, butter (from Finland), juice (from Florida), a mousse-like dessert, and coffee. I didn't eat the meat; it tasted really strong. But the rest was O.K.

We arrive in in Moscow about 4:00 p.m. Now having landed safely in Russia, everything looks a lot like Romania. The thick diesel fumes, the rough roads, the crazy drivers, crowded buses, people walking everywhere with their little shopping bags always hoping to find something worth buying. The few cars we see on the roads are Ladas or some other cheaply made vehicle. There are still lots of Lenin statues. We see large fields where people are planting gardens. There are, however, some beautiful and interesting structures along the way. They look new, and we assume they might be official buildings.

At 4:35, we reached the hotel Belgrade. We've paid $200.00 per night for this place, and it's comparable to the one we paid $10.00 for last time in Minsk! Not even any hot water!! And the noise from traffic thru the night was awful.

Al scouts around the hotel to see about water being available, etc. We're on the sixteenth floor, and the elevator isn't real efficient, so it takes a while to get around. He learns that one of the cafés is really grody—lots of smoke and real crowded. The other one isn't open. And the third one is now serving dinner from 6:00 to 10:00 p.m. So even though we're not real hungry, we decide to go now and risk our chances at being served. What's supposed to be open and available according to signs isn't always the way it is.

The dinner menu was many pages long with all kinds of exotic dishes listed, but alas, only a few things available, and they must be given the "smell test" to try to distinguish its safety. There is, however, always tea. It may not be very good, but at least, one won't likely get food poisoning from it. We ended up ordering stroganoff, because that's one of the few things they had. But the meat smelled so bad I couldn't eat it. I ate the potatoes and carrots and my cucumbers. Then we enjoyed some tea and the rest of our beverages.

The one good part about eating out is that we can pay in rubles, so our meal—all drinks and everything included—came to about $3.00 for the two of us! If only we could pay for our room that way instead of hard currency.

It's still light here. We're much farther north now, so we're close to the time of "white nights." I'm glad to have my sleep mask.

Wednesday, May 15, 1991   Sunny-Warm

Woke up very early—4:00 a.m.—and had a hard time going back to sleep. The bed is fairly good, but we're not used to all this early morning daylight.

Went to breakfast around 8:15. It was pretty depressing—a lot like Romania: some poor-quality cold cuts that looked to be mostly fat, a boiled egg, some sawdust-like bread, jam, butter, and lukewarm tea. It all wouldn't be so bad, but the attitude of service (or lack thereof) makes one feel like you're imposing. It's so degrading and humiliating. We ate what we could and then went on our sightseeing tour.

We walked and walked and walked today! My poor feet. Our tour of the Kremlin and the adjoining cathedrals was very interesting. Our tour guide, Rita, is real nice and very well informed. She gives us lots of info about her country, their government, their religion, etc. Some tidbits of information she gives us:

1. Lines to Lenin's tomb now shorter than the line to McDonald's.
2. Astrology is very popular—prediction now is for a younger man to replace Gorbachev in three years.
3. Second bar on Russian Orthodox cross means their religion is open to all.
4. Half-moon under cross means it carries believers to Christ.
5. Cross absorbs positive energy from Jerusalem and imparts it to believers.
6. Women separated from men in church for they are the source of sin (Eve).
7. One visit to Orthodox service can absolve all your sin.
8. Icon equals evidence of miracle.

My heart aches for all the misconceptions and myths that people believe. I keep praising the Lord for allowing us to be born in

America, where we have the freedom to learn truth and to worship freely. We learn a lot from the guide showing us around the city. She points out huge buildings, still occupied strictly by the KGB. Yes, they are still very active.

Another interesting thing she told us is that the body in Lenin's tomb is not really Lenin! The story is that Lenin died from poison mushrooms. This poison stays in the roots of the hair, so people were afraid. Therefore, they had a replica made to honor and worship him, but had the real Lenin buried.

Well, we've now collected two full days of sweat and dirt and no hot water to bathe. Phew! It's hot in our room, and I'm miserably hot and stinky, but nothing to do.

Thursday, May 16, 1991   Hot-Sunny

We go down for breakfast: sardines, wieners, canned peas, bread, jam, butter, tea. Coffee costs an extra ruble—all of three and a half cents.

We end up sitting with a couple from Australia, and it's funny to hear them complain about no hot water. I guess we've gotten used to these things.

Our tourist guide picks us up from the hotel at 6:00 p.m. and transports us to the train station. We board a train to Estonia, a republic that is in the Western part of the Soviet Union. It's a fourteen-hour train trip, and I must say the accommodations are not at all like they are in America! My stomach is starting to become very unsettled this morning. I have some tea, but I'll be very happy to deboard this train and get my feet back on solid ground. I'll be careful not to eat much meat, since it seems that is where the problems typically lie in contracting food poisoning.

Our train is fairly clean and comfortable, but oh I'm so hot, hot! I try to sleep, but it's pretty "rocky" and "wavy."

Friday, May 17, 1991 — Sunny-Cool

We arrive in Tallinn at 9:15 a.m. Al calls Viktor, but he has not been able to arrange a room for us in the hotel. However, Pastor N. has found a room in a local guesthouse for us. They take us there, but the room is not yet ready. We have to wait till noon. Oh I'm so tired! How I long to bathe, to rest.

Finally, at noon, we are able to enter a room. Oh how wonderful to have a bed, to have hot water (even though it's a community toilet and tub). First thing I do is wash my hair and take a bath.

At 5:30, Pastor N. comes to take us to the Russian Baptist group for our first seminar. These are a very special group of men—mostly young. They are very interested and eager to learn. Nicholai (a student) asks about my health and tells us they had been praying for me.

We finish up around 10:00 p.m. It seems strange to see how light it still is as we find ourselves even farther north. Viktor (who we learned later was likely a KGB plant reporting on the church activities) drives us back to our hotel.

Saturday, May 18, 1991 — Sunny-Cold

The next morning, we're prepared to begin a long day of seminars. Many of these dear saints have come great distances for the teaching, and we don't want to disappoint them.

We learn that Stefan speaks some German, so we are able to visit a bit. He showed us the place they hope to move to soon. It's a larger flat in an apartment building under construction. Stefan says they have waited ten years for this!

We tour the church while we wait. It was built back in the tenth century and now serves this congregation of about 1300.

It's interesting to see the symbols of lion, ox, man, and eagle on the pulpit. The very symbols Al was teaching on last night. *Thank You, Father, for this follow-up of encouragement.*

We finish the seminar at 11:30. Our translator, Jon, takes us to the train station to buy tickets for our travel to Riga tomorrow. We walk thru the old city as Jon points out various sites. I'm absolutely frozen to the bone. My ears are hurting, my hands are numb, and my head is hurting. And all of a sudden, I see this little old lady sitting along the curb, selling her homemade woolen caps! *Thank You, Father!* I quickly buy her best cap for all of 70¢! Oh what an answer to prayer!

After lunch, we hurry over to another church for our next seminar. They are ready and waiting for us. It's a very emotional time as we meet now for the first time since my cancer surgery. They have been praying, earnestly, for my health and are giving praise for my return to health. *What a wonderful gift from You, Father, to have these dear brothers and sisters caring, praying, and loving me all across the miles and holding me up to You on arms of prayer.*

The seminar continues. Oleg shares that he was invited to university to speak and used our BEE World course materials to address these students. After two hours of sharing with these students, they asked for more!

At 6:45, we arrive back at our room. I take a bath. We eat some of our food and prepare for an early departure to Riga in the morning. And now I gratefully sink into bed, sleeping almost straight thru from exhaustion.

Sunday, May 19, 1991 Sunny-Cool

We get up at 5:00 a.m. Stefan gets us at 6:15 and takes us to the train station. We board the train to Riga. It's freezing cold—no heat at all! It isn't long, though, before my muscle relaxant takes hold, and I fall asleep in spite of how cold I am. The blankets and pillows here on the train are too grody to use, but Al covers me with his coat, so that helps a lot. I sleep with my cap on.

We arrive in Riga at noon. Helena meets us and takes us to the Hotel Riga, where they have reserved a room for us.

I'm not looking forward to sitting thru another seminar tonight, but I'll probably not be making trips like this again, so feel I want to participate as much as possible. If we do end up moving here, I probably won't be attending the seminars. And if my health gives out and we're not able to live here, then I won't be doing it either.

At 5:10, we leave our hotel for the evening seminar. It's raining and cold, and we have to walk a long ways to catch our tram. As is always the case, the tram is packed, beyond capacity, so it's push and shove all the way. Al pushes his way onto the tram, but I nearly get caught in the doors! I end up on the steps. So much for chivalry.

The translator is coughing, Al has a headache, and others (including me) are hacking away. But we are all excited about being together, so we enjoy fellowship and learning in spite of not feeling well.

At one point during the seminar, Al asks if the material they are studying thru BEE World has been helpful. Igor says, "There are no words to describe how helpful it is been! Now I have the info to share with people my faith, especially about Christ's return." Alex says, "Very helpful from the historical aspect."

Last night, at our meeting, one student expressed very emotional gratitude for our coming to the Latvian people. In every group, this has been a common thread. And this is what makes all our work, and all we go thru to get it done, worthwhile. These people are so deeply grateful for teaching which helps them understand God's Word.

We close the seminar with prayer at 9:30 and say our good-byes for this month, and Viktor gives us a ride back to our hotel.

Tuesday, May 21, 1991   Mostly Sunny – Also Rain

Thank You, Father, for a good night's rest. It was an encouragement to be with the group last night. Our problems and the things I was wasting energy on just didn't seem too important after putting things into eternal perspective. I get so hung up on the "daily" things that I forget what my journey thru this life is all about and what it's leading to.

Wednesday, May 22, 1991   Mostly Sunny – Mild

Walked over to Hotel Latvia to get our airline tickets for tomorrow. We're booked on a real small forty-eight passenger aircraft. It could be another experience like our crossing the Aegean Sea on the small fishing boat named *Diana*.

For our evening seminar, we meet our translator Julia at 5:30, and then Nicholai G. picks us up in an old, rickety farm truck. So here we are, riding down the highway next to the Daugava River in Riga in this bumpy old truck. But our hearts are joyful as we look forward to meeting with dear brothers and sisters to study and fellowship.

We arrive at Nicholai's apartment at 6:00 p.m. Julia translates for the seminar and does a very good job. During the evening, I ask her about her English. I asked her what kinds of literature she likes most and would desire in English. "Of course, I like most of all the Bible," she says. Would this have been my answer? I probably would've mentioned Christian books, but I'm saddened to think that I probably wouldn't have mentioned the Bible as being my most enjoyable book to read.

After the seminar, Tamara brings on a huge feast for us all: meat and potato soup served with a glob of sour cream. After the soup, we have the main courses of fried chicken, mashed potatoes, cabbage salad, pickles, cheese, cold sausage, bread, butter, tea, and coffee cake.

After our feast we visited over photos I had brought of the kids and our families. I'm so thankful that Nicholai speaks some German. It's such a strain when one can't communicate. But his German is a great help.

Before we leave, Nicholai gets out his guitar and sings and plays for us. He does songs in Finnish, Ukrainian, Latvian, Russian, and Polish. It's obvious he's extremely tired (as are all of us), but it doesn't matter. We enjoy sweet worship of our Lord together with this dear family and count it a precious privilege to have this experience.

During our visiting with Julia, Nicholai, and Tamara, we learn many interesting cultural and spiritual insights:

They tell us all water here in Riga must be boiled before it is fit for consumption.

The average income of people here and in Latvia is 180 rubles per month, which equals $6.00 per month!

Nicholai shares that his church has six hundred to seven hundred members, and baptisms are a frequent happening.

After exchanging gifts, we finally pile back into the truck, and Nicholai takes us back to our hotel. It is 11:30 p.m., and we are very tired, but it's been a rich evening of worship, learning, and fellowship with our friends here in Riga.

It was hard saying good-bye to these wonderful people. They told us how they have been diligently praying for my surgery and subsequent treatment. Here in the Baltics, a diagnosis of cancer pretty much means a death sentence, so they are sad about my illness. We try to reassure them that we are trusting the Lord, and if His will is for me to continue on here in the ministry, that He will make it possible, and I'll be back again.

Thursday, May 23, 1991   Rain – Cold

Today, we need to get up early to catch our plane to Minsk. Before we head down to breakfast, Helena calls and tells us that all things are in order for us to obtain a visa. This is a special answer to prayer. And the other news she has is an additional answer to prayer—they have spotted an available five-room flat for us in a nice area of Riga. And this is renting for $360 per month, including utilities! Praise the Lord!

At 9:30, Al hails us a taxi, and we are now off to the Riga airport to catch our flight to Minsk. Total cost for the two of us for cab to the airport was six rubles, which is 50¢.

We have quite a long wait at the airport, but time goes fast as we watch a Russian soldier and his family of wife, young son, and typical little Russian girl. This little girl is darling—big round face, blue eyes, and all dressed up in her homemade knitted sweater and cap.

The cleaning ladies are busy mopping the old, worn-out floors. People are scurrying to and fro; some sit and wait and munch on their dry bread and boiled eggs. There are no ice cream shops, no hot dog stands, no pop machines, and no coffee bars! Life is barren and void of all Western comforts. The place is dark and gloomy, but one really needs to give them credit for their efforts in attempting to make their surroundings tolerable. The one thing that is always in abundant supply is fresh flowers. Too bad they aren't very nourishing.

We, as foreigners, are asked to board this small plane first. They tell us to pick wherever we like to sit. And then all the nationals are allowed to get on board. The plane is actually pretty decent, but no heat. It's freezing cold! Al gives me his coat to wrap around my legs, and that helps.

Once the plane starts warming up, I'm not so sure I want to stay on board! It's terribly noisy, and the vibrations are so bad it makes one's teeth rattle. Our take off and whole trip generally is pretty good, though. Really not as much turbulence as we'd expected.

Arkady and Nicholai are waiting for us at the Minsk airport to pick us up. Arkady and Nicholai seem genuinely happy to see that I have been able to make the trip. How precious it is to have brothers and sisters concerned and caring for me as I face this challenge of on-going cancer check-ups and treatments.

It's a joyous reunion with Alla and the children—Tanya, Natasha, Nadia, and Helene—as we enter Arkady's apartment. They always seem genuinely thrilled to have us, no matter how much work it means.

At 2:00 p.m., we are served a big feast of chicken, mashed potatoes, cukes, Russian beet salad, veg soup, radishes prepared with sour cream, cream cheese with sour cream, and cheesecake with sour cream. They make most of their dishes with sour cream.

I'm really thankful I bathed and did my hair in Riga, though. One of the first things Arkady announces is that they have no hot water in their flat. This seems to be a common occurrence.

After our big feast, we take a rest and then prepare for this evening's seminar.

We leave at 5:30. Arkady is just learning to drive his Lada, so our trip to the church was pretty interesting, to say the least. Nikolai is a very patient driver's instructor, but the whole thing is pretty hilarious as we chug along with Arkady's efforts in learning to shift. At one point, it wasn't really too funny—we narrowly missed being hit by a truck and a bus. We finally arrive at 6:20 p.m. There are only five group members present tonight, but about six observers, so it's a good size group anyway.

There is a worship service going on upstairs; there are people coming and going, and we hear the singing from the service upstairs.

At one point, I hear clearly and beautifully the strains of the well-known hymn, "I Know Whom I Have Believed." The singing here is glorious and soul searing. "Heavenly" is the only way I can describe it. Luba notices my interest in the service upstairs, so she motions for me to go upstairs with her.

Walking into this large room with the huge white columns, stained window above the pulpit, simple decor of pale blue and white, and a simple cross on the pulpit is a marvelous feeling that this is truly a taste of heaven and how we might worship before God's throne. The singing is done mostly from memory—all verses—and everyone is dressed modestly, most women wearing headscarves. This is clearly no fashion show as is often the case in America. There are five speakers on the platform, and they all take their turns bringing a message. No one seems in any hurry to finish. This whole church setting is actually rather plain, but regal in its sincerity.

During the seminar, I need to make a trip out back to the toilet. I have yet to see a church here in the Soviet Union with a toilet indoors. It's always a plain outhouse with holes in the floor, and so smelly you don't even need to ask where it is; you just follow your nose.

Friday, May 24, 1991   Rainy-Cold

It's a yukky, cold, damp day outside, and there's a reason to be gloomy, but being around Alla and her bright smile lifts my spirits. She serves us all a delicious breakfast: egg soufflé, mashed potatoes, chicken, cold meat and cheese, bread, cookies, and tea.

Since they have no hot water, after breakfast, Arkady takes us to a genuine Russian sauna to get cleaned up. This is a first for us, and an experience we won't forget. (Complete attire for the sauna consisted of a wool stocking cap. Period.) Alla sends soap, towels, shampoo, etc. with us. They take such good care of us!

This complex—a sports hall of sorts—is very crude, with a plain wooden sauna room (100°C), a square cooling tank filled with water, very crude showers, toilet, and lounge room. But we enjoy this treat and chance to get clean, relax, and appreciate Arkady's very sensitive thoughtfulness in bringing us here. The little Russian lady attendant brings us four glasses of tea, and then Arkady brings us a BIG treat—a bottle of Pepsi!

These things are all so much more precious because they are simply not so readily available. We spend two hours here in the sauna. I feel like a new person! *Thank You, Father, for these dear brothers and sisters who give so freely of themselves and what they have.* Now we go back to the flat, and rest for a couple hours.

After dinner, we look at photos we brought of our families, and then we exchange gifts. Arkady's mom (the babushka) gives us some national dolls; Nicholai gives us an ornament made out of cow horns.

Al begins to feel quite ill. But we have another seminar this afternoon at six o'clock.

The room for meeting is freezing! I can't believe how Europeans love to have windows open! Elenora (teacher of English at the university) is translating tonight. I had a chance to talk to her a bit about accepting Christ. Her response: "I think Satan is stopping me from accepting Jesus in my heart. I believe in God, but all my life, I have been told this is foolishness, and I'm afraid to take this step of faith. I am constantly fighting within myself over this." I must pray for Elenora. She cares for her blind mother, she is raising her son by herself, and she needs Jesus.

The seminar goes on with much discussion, but most are really quite obviously tired and are nearly falling asleep. Arkady is one; he does so much for us and others, so it's no wonder he's tired.

After the seminar, Al goes right to bed. He's really feeling flu-ish—nauseous and headachy.

Alla has another meal prepared, so even though I don't feel so terrific, I feel I must accept their urgings to eat. I can't believe all the food that Alla has prepared these two days. It's all been pretty good, but oh so rich. My poor tummy! That was a bit much, but I can only pray, "Where He leads me, I will follow; what He feeds me, I will swallow."

All night long, I feel quite sick. All this rich food and so late at night, it's more than we can handle. Al and I try to lie quietly, and soon we do fall into a rather fitful sleep. We do manage to get by without vomiting, but it's been touch and go, and our plastic barf bags are close at hand.

Saturday, May 25, 1991   Sunny-Cool

At 7:15 a.m., Arkady gives us a ride to the train station. Vladimir meets us at the station and goes with us to Brest to serve as our translator.

There are five children in V.'s family, so there are seven people living in a small three-room flat. But the waiting list is long for a larger one, and they expect it will be the next generation before they realize this.

This train is really yukky; the windows are so filthy you can't even see out. We arrive in Brest at 11:30 a.m. Pastor Jakob meets us, and it's a joyous reunion of seeing him again. He assures us he and his family have been praying, constantly, for my health to be restored.

The seminar is a bit late getting started. But there are seventeen men present—the largest group on the circuit. They're all very eager to learn. It's a joy to be with these dear brothers. Their big, work-calloused hands and their gold-crowned teeth are an ever-present symbol of people here in the East—along with their thoughtful and caring ways.

At 6:15, we end the seminar, and Jakob takes us over to his place for tea. Their house is freezing—windows wide open—toilet out back. But they seem to be perfectly comfortable. I feel like I'm never going to get warm again.

Jakob tells us about his house and how when they first built it twenty years ago they used to have church right here. There would be upwards of two hundred people packed into this four-room house! But it was safer and the only meeting place they had. Now they have more than one thousand at their church. And Jakob says there are many new village churches also.

At 7:30, we say our good-byes. Pastor Jakob takes us back to our hotel where we prepare to leave early in the morning. Our taxi will come at 4:45, so we better sleep fast!

Sunday, May 26, 1991   Cool

The alarm was set wrong, but fortunately, I woke up at 4:15. Yikes! Thirty minutes to get down and catch our taxi to the train station. No time for makeup or hair curling.

The other passenger in the cab was really drunk—obviously been out all night. We arrive at the train station at 5:00 a.m. and now begins the challenge of customs, passport control, and trying to get all our luggage on the train in time.

We enter the cold, dark station with people draped over benches and luggage, trying to get some sleep. Al scouts around looking for the Intourist guide who is supposed to help us. But no one answers the doors, and time is slipping by. How are we ever going to get thru controls in time to catch our train?

As I sit here and wait, my eyes come to rest on an unreal sight that can only occur here in the East. There is a huge mob of people jammed in front of the cashier's door—people pressing and shoving, many are yelling, some are crying. Every once in a while, there's a loud scream from one of the people squeezed in this mob. Many are holding their passports above their heads, so they won't be destroyed by the mad chaos—or maybe just trying to get attention. I can't imagine this is just the "regular" line of people waiting for service.

Finally, the Intourist fellow appears from behind locked doors. We have no idea if this is the fellow we need to help us, but with time passing quickly, we are desperately praying for the right contact. Al just "happens" to approach this young man for help, and lo and behold, he's the one we've been searching for! In this chaotic scene—not knowing the language or even where to begin looking—here he suddenly appears and is ready to show us what to do! *Thank You, Father, for once again showing us Your tender careful concern and Your faithful leading.*

As we are shown where to go, what forms to complete, which doors to go thru, we look wonderingly at this mob scene in front of the cashier's door. The young Intourist fellow nods toward the mob and—in German—explains these are Romanians waiting and hoping desperately to get tickets out to the West.

As I look back at this desperate scene of people waiting to get tickets, suddenly, a woman in her forties, perhaps, breaks thru and makes it thru the door. She falls to her knees and begins to weep and weep. Her young son gathers their belongings around her and attempts to comfort his mother, but she's simply a broken woman—physically, emotionally—and cannot control her emotions. The weeping continues as we leave this area.

As I turned around, I came face to face with a young Russian girl. And with tears in her eyes and some escaping down her cheeks, she says in German, "I guess you know my country." Yes, we know "her" country, and we know the rest of the Soviet Union and former East Bloc as well. It's a "prison" where desperate souls are struggling for survival and hoping against hope to reach another land where they can gain some semblance of humanity again.

At 6:45, Al and I finally reach the railway car we're assigned to, and we board a very crowded train heading for Poland—the Gateway to the West.

The train is icy cold; it's so cold we can see our breath! This is going to be one long ride. I keep on my cap, gloves, and coat. Al covers me with his coat also, and finally, I'm able to drift off to sleep for a while. At 9:30, the train comes to a stop; we can see we haven't reached our destination yet. There's no explanation; everyone is simply ordered to deboard the train. So people start unloading, handing box after box, bag after bag, out the windows to the waiting arms of their travel partners. Everyone just stands around wondering what to do. We're literally in the middle of nowhere, so how can we get to the airport?!

We finally decide we must try, so pushing/shoving/carrying our bags, we begin to walk. We finally reach a station and try to get a taxi, but its Sunday, so they're charging double today! Twenty dollars for a lift to the airport! It's too far to walk, so we have no choice but to pay the guy.

Al secures tickets for us to get to Vienna, so now all we have to do is wait the three hours till flight time. We read, snack, walk, and finally, get warmed up. The time goes pretty fast.

At 1:30, we board this beautiful, wonderfully, clean plane with cheery, smiling flight attendants, and we're on our last leg of our journey home to Vienna! How grateful we are for all the care God has shown us! For the many marvelous experiences of learning and fellowship and for the anticipated visa and apartment for us in Riga.

Chapter 28

BACK IN WIENER NEUDORF AFTER USSR TRIP

Encouragement

It was encouraging for us to see the serious dedication of the Biblical Education by Extension students. Some of these pastors and lay leaders shared, with choked voices and tears in their eyes, how grateful they were for the BEE World study program. Many shared how God had immediately used what they were learning. One told of being invited down to the KGB headquarters in his city to explain to them what the Bible teaches. Others were immediately passing on the things they had been learning by speaking in public schools and universities, in hospitals, and in prisons. Some were even taking their training far into unreached areas of Siberia and Soviet Central Asia, where they preached the gospel and taught the fundamentals of Christianity.

Some of the concerns we had for our BEE World students we shared with our supporters:

- Many of God's faithful servants will be tempted by the lure of material wealth and personal comfort as new opportunities arise.

- They'll face a flood of false teachers and a multitude of missionaries from all over the world, often leading to divisions within their churches as some follow one group and some follow others.

Once we reached Vienna, we experienced sunny, warm weather. We still had an hour and a half trip on public transportation to reach our home in Wiener Neudorf, but adrenaline helped us keep on going. We'd been traveling for about thirteen to fourteen hours, so we were beat when we got home.

It looked like things were well at home. There was quite a bit of mail and no emergency's while we were gone. I (Betty) unpacked, bathed, had a bite, and then fell thankfully into our own bed.

I was itching—must have picked up some kind of bugs again.

It was good to be back home in Wiener Neudorf, but even more than that, I was looking forward to getting back to the States again. I was experiencing so much pain under my arm, in my breast area, and kept wondering just what was going on. Without the use of a physician here in Europe, one's imaginings could get away with one, so I was looking forward to some "after-care" from my surgery. My back bothered me a lot—all kinds of pain. Little did I know what lay ahead in this area.

We were so thankful that a five-room flat had been spotted for us in Riga, which was almost unheard of, especially for only two people. That would allow us to dedicate one room for an office and one room for a guest room. God provided so beautifully, and it was a wonderful testimony of His grace to all those who would hear of this gift. So it seemed things were falling into place for us to move to Riga. I don't mind saying I was more than a little nervous about this; however, in seeing how God was moving out before us, it was hard not to have confidence in His leading.

We had about a week left here in Austria before some time in the States, and then moving into Latvia, a republic of the Soviet Union. *I love this home in the village of Wiener Neudorf, and it's going to be very hard to leave it, but I'm trusting you, Father.* I spent most of the morning after our return in my office, writing a simple, evangelistic letter to family members. I wanted everyone to really know how to come to know our Lord Jesus. How I prayed it might touch even one heart and change that life from turmoil to peace. I was feeling so rotten again, but dearly desired to finish this letter.

Oh Father, I pray You will work through these letters to bring glory to Yourself. I thank You for the possibility of a flat in Riga, and I pray it will meet our needs. Thank You for the devotions this morning, which spoke of courage in You. Not that we are brave, but we can say "no" to our fears because we know the Source of true courage.

Biblical Education by Extension Retreat in Germany

BEE World held a retreat near Berchtesgaden, Germany. It was the place where Adolph Hitler had his Eagle's Nest Chalet during WWII.

The mountains around Berchtesgaden were glorious in their majestic splendor. The trees were absolutely exquisite with their covering of snow and frost. Everything looked so picturesque and hardly seemed real. We spent quite a lot of time with Hans and Helen S. at the retreat and got to know them a bit better. They were a wonderful, servant-like couple, who were invaluable to

Gathering with Our Teammates — May 1991

us a bit farther down the way. How marvelous of God to put us together with other believers who were ready and willing to serve one another.

After the retreat, Al went to the office. He brought home a list of items we might need in the Soviet Union that would be hard to obtain. It seemed the hard currency shops were exorbitantly high—like forty-eight dollars for a two-pound beef roast! *May I take just one day at a time, and not worry today about the problems we may face in the future.*

I was being bothered again with what felt like either lice, mites, or whatever. I was itching like crazy and had bites on various parts of my body. I gave myself a "treatment" with an emollient, but it didn't help much. I suspected the cap I bought to warm my cold head in Tallinn, Estonia, of being infested. Much as I hated to do so, I threw it in the garbage.

Suddenly, it was moving day! This was the day when all our furniture was moved from our home into warehouse storage, and our transition actually became a reality. It was a strange feeling. I was excited about the future, and yet I was somewhat anxious as well. We'd been so blessed here in Austria—such nice, comfortable surroundings in a convenient location. It felt like home already. We'd been here eight and a half years, so it was going to take some mental and emotional adjusting in order to switch gears for another land.

Summer Schedule

Our recent meetings in Latvia led to a decision to make Riga, in the Soviet Republic of Latvia, our new home, instead of Moscow. So, we made plans for a time in the States that summer to prepare for our upcoming new life.

While in the States (June 14–August 31), we took care of various medical and dental needs, made out-of-state visits that we were unable to do the prior winter, began Russian language studies, prepared for fall teaching seminars, purchased things we needed in Riga but couldn't buy there, and made many other necessary preparations for living and ministering in the Soviet Union.

Mail

One of the things we'd miss in Riga was the dependable mail and telephone service we enjoyed in Austria. Now our mail would have to be carried in from Austria via our colleagues from Vienna, who were usually pretty well burdened with their own things and the various books, medicines, and other things they would bring in for our students.

We'd request our supporters to send lightweight items, such as herbs, marshmallows, popcorn, rice, bar soap. Duplicated items were never a problem as the store shelves were often bare. Flour and sugar were rationed items, which meant we couldn't buy them without ration cards. A favorite useful and appreciated item was coffee, especially decaf.

Chapter 29

SUMMER IN USA

Return to America — June 14–August 31, 1991

Prior to our move into the Soviet Union, we made one more trip back to America. Travel was always stressful—the plane was crowded, it was hot in the cabin, the handle of my suitcase broke, we barely made our connection in Minneapolis to Fargo.

We flew parallel to a thunderstorm, with an incredible lightning display all the way from Minneapolis to Fargo. I (Betty) recognized afresh just how insignificant we humans were in God's big world. But then I remembered that God was my Refuge, a present help in every storm.

When we arrived in Fargo, we were there only minutes when Hans S. called from Vienna and said he'd pick us up at the Vienna Airport when we returned. But that wasn't all! Hans also said that he and Helen would haul our things to Riga in the "Bee Mobile" (a large black and yellow all-purpose Mercedes van owned by our Vienna mission office)! All this without our even requesting it. How good God is! God's timing is so perfect. We'd been wondering all along how we were going to manage, but God knew.

Thank you, Father, for Your wonderful way of letting us see You at work in our lives. It is a tremendous strength and comfort to know that You are there and so capable of providing for our every need. We'll need Your help in arranging all these visits, Lord. I get so weary just thinking about it all.

I felt so terribly stretched. But first, I needed to get rid of this itchy stuff on my head. I saw Dr. M., who said I'd been bitten by spiders! They had left their residue behind, and that was what was making me itch. Dr. M. prescribed some antihistamines and some shampoo to get rid of this yukky stuff. Oh the price of following Jesus!

My next item of business was to complete all my medical tests. The scan, mammogram, chest x-ray, and lab work all turned out negative. *Oh, praise You, Heavenly Father!* My heart soared with gratitude for this gift of grace. Dr. M. said the pain I felt seemed to be coming from the scarring and nerve damage.

Then we made our way out to the cottage on Lake Cormorant, which had been made available to us as our "headquarters" for the next ten weeks. The spot here on the lake was so beautiful. The accommodations were rather simple, but it was private. We didn't have to share with anyone else! *Another one of Your precious gifts, Lord. The calm quiet of this serene evening here at the lake is almost more than we can take in! Thank You, dear Father, for Your goodness through these dear saints.*

It was cool in the cabin, but the spectacular sunrise coming up over the lake in the morning was totally worth it. It was so pretty, a natural beauty that far exceeded anything we could have ever imagined. We used this haven as a respite and for meetings throughout our time in America. It was such a cool and lovely comfort to our aching souls. All too soon, we'd be back in the huge, noisy, bustling cities of Europe, so we tried hard to soak in this wonderful, peaceful lakeside setting in Minnesota.

Chapter 30

BEGINNING OUR MOVE— AUSTRIA TO LATVIA

All too soon, we were saying our good-byes again as we prepared to leave the States. It seemed that was all we ever did—greet people after long absences, then say good-bye as we left again. The trip was a long one—thirty-five hours from the time we left the lake till our reception at the guest house in lower Austria.

Jeff, Hans, and Helen were at the airport in Vienna to meet us when we arrived. They took us, along with all our luggage, to a guest house run by another mission organization. It was so nice to have some privacy, and the cost was only a few dollars a night, including breakfast.

We got to bed about 1:00 a.m., but being so exhausted and dealing with the seven-hour time difference, I ended up sleeping until 3:15 p.m. the next day! I had never in my life slept so many hours at one time before!

We spent most of the next day shopping for last-minute items to take to Riga with us. However, we were already so overloaded, so I tried to limit our purchases to only the most essential items not already prepared for loading onto the van. I just prayed we didn't leave anything too important behind. Here I was concerned about how much flour to bring, and Al was the one concerned about more immediate things, like border crossings in these tumultuous times.

What follows are Betty's journal entries chronicling our move from Vienna to Lithuania in October 1991.

Sunday, October 6, 1991   Sunny–Mild

What in the world would we have done if Hans and Helen had not offered to transport our belongings to Latvia in this large van? My emotions are pretty frazzled right now; how I longed to settle down in one spot for a time. *How grateful we are, Lord, that You are sovereign. Give us the grace and the confidence to know that You are in control, no matter what.*

The Enemy has been having a heyday with me lately. I keep wondering what I'm actually doing here and what good it will be for me to live in Latvia. Yes, Al has his work, but my "job" is totally different. A dear, dear sister in the Lord gave me a wonderful boost of encouragement by saying to me, "Just your presence, alone, is a tremendous ministry to these people." Oh, how that lifted my spirits and gave me new and inspired faith.

We're going to need a great faith to believe that this old van can, indeed, hold together with such an overload of our things and on such rough roads.

Bless us with Your arm of safety, Lord. How thankful I am that we can depend on You, Father. Al was working so hard. He's loaded it all himself, and he's had to rearrange a lot of what's left too. He's beat. Protect him from injury, Lord.

Al seemed led to call our German diplomat friend. Manfred expressed great concern for our proposed plan and route to Riga. He told us that even he could not get through to Poland and Lithuania. He said people were waiting for days in Belorussia to cross into Lithuania and Latvia. Things were simply chaotic, this being the tail end of the revolution. Everyone is confused. These republics (now in the process of becoming independent countries) are in many cases, having to create international borders where none existed before. Manfred suggests that our best hope of getting into Latvia, with all our belongings, is to go up through Czechoslovakia, on to former East Germany, take a ferry across the Baltic Sea (a twenty-one-hour trip) to Lithuania, and then on into Latvia.

Monday, October 7, 1991   Sunny–Mild

One step forward and two steps back! Our departure time was scheduled for 7:00 a.m. this morning; however, just last night, when we spoke with our German diplomat friend, we learned that Poland is not allowing people to cross over into Lithuania. So now what? We call Hans and Helen and tell them about these latest developments and decide to delay our departure until we can seek God's mind further on all this. It's a long, restless night for us.

After a full morning together with Hans and Helen, praying, making phone calls, studying maps for various possibilities, we determine that the route through Czechoslovakia, East Germany, and then the twenty-one-hour ferry across the Baltic Sea to Lithuania will be our best option, thereby avoiding Poland and Belorussia altogether. Reports have it that people are waiting three to four days at their borders with very limited facilities while you wait! You simply stay in your car.

Our next challenge is trying to book passage on a ferry. After many tries, we are told they had room for the two vehicles and two persons, but we need to be there by 9:00 a.m., October 9. It's already midday on the seventh. And what do we do about the booking for the third and fourth person? In a split-second decision (while on the phone to East Germany), we decide to go ahead and book for the available space and pray that somehow we can talk our way through their letting Helen and me come along too.

So now we decide to leave Vienna within a couple of hours and drive as far as Dresden, and then hopefully, make it to the port by 9:00 a.m. on the ninth. We are all frazzled and we haven't even left Austria yet! We spend time in prayer. Oh, how we need God's strength for this trip.

At 3:00 p.m., we meet Hans and Helen, load their things onto an already overloaded van and car, and head out to Prague,

Czechoslovakia. It's slow driving on a two-lane highway. The van is packed to capacity, so that is also slowing us down. We average thirty to forty miles per hour max.

We drive into the Prague area around 9:30/10:00 p.m. We are soooooooooo tired, but in order to make the port on time, we need to keep on. We cross the border into East Germany and finally reach Dresden about 1:30 a.m. We pounded on the doors of four different hotels, but only one responded. She told us very bluntly and explicitly, "There is no room in the inn." However, Hans knows a Christian brother in Dresden (one of our BEE World students). We call him, and he welcomes us to come and stay with them, no matter what time. *Thank you, Jesus!*

The border crossings have all been easy thus far. They haven't made us unload anything yet, praise God. Two scenes that will remain forever in my mind are: 1) Twelve to fifteen miles of trucks lined up and waiting to cross the border into East Germany, and 2) Hordes of prostitutes "working" the highway, especially around the waiting trucks. They all look so young!

Now it's 3:30 a.m., and we're just reaching our Christian friend in Dresden. Gottfried welcomes us into their flat and shows us into their dining room and living room, where the couches have been prepared for us to spread our sleeping bags. Our "bed" is narrow, so Al spreads his bag on the floor and quickly drops off into an exhausted sleep. My mind goes over the events of this long day. I thank God with a grateful heart for His protection on very rough, narrow roads. With our heavy load, there are so many things that could have gone wrong, and we have no clue as to what lies ahead of us.

With Al and Hans driving to the point of utter exhaustion, we KNOW it was God's holy angels giving us watchful care.

We're back out on the road the next day with all our wares. All of a sudden, I hear this loud bang in front of us. Hans has just had a blow out on the van. The van is out of control, weaving and

BEGINNING OUR MOVE—AUSTRIA TO LATVIA

swaying all over the place. I frantically pray, *God, help us! Oh God, give Hans Your strength! We're in Your hands Oh, God!*

In a matter of seconds (it seemed like days to me!), Hans maneuvered the van out of oncoming traffic, regained control of the high and heavy load which threatened to overturn the van, and was able to get it over to the right shoulder, where he stopped. WHEW! Only the Lord's quick and mighty hand could have spared us a tragic accident in these last few minutes. Our hearts are pounding as we get out and survey the shredded mass of rubber, which just moments ago was our tire. Thank God for His protection!

The spare tire is very old, dried out, and smaller than the original, but our prayer is that it will get us to a place where we can have it replaced. We need to drive even more slowly now with this old tire and no spare tire. Before starting out again, we all stand beside the van here on this busy highway, heads bowed, thanking God for His mercy, and asking for His care and guidance in leading us to a tire store where we can have our spare replaced. We know that this will require another miracle, since to find a tire store out here in the middle of nowhere before we arrive in Berlin will take God's

Thanking God for Safety After Highway Tire Blowout

intervention. If we have to stop in Berlin to find another tire, we'll never make our ferry on time.

We decide to get back on the road. We drive only a short distance in the open countryside when we see a small sign along the road that says, "Reifen" (tires), pointing to a tire warehouse in a patch of trees down a side road! Oh, how marvelous are His mercies—new every morning and continuous beyond belief. Our hearts rejoiced!

We rejoice over God's provision of a new tire, but it is already 4:00 p.m., and we have nearly three hundred kilometers to drive before reaching our destination for the night. Now that might not sound like much of a challenge until you realize that we can only drive thirty-five to forty-five miles per hour. But God is with us, so we confidently resume our journey. The drive is exhausting, hard, and intense, with extremely fast traffic, but our hearts are full, for we have seen the Lord in His protection and provision of a new tire!

I'm so grateful that Hans, with his fluency in German, his boldness, and his connections, is able to secure a room for us that night. Never in a million years could we have arranged for a better couple to help us move!

We reach our destination at 11:30 p.m. The hotel is merely adequate despite the high rate, but we're so thankful to have it that we gladly put up with the four lumpy, horsehair beds in one room, the noisy street sounds, the filthy carpets, and the mold on the walls.

In the morning, we prayed without ceasing as we drove to the port, asking God for passage on this ferry to Lithuania. We desperately need passage on this vessel. The complications would be endless if we were refused. We are also praying for grace to accept whatever plan God has in mind for us, regardless of what that might mean. Soon, we will know what the outcome will be.

Arriving at the ferry office, we saw Frau Stenzel almost immediately. She came at us with a scowl on her face and with a loud voice, said in German, "I told you very plainly that there is room only for two people!" Hans replied, "Yes, we understand that, but we thought perhaps some of your reservations would not show up." She quickly looks over to her colleague and says, "What shall we do?" While it's true that the cabins have been reserved, the people aren't here yet.

We are all storming the gates of heaven with silent prayer during this decision making. "Shall we turn these people down and take a chance on not filling the available space? Or should we accept these people because they are here first?" She answers herself and in her crisp official German says, "Güte! We shall accept these people since they are already here first."

> *Hallelujah! Thank You, Jesus! Praise to Your mighty power, which we have just now clearly witnessed again. How can our hearts do anything but rejoice? Step by precious step, our great God has provided immeasurably more than all we ask or imagine, according to His power (Ephesians 3:20).*

We leave the dock office floating on air and spiritually buoyed up, once again stopping and bowing in grateful prayer beside our vehicles.

Another stressful period of time now as we wait for customs control officials to check our load to determine whether to let us pass without unloading everything for inspection and paying customs fees before we are permitted to drive onboard the ship. At first, they insist we unload everything. However, Hans argues with them until they agree to let us through without unloading anything—as long as we promise we would never come back through here again. So again, we are spared as they waved us on through and on to the ferry. *Thank You, Jesus!*

This ship is massive. There are all kinds of Russian vehicles aboard—all going back to Russia. The attendant took us upstairs. Surprise! Our quarters are clean, attractive, roomy, and very pleasant. Meals are all included. What a gift! This ship is actually nicer than our hotel rooms typically are. We have nice private quarters, a shower, a toilet, and very comfortable beds!

Thursday, October 10, 1991　　　　　　　　　Sunny-Mild

The steward calls us to wake us up at 5:30 a.m. to prepare for landing in Lithuania. While we had some anxious moments after debarking from the East German ferry, we were now ready to officially enter Lithuania. Finally, the last guard looks at our passports and visas, lifts the gate, and waves us on through.

We relax a bit, but we still have one more border to cross—that between Lithuania and Latvia, some hundred miles farther on. Reaching the border, we hold our breath and continue praying as we pull up to the barriers. The Lithuanian guard glanced at our passports and waved us through. The Latvian guards didn't even bother to get off their stools. They just sat there, watching our big black-and-yellow van and Austrian car cautiously moving through the border controls as though they were seeing some kind of apparition. With chin in hands, they simply waved us on through! How can it be? It can and IS so only because of the powerful God we serve who can do what no man can do. *Hallelujah, Lord, we praise and thank You for Your great control and most of all for Your love.*

We are literally home free now, since this border is the one we had the most concern over. We continue on, driving about six more hours to our final destination, Riga, Latvia. The huge potholes in the roads, and so many cars driving without lights, keep us mindful of just how dangerous it is to be driving here. So, we continue on at a slow rate, until we finally see the lights of Riga! Little did we know what challenges awaited us there.

It takes us two and a half hours of searching in the dark to find the apartment secured for us. But when we entered the gloomy, dark, rundown building with hallways covered with grime and opened the door to what was supposed to be our new home, our hearts sank. *Oh God, strengthen me. Help me hold up, for Al's sake, as well as my own.*

Hans and Helen are the support God sent with us to this forlorn land. How terribly grateful I am for their presence. We're in shock.

Al & Betty Arrive Safe in Latvia — October 1991

I turn to Helen with tears in my eyes and say, "It's soooooooooo gross!" Helen responds with, "I know." *Thank You, again, Father, for these dear angels of mercy.* Helen's response means more to me than anything else could have meant at this time, because I could see that she was truly identifying with my despair.

The Lord somehow gave us the courage to unload all our things tonight, even when every fiber in our bodies wants desperately to turn around and run back to Austria. All four of us are completely exhausted, emotionally and physically, by the time we finish, but we find some bread and tea in our belongings and, before going to bed, spend time thanking God for our safe arrival. Hans then shares with us how Al and I have had been an inspiration to THEM, to go where God would have THEM go. This is what led them to offer to help us with our move to Latvia.

Friday, October 11, 1991   Sunny – Mild

The next morning brought some sunshine and lovely weather, which hasn't changed the ugliness of our flat, but I got up and prepared a bite to eat for us all with the bread, cheese, and coffee we'd brought along. We spend time with Hans and Helen surveying this place and brainstorming possibilities for making this place a bit more livable. After a time of sharing and prayer, these dear angels turn to us and tell us that they had decided not to return to Vienna immediately, but to stay here and help us get settled. How precious! God knew we'd need someone like Hans and Helen. Hans has handyman skills, and he never goes anyplace without his tools, so we were ready almost immediately to begin refurbishing this place.

    We then took some time to decide what took priority. We all concur that a working fridge is important. But for today, we put on our work clothes, unpack the soaps and disinfectants, and begin scraping, scrubbing, and scouring. It takes knives and diesel fuel to cut the thick layers of grime—nothing else works. We all have raw hands and aching backs by days end and arms so sore we can't wait to get to bed. We are so weary, but the place smells a bit better, and there are a few less roaches in sight. Night is a time to rest, but not for the roaches. This is their time to scrounge, so they start appearing all over the place. We set a bunch of traps and pray that there will be fewer by morning.

Saturday, October 12, 1991   Sunny – Warm – Lovely

We can't wait to get downtown and see if we can find a refrigerator! We start at the little mission office, where Helena and Genady have their work. There is a little store in the basement of their building, so after stumbling down the broken-down steps to the store part, we go in and find one little refrigerator. Refrigerators here are the small, apartment-size ones that fit under the counter, but that is fine. Would you believe that this is the only one we ever saw for sale in a city of over a million people? These are Soviet times, so merchandise in stores is merely stuff that they weren't able to sell to the West. *Thank you, Jesus, for yet another provision.*

But now what? There is no delivery service here. Suddenly, a Norwegian evangelist appears at the ministry office. Guess what? He's driving a van! Yes! He readily agreed to haul our new fridge. Not only that, but he led the way as he'd been at our apartment on previous trips, so we didn't have to get lost! How good is our Father?!

This same evangelist also gave us some tips about living in Riga, which turned out to be extremely valuable.

Sunday, October 13, 1991 — Sunny-Cool

It's Sunday, and a lovely day with lots of sunshine and a crisp feel in the air. We found a church with a German language service, which was a blessing. My, how my German background is coming into play, a gift from our Father.

We met a doctor at this church, who told us that most of the Germans were hauled off to Siberia and other parts during the war. That's why there are now very few left in Riga. I'm thankful, however, for the ones that are here. It's an awfully lonely feeling to be so isolated and not be able to understand or communicate in worship and fellowship with the Latvians and Russians.

After church, we wandered around the city and came onto an open-air market. It was encouraging to find some fresh veggies and various other items. Meat, eggs, cheese, etc. are virtually non-existent, but we found some cabbage, carrots, peppers, and onions. Even though these things don't look really great, they should still make some edible soup.

It's getting cold in our flat. The rule is that we didn't get any heat until the fifteenth; so hopefully, it will be turned on today. We've been supplementing with a little space heater. I made some hot chocolate for our breakfast with milk from the store—fresh from the farmer's barn. We hadn't gotten sick yet, but don't know the long-term effects of what we're eating and

Buying Milk in Latvia — 1991. Bring Your Own Bottle

drinking yet. Our purchases are limited, since we don't have citizenship cards, which are necessary to get ration cards to make purchases.

Finally, we hit the jackpot! A store with paint, turpentine, and an acceptable pattern of wallpaper. The paint cans are rusty and smeared with paint, and the paper is very poor quality, but at least, we can have some clean walls.

Helen is an angel from the Lord. She scrubs and scrubs, never complaining, taking the worst jobs, and always ready for more. *How I praise You, Lord, for this devoted servant of Yours, and that You have given her to us as a sister in You.*

As I watch people going in and out of the little store across the street, it suddenly hits me that all day long there is a steady stream of people coming out with the same thing—bread! That's pretty much all there is. I did find a little store today where I bought a couple things I couldn't identify. When I got it home, I discovered it was some kind of soft, mushy cheese. If we get sick from it, we'll know it's not safe to eat. There was a long line waiting for some fatty, bony pork, but it looked so bad, I didn't feel it worth taking a chance. With all the flies on it, it didn't exactly enhance my appetite.

The heat is on! *Thank You, Lord, for this blessing.* It was really getting pretty cold in here, and it's going to take a while to heat up all these concrete walls and floors. Hans and Al are installing our new cupboards. It's quite a task, since nothing is even. They have to cut out and make adjustments for all kinds of water and gas pipes. I am so grateful for their support. Even with these dear friends, it's still an overwhelming task to get this flat livable.

Saturday, October 20, 1991   Cloudy-Cold-Windy-Rain

After eight days of helping us get our flat livable, it's time for Hans and Helen to go back to Vienna. Oh, it was such a hard thing to have them go. They have been my support, my strength, my encouragement. *Father, they have been the embodiment of Your Son. Thank You, precious Father, for this week of showing Yourself to me so clearly through Hans and Helen. But now I must lean wholly on You, Lord. Give me the faith to go on, Lord. Help me yield to Your molding, Lord.*

There's still no washing machine hook up. It's so hard communicating the things we want to have done. So, we use our clean clothes sparingly and pray for a plumber who might be able to understand our sign language.

Tuesday, October 22, 1991

This morning, we awoke to a surprise we hope never to encounter again as long as we live here. A flood of sewage is coming out of our bathroom! The sewer is plugged, so all the yukky sewage from the eight floors above us is coming into our kitchen sink and toilets, across our hallway and into our living room. We bail with buckets and mop until a reasonable hour to call our friends. They get in touch with the building maintenance person, but she says the plumber can't come until noon or later!

Our dear Lord, however, came to our rescue through the visit of a pastor friend from America. Now you would think that with a pastor coming to visit that about all we'd do is sit in the parlor and drink tea. But not Pastor Don! After coming in and greeting everyone, he immediately rolled up his white shirt sleeves and his pant legs and began mopping right along with us. What a blessing! What an encouragement to see his example of demonstrated love. *Thank You, Father, for Your people, who see themselves as not beneath such a job as this.*

At 2:00 p.m., we are all still mopping and scrubbing. Once our Latvian friend arrived, he was able to notify all the tenants and have them stop using the toilets and sinks until we got this problem resolved. So finally, at 4:30 p.m., the plumber arrived. His eyes were big as saucers when he saw our mess. It's dark and late, but the plumbers are still working. At long last, our sewage overflow has been stopped.

After eleven hours of fighting this sewer problem, and endless frustrations with not being able to get help, we now face the gruesome task of cleaning up the mess. We have been initiated, royally, into what we hear so often from people here, "Here in our system."

The worst of it all is that having a flat on the first floor of the building makes us vulnerable for frequent reoccurrences of this problem. Not a pleasant thought to look forward to. Tonight, our hands are raw, our backs and legs ache, and our flat reeks like a sewer, but we are so grateful that the problem has come to a halt.

That night, I fell into our not so good bed and, in spite of being tired and sore, made good use of this European bed with the two singles shoved together, with that "hump," or gap, in the middle of the twins to contend with.

We've been working nearly two weeks now, and while we've made a lot of progress, there is still so terribly much to do. *Lord Jesus, help me walk in Your Spirit. Help me be strong and patient. Give me up-building thoughts to help Al. Right now, it all seems too hard, and future days look black.*

For the most part, we've been assured that living in this apartment building is as safe as it gets in Riga. We have not seen any sign of things that might frighten us so far. But one day, the plumber, whom we desperately needed, knocked on our door. Al wasn't home, so I answered. Lo and behold, it was the plumber, alright; however, he was totally drunk, wobbling and swaying all over the place. He backed me into the kitchen, and about that time, I got very scared. I called out to Al, under the guise that he was there with me, and pushed my way around the plumber to the hallway. Then I pointed to his tools and then to the door. He got the message and left. It was an anxious time for me. It made me realize just how vulnerable I was there by myself.

Thursday, October 24, 1991   Cloudy-Cold-Grey

Our newly gained friends, along with the ones who are more "friendly" than necessary, are surely a motley lot of people, and it reminds me of the many whom Christ befriended and gathered unto himself.

I'll tell you about Mr. B. He was a funny little man—short, balding, flighty, and almost frail in his construction. But he scurries around and gets things done—the Russian way! He's been hanging paper for us, which isn't an easy task with all the bumps and crevices on these rough walls. But it's so grossly dirty that anything would be a 50 percent improvement. He's teaching us a lot about conserving materials. His piecing all the small stuff together in order to make the paper "stretch" is a classic example of how they make things last. Everything is so hard to come by that they save wherever they can. Matching the pattern in installation would waste paper, so he doesn't worry about making it match! Fortunately, it's not a large pattern, so it doesn't show too much.

Mr. B. is so desirous of doing his best, though, that one cannot help but appreciate and be grateful for his help.

Just a bit about trying to make a meal here. It's lunchtime, and I want to feed Mr. B. before he heads home on that long trolley ride. I fix some potatoes, a little ham, some pickles, and Kool-Aid to drink. Mr. B. was quite impressed, especially with the meat. He said they rarely buy meat; it's just too expensive. For us, it costs about a dollar for two pounds, but for nationals, it costs about a sixth of their monthly wage. The meat isn't good, and one always wonders whether it's spoiled or contaminated, but I try to cook the daylights out of it to kill as much bacteria as possible. (The *Wycliffe International Cookbook* has been very helpful.)

Mr. B. told us about his father being shipped off to Siberia during the war. His mom and the children were sent to Moscow. Then he was conscripted into the army. In his broken English and emotional state, he expressed deep sadness over the war and the oppression by the Russians. It must have been so horrible. Every family here seems to have a similar story, and none can share without weeping as they remember the horror of it all.

After lunch, I walk to the store and am happy to find what appears to be oatmeal. The stores are dirty, old, dark, with bare cement floors and rusty bins for the bread. The bread is mostly stale, but they have a spoon hanging by the bins that people can use to "test" the bread for hardness. The loaves, of course, aren't wrapped, so instead of punching with fingers, one has to do the "spoon test." The ingredients are poor, and there are, of course, no preservatives, so the bread dries out really fast. Today, though, they have chicken! All intact—head and comb and feet still on and innards all in place—and thank goodness, dead.

There was this snazzy looking lady, all decked out in a nice coat and hat, who came in and bought her chicken—only partially plucked and still with head and feet intact. Nonchalantly, she stuck this thing right into her purse! Off she walked in her uppity manner with the chicken feet sticking out of her nice handbag. In this country, one's dignity and pride go right out the window in a hurry in view of survival and putting food on the table.

Wednesday, October 23, 1991   Cold-Dreary-Grey

As we continue adjusting to our new home in this very different culture, we often praise God for our success in finding food. Food is indeed scarce, but by making the rounds of various stores and markets each day, we've been able to find an adequate number of items such as potatoes, cabbages, carrots, cheese, tea, bread, oatmeal, and "manna," which is like our Cream of Wheat. We have also brought a lot of staples, like flour, rice, cooking oil, and dried soup mixes, from Vienna.

We praise God for our German language ability. We've found that the people here who speak no English often speak German, and this has allowed us to communicate in a number of important situations. PRAY for our acquisition of some basic Russian and Latvian language ability for everyday situations where neither English nor German is spoken.

The plumber finally came today and installed our new kitchen sink. But the workmanship is so shoddy that as I wipe around the faucet, a whole bunch of enamel chips come with my rag! As I said, the workmanship is shoddy, and that's not all. Our kitchen sink now has hot water in BOTH faucets! The reality of life here is beginning to settle in.

Mr. B. finally finished the wallpapering today, and we wanted to settle up with him, but he refused to give us a price. He simply said, "You needed help, and I come. It comes from my heart." And all this from a non-believer (his daughter is one of our students).

After pressing him a bit, he finally said, "You can get me some of those instruments [tools]." He was awed by the equipment Al was using and was amazed at the quality. No such things are available here. We told him we'd try to get some tools for him. His response was that of one given a million dollars! He hugged and kissed Al I don't know how many times and, with tears in his eyes, tried to express his gratitude. Our whole experience with Mr. B. has been rich in so many ways, and I just pray that he is closer to the Lord's Kingdom as a result of our time together.

December 1991

It's Sunday again today, and we attend the worship service at the Church of the Cross, where Al is involved in training a group of their young men. Worship was SO good! A lot of special music… they don't worry about the time element here…however long it takes is alright. The pastor asked Al to share. He wasn't anticipating this and wasn't prepared, but we've learned to have at least preparations for brief greetings and a mini-sermon in our back pocket ready to use, so that we are able to at least bring greetings from our brothers and sisters in America. It's such an encouragement to the believers here to know that others are praying for them and not forgetting the hardships they face.

We had a chance to visit, briefly, with Pastor J. It's obvious he has been through much suffering during his many years in prison, since he has such a compassionate spirit. We also visited with Victor P., who has just returned from Siberia, and he told us that believers are growing by leaps and bounds there and churches are being established, but literature is so scarce, especially Bibles. No Westerners ever get that far east.

Chapter 31

HEROES IN LATVIA— NEW MINISTRY ROLE

FIFTY RED DOTS CHALLENGE

October 1991 Heroes in Latvia

[This story is a prayer letter written by Al to our supporters back in the States.]

The old white-haired Russian preacher was frail, and he had to hold his Bible just inches from his eyes in order to read his text. This small church on the outskirts of Riga, Latvia, was packed with perhaps four hundred people this cool October morning. The ceiling was decorated with strings of brightly colored autumn leaves, and branches full of fall foliage had been placed around the walls. The singing of these believers was unbelievably beautiful. It clearly came from deep within their souls.

With life here so difficult and dreary, we could understand their enthusiasm and sense of praise earlier in the service as they sang, "When the Roll Is Called Up Yonder, I'll be There." What a contrast to compare this present world with the glorious future God has promised to His beloved children!

At one point during the service, our translator leaned over and asked, "How long will you be in Riga?" "We live here! This is now our home," I responded. His eyes got as big as saucers as he considered this. "You are heroes to come and live here!" he exclaimed. Well, we knew we were not heroes; we were simply doing what God had called us to do. Nevertheless, by living here and sharing in their everyday problems, we could better relate to them and better impact their lives.

The old preacher's message was the third full-length sermon this Sunday morning. His text was Matthew 5:1-5, with his message centered on verse 4: "Blessed are those who mourn, for they will be comforted." He pointed out how so many in Latvia mourned because of sin and hardship in this present world. "Jesus is the only answer," he said, and if we knew Him and the comfort He gives, then we must tell others about Him.

That was why we were there. We believed that God wanted to use us to encourage and equip His people in the Baltics as together we worked to make the gospel of Christ Jesus known. Since we arrived on October 10, we'd been busy getting settled. At the same time, we were beginning to work with various church leaders to help establish training centers for pastors and other Christian workers. It was not going to be easy.

Al's Changing Role

After weeks of focusing mainly on making our apartment livable and learning how to survive, we now turned our attention to the work God had given to us here in the Baltics. One of the remarkable changes was the freedom to do open ministry. We could move our seminary books around openly; we could meet openly with our church leader study groups in homes or in their churches, with no fear of arrests for "illegal" activities. In our new location and in these changed circumstances, our role was somewhat different from our cloak-and-dagger days.

JOB TITLE: Biblical Education by Extension Co-Coordinator for Estonia, Latvia, Lithuania, and Belarus.

PURPOSE: Help to establish new Christian training centers, Bible Institutes, and seminaries and to provide assistance to existing ones.

GOAL: Equip present and future church leaders to better shepherd the church and to expand the church through evangelism, discipleship, and the planting of new churches.

MAJOR AREAS OF RESPONSIBILITY: Promote and demonstrate a life of faith and spirituality in ourselves, through our teaching, and in our ministry.

Assist in the design and establishment of the various training centers being started.

Plan and lead approximately one-fourth of the seminars for the courses being taught by BEE World this fall and winter; courses include Evangelism and Discipleship, Galatians/Romans, New Testament Survey, and Old Testament Survey.

As we sought to equip God's people for ministry, they sometimes challenged us by saying, "Don't only tell us how to do these things; show us how!" Perhaps more was conveyed by what they saw in us and in our lives, than by what was taught in the classroom. Our prayer was that the Holy Spirit's power would effectively work in and through us to accomplish His purpose in all our relationships and in all that we said and did.

Fifty Red Dots—New Challenge

One of our key church leaders in Latvia was already ahead of us in his thoughts about the new opportunities.

We had been settled in Riga only about a month when I (Al) stopped into his tiny office one mid-November morning and saw him sitting at his desk, placing little red dots all over his open map of Latvia. I asked, "Genadij, what are you doing?" He looked up at me and explained, "I'm planning where we're going to plant the first fifty new churches in Latvia." I was a bit taken aback at the boldness of that picture, so I asked, "That's a great idea, but do you have capable men equipped to go out and plant fifty new churches?" He looked at me with a big grin and said, "No, we don't, but you're going to train them."

Needless to say, I was at first not ready for this challenge, but it turned out to be the impetus for beginning a plan to make it happen. He soon had the necessary government papers in hand for beginning the Riga International Bible Institute. The Bible Institute was not going to specifically train church planters only, but it was the beginning of providing Bible training which had not been possible before.

We had no money, no classroom space, no teachers, and very few books to use for such a purpose. Trusting the Lord was in it, I accepted the challenge and shared it with our people back in America and with our team in Vienna. Less than ninety days later, the Riga International Bible Institute miraculously opened its doors for the very first school of its kind allowed in Latvia in fifty years.

Chapter 32

FIRST CHRISTMAS IN LATVIA

Al preached on a national TV broadcast that went throughout all of Latvia on Christmas Eve 1991. We had many new experiences and many beautiful times with friends during the Christmas season. But perhaps one of the most impressive, in regards to how things had changed here, was Al's opportunity to speak, openly, in a church of over four hundred people and bring a message on Christmas Eve.

We were invited to Revival Baptist Church for their special service. The church was decorated so beautifully with a lighted tree and streamers of colored lights. The choir looked nice in their white blouses and black skirts and pants. No finery was on display in the congregation tonight, merely a deep, genuinely worshipping spirit of believers commemorating the first coming of Christ to earth.

We were immediately whisked away to the pastor's study. Sitting in the small room were eight church fathers gathered together to pray and prepare for the service. Al was one of the men who would be preaching that night.

The whole service was being videotaped for use on TV around the country. It seemed so awesome to sit there with the hot lights all around and cameras rolling and realize that this service—this privilege which the Lord had given us to participate in—would be

June 2014 — Al Revisiting the Pulpit Where He Spoke on Christmas Eve 1991

beamed, not once, but twice, on national TV. Who would have ever thought this possible? It was truly a miracle. To think that God's message of love and hope through the coming of the Christ child went out to all of Latvia, as far as we know, for the first time ever.

The service was sober, deeply moving, and tremendously uplifting in its gravity of spirit. There were messages from several of the "old warriors" (I'm sure that term is literal in all that they'd undergone for their faith under Communism). The music lifted the heart to the portals of heaven, and the prayer times brought one quickly to tears, the whole body falling to their knees as one, with long outpourings of the heart in worship and contrition and voices lifted in joyful praise while still on their knees. These people must surely be a sweet fragrance in the Lord's nostrils. And for us to be a part of this was totally a gift from the Master, Himself.

This privilege was one we could only dream of in earlier times, but God had opened the doors for the second time now. Think of it! The opportunity to tell all of Latvia about Jesus!

After the service on Christmas Eve, we were invited to spend the rest of the evening with some Russian friends. It was an exciting privilege, but also a bit stressful in not knowing the customs or what was expected. All we could do was try to watch and be sensitive as the activities unfolded. Michail spoke English quite well, but Valla, his wife, spoke very little English. And our Russian consisted of very few words, so there was a lot of sign and body language going on. Their four children were learning English in school, so that was helpful. It was also very precious to have children around to help us celebrate the Lord's birth.

There were few packages under our tree that year, but enough to know we were loved and to remind us of the REAL gift of Christmas. Having a simple Christmas was in itself very special, because it placed our focus on the true Gift, the Lord Jesus Himself. It seemed rather strange to see business as usual going on all around us on the twenty-fifth. The primary recognition of Christmas wasn't held until January 7—the Orthodox day of celebration.

The day after Christmas, we had some Russian friends in for a meal and a good visit. In this case, the gal was learning English, so we could communicate some. And the man spoke some German, so that helped. The Russian people loved to give gifts, so they came with homegrown apples and some homemade jam. I (Betty) had fun getting Rema started on some cross stitching and a few other little gifts. My cross stitching was now spread out over Ukraine, Belarus, and Latvia! It was such a special bridge builder in developing relationships.

Later in the week after Christmas, we enjoyed another Russian family visit. They were most interested in the meal I served, never having had jello or angel food cake before.

As was customary here, this family brought gifts for us—fresh flowers, always! Then also a tablecloth and a ceramic basket. All were very pretty, and surely cost them their week's grocery budget. I got Valla started on some counted cross stitching, which was very interesting and so fun. I gave her a pattern book and the materials to make a few pieces. I also sent home some potato salad and some cake for the children left at home. I gave them some bracelets for their girls. It was a good evening, but communicating through a language we were unfamiliar with wore me out! It seemed that typically people stayed for seven to eight hours, and I really felt the effects of sitting so long.

Just a few comments on the current status of things here: The sewer problem seemed to be fixed. Our faithful friends and coworkers from Vienna brought in a "trap" they installed that permitted all outgoing sewage to go through as designed, but it prevented all sewage from backing up into our apartment in case of stoppage. Whew! What a relief!

As for our heat, we'd managed to stay pretty comfortable even though it was not as warm as we'd like at times. Sometimes, it got down to fifty-six or so, but more typically, the temperature hovered around sixty. We put on more layers, lit the kitchen oven, and managed to get by. This might sound funny, but my head got very cold at night. I bought a night cap like what one sees the old pioneers wearing on TV. Wouldn't you just love to have a picture of that!

The winter had actually been milder than we expected. We'd had some snow, lots of ice, and even rain. The strong winds and damp air from the sea were really penetrating, but it wasn't as bad as we'd anticipated. The food supply had been adequate. We even found rice in the store not long ago.

Even though the increases have been up to 800 percent on many items, we were still in pretty good shape as far as buying power was concerned as we were working with dollars. Now if there were only more to buy! Every once in a while, we found special new discoveries, but the thing I missed the most were the greens. The fresh stuff! How I'd have loved a huge lettuce salad! The mainstay of the people here was potatoes.

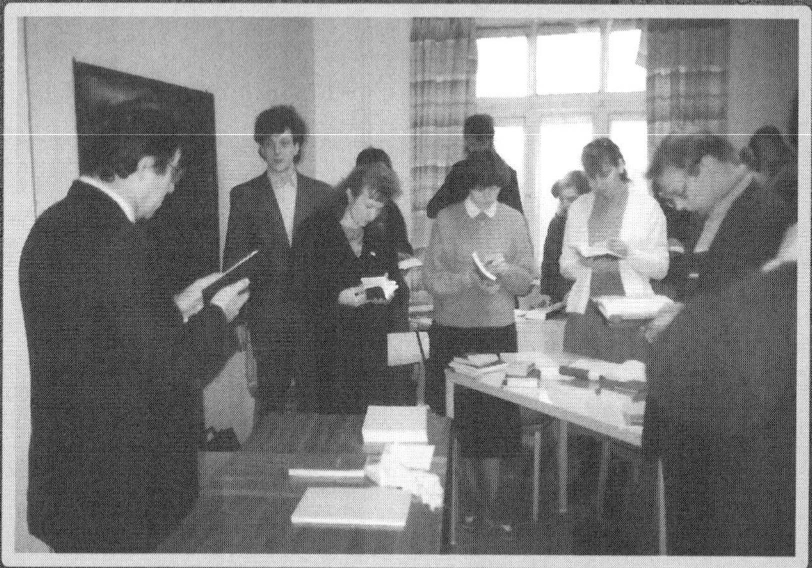

Part Five

Chapter 33

BEGINNING A NEW YEAR—1992

New Year's Eve — Riga, Latvia

Today was another new year. How could it be?! Another year had passed! It was now 1992. Last year at this time, as I (Betty) was finishing up radiation treatments, I was not sure whether I'd see another year on this earth. *But Father, You have been so gracious and tender in caring for me. You have given me many new experiences, as well as many new opportunities. Teach me more and more of Yourself, precious Lord. Conform me more and more into the image of the Lord Jesus.*

For our New Year's Eve celebration, we made a taco salad for our supper. One learned very quickly how to improvise. Since there was no lettuce or tomatoes or taco sauce here, we just made do with shredded cabbage, chopped onions, and some sour cream, but oh, it tasted so good! I had to grind meat for the hamburger, but at least, we had a little meat. This evening, we saw some fireworks going off in the distance, so I guessed that was the way they celebrated here.

Car Vandalized

Now in early January, it was so cold in our flat —down to about the low fifties. With the cold and these awful mouth sores, it was hard to think about much else. Well, it wasn't long before we had far greater things to occupy our thoughts. A fellow tenant from our building alerted us that our car door was ajar! When Al went out, he discovered the windshield had been destroyed (we found it later in a ditch nearby, with many cracks, but hopefully still usable to keep out the snow and rain until we could get it replaced). The door locks on both doors were destroyed, the tape deck and radio had been ripped out, and the electrical system was all messed up. The big challenge now was finding parts and then a qualified repairman to do the work.

The heaviness of lost people who would do such a heinous thing weighed on me. This incident all hit me hard in such a desperate way, and I simply had to get away and speak to the Lord.

Our dear friend Victor P. found a fenced-in yard where we could rent space for our car where it would be more secure. The owners also had a big intimidating dog to guard the car! Parking five blocks away was a rather inconvenient arrangement, but we just couldn't leave the car out as open prey for these gangsters any longer. This was no guarantee for safe keeping, but it would probably discourage thugs a bit at least. From what we'd been told, things were really getting desperate.

The crime rate was skyrocketing, and we'd been warned not to even go out alone, especially at night. We thanked God for this provision. It was still hard to let go, since our place was on the first floor and an easy target for burglars.

Children's Orphanage — Orthodox Christmas Visit

The morning of January 8, 1992, it was dark and gloomy and drizzling. Al went back to the foreign ministry office to register our presence here in Latvia. Since we had entered Latvia back in October on a Soviet visa, we now had to go through a long list of requirements to be properly registered as residents in the newly independent Latvia. Everything was in such a state of confusion just now.

That afternoon, Al and I visited an orphanage here in Riga to bring them toys and sweets for Christmas. I was so deeply grateful we were able to visit this home, but oh, how my heart bled for these seventy-three little children. Each one had their own story of pain and grief.

Riga Orphanage Visit — January 1992

Evita and her brother, Victor, were just two of the sweetest kids this side of heaven. But they were orphans now because their mom killed their father and was now in prison, leaving Evita and Victor behind on their own.

The home was fairly clean and orderly, and the workers appeared to be genuinely concerned and caring. Many of the children had obvious eye problems. Some were mentally handicapped, and it was obvious that all were acting by rote and used to group settings, not individual experiences. We were told that shoes were the greatest need. After that would come blankets, sheets, and interestingly enough, a knitting machine. We learned that volunteers would come in and knit clothes if there was a machine.

The saddest fact of all was that at age sixteen, these kids were handed a thousand or so rubles (ten to fifteen dollars) and shoved out the door. They were on their own without job skills, living skills, or even the ability to cook a meal for themselves! The majority of them ended up behind bars—the girls became prostitutes, and the boys became thieves.

It had been a long day with many emotions on the surface, so it was hard getting to sleep that night. The scenes from the children's home kept haunting me all night. The little hands reaching out to us for sweets. The vacant, guarded eyes looking out onto a world that had dealt them a bitterly, painful blow. It was all so unfair and difficult to erase from my mind's eye.

Harvest Is Ready — January 9, 1992

My heart was weighed down this morning, though. I just had to get out for a while. I took a long walk through the woods and had a good talk with the Lord over all the things that were troubling me. I just felt so pained and perplexed over all that I'd seen and experienced these past few weeks. It wasn't often I felt so much compassion for my "enemies," but the horrible hopelessness of those who didn't know our Lord just seemed so oppressive. And as I brought these things to mind—our car being vandalized, the sadness I felt in visiting the orphanage, the everyday struggle of survival, just the injustice of it all—before our Lord, it seemed to be more disturbing than usual.

But God, in His gentle, loving way, pointed out that it was just such times as these that people were more inclined to seek Him. Oh, how I prayed that I would be ready. Each day brought such precious opportunities of witnessing to the Lord's great love. Sometimes, it was in a very simple way like sharing with a German-speaking lady while standing in line (something we did a lot of!). Other times, it was far more dramatic, like Christmas Eve, when Al was asked to speak at a church of about four hundred, which was then televised on Latvian national TV twice. The possibilities were abundant, the harvest was truly ready, and we prayed that we would be faithful in all that God entrusted us to do.

Learning a New Culture

As we began a new year in newly independent Latvia, we were adapting to a very different culture from our previous home in Vienna, Austria.

Latvia has a long history. Riga lies on the Daugava River, which empties into the Baltic Sea. In the early Middle Ages, it was a center of Viking trade. Over the ensuing centuries, Latvia was under many different empires—Polish, Lithuanian, Swedish, German, then part of the Russian empire from 1721-1917. It was then part of the German Empire from 1917 until 1918. They then enjoyed a period of freedom as the independent Republic of Latvia from 1918 until 1940, when the Soviet Union invaded and took control for two years during WWII. Then Nazi Germany took over until 1944, when the Soviet Union regained control until 1991. What a history! All of these periods left an impact on the culture.

Geographically, Riga is situated across the Baltic Sea from Stockholm, Sweden, so we experienced the long daylight hours in the summers (the "white nights"), and the long hours of darkness in the wintertime.

We heard from friends about how the inflation brought about by the disintegration of the Soviet Union had affected people, especially older ones on a pension. They couldn't even go to church, since the trolley tickets were more than they could afford. Some of the churches were giving their members a gift package of some cash, plus food items.

We told some of our friends about our earlier Eastern European travels and how grateful people had been for the Christian teaching materials we were able to bring. Helene's eyes filled with tears when she heard this and thanked us for the risk we took.

About all that had changed since the walls came down was that people could now openly complain instead of secretly. Everyone was quite concerned about the possibility of returning to Stalinist ways again. The same old Communists were still in office, and the election wouldn't be until the next August.

While life in immediate post-Soviet times had its challenges, Riga came to have a very special place in our hearts. Betty especially had a heart for the people we served and came to know and love in the Baltics. At one point, near the end of her life, she even suggested she'd like to return to Latvia to live out the remaining days of her earthly life.

Here are some of the cultural differences Betty observed in Latvia:

- Small dessert plates for serving the main meal.
- Wallpapered ceilings.
- Three-foot broom handles (killer on the back!).
- Men kissing men on the lips for greetings and farewells!
- Always standing for prayer before AND after meals.
- Kneeling for prayer in churches.
- Eggs in plastic bags (careful!).
- Spoon hanging next to bread bins to check for freshness.

Political Situation—Early 1992

Al and I became more and more "gun shy" as time went on. We heard bits and pieces of how the KGB was definitely still around, keeping a low profile, just biding their time. Things really hadn't changed all that much. The many and obvious frustrations of the people we were involved with grieved us deeply. Living right here in a newly post-Communist country gave us great insight and empathy as we were able to relate to all that they experienced. These were some interesting, fascinating, absorbing, and all too often, difficult and painful times. But opportunities abounded, and God graciously gave us special glimpses of how He used us, so we felt at peace despite the uncertainty in everything around us.

Adapting to Life in Riga

Much remained the same from the recently ended Soviet times. The heat was still controlled by the government, and they provided very minimal heating. But God helped us to adapt to these incongruous and outrageous inequities. We did find the first English newspaper we'd seen since our arrival in Latvia several weeks before, and we snatched it up with hungry hearts to learn about what had been happening in the world. The paper was ten days old, but it was still news to us here in Latvia.

The stores had no refrigeration, so hunks of meat lay out on an open counter with flies buzzing all around. The only hope of getting "safe" meat was to buy it and cook the daylights out of it as quickly as possible. I (Betty) wished I could have brought more food items along with us from Austria, but we just didn't have room. Thankfully, I did bring clothing items for some of the believers. There was virtually nothing in the stores, and what was there was old and far more expensive than most could afford.

It had been as grey inside of me as it was outdoors. But oh, how gracious of the Lord to bring a courier from Vienna with some much-needed items for repair and, best of all, our mail! Encouraging letters from home as friends and family attempted to keep us up to date on what was going on. We always breathed a sigh of relief after scanning the letters and realizing there were no emergencies. *Father God, You have sent us here, so please mold us and shape us into useable vessels for bringing the good news. Crush our haughty spirits if need be that we might become pure and blameless in our task for You.*

The water was still off today in our flat. This was just one of the everyday challenges we faced. Things were generally pretty chaotic as people attempted to adjust to their newly acquired freedom. People were buying up everything! Stockpiling was the name of the game for survival, and with imminent hard times coming, and the currency changing from Russian rubles to Latvian lats, people were going crazy trying to spend their rubles. It didn't seem to matter what they bought—everything from paint and furniture to just plain useless junk. Even the souvenirs became scarce.

Angel in a Fur Hat

During the early and mid 1990s, we continued our travels to conduct training seminars in the other cities on our circuit. During this unsettled time, there were many travel uncertainties, of which law and order was one. We had been warned about the train station in Minsk, Belarus, being less than safe for Western travelers like us.

We asked our people in the USA and Vienna to pray for our safety as we headed out on a trip to Belarus with Minsk as one of our stops where we needed to change trains. In answer to their prayers, the Lord provided an angel in a fur hat to meet us there and help us during our stopover.

I (Al) had just fallen down the steep metal steps getting off the train with our two heaviest suitcases. Picking myself up, I stacked all of our luggage under a concrete staircase where the muddy slush was not so deep. Betty stationed herself by the luggage away from the crowds of people pushing their way along on Platform 5 at the Minsk, Belarus, train station.

Rubbing my back, which I had painfully wrenched in my fall off the train, I looked around to figure out how I was going to get everything safely up the long two-story high incline to the dark, dingy, cavernous waiting room. We had three hours to wait for our next train, which would take us to the city of Brest. Suddenly, a somewhat rough-looking Russian man with a fur hat was standing in front of our luggage. With a wide smile, he asked Betty haltingly in English, "Can I help you?"

Betty had just a moment to discern whether or not to trust this man, as muggers and thieves favor train stations as a source of easy victims. She sensed immediately that this was not a mugger, but God's provision for our safety and help. We not only had a lot

Our Angel in a Fur Hat at Minsk Train Station

of luggage, full of gifts for God's people in Belarus, but we were also carrying a lot of cash provided by individuals and churches in America for various mission projects on this trip. We were concerned about being alone as Westerners in situations such as this. We had asked people to pray for God's help and protection. All along the way, from Moscow to Tallinn to Riga, and now Minsk, God was clearly and beautifully answering prayer.

Our "angel in a fur hat" cheerfully helped us get our luggage up the long incline to the waiting room. In Russian, he informed the people around us that we were Americans and he was going to keep an eye on us and help us. He wanted to buy us coffee, but we knew he had little money and we didn't want him to spend it on us. Our protests were futile. Off we went, arm in arm, to the little cafe at one end of the room where hot water was dispensed from a large silver samovar and Russian instant coffee mixed in. The cups were dirty and cracked, and the "coffee" was lukewarm and bitter, but the pleasure that showed on the face of our angel made it a memorable treat.

Later, he helped us get our luggage back down the long slippery incline and out onto the muddy platform where wet snow was still falling. Soon, our train screeched to a stop in front of us, and he helped carry our luggage onto the train. We offered him some money for his help, but he refused. As suddenly as he had appeared, he was gone, and we were safely on our way to Brest. Because of his limited English and our limited Russian, we were unable to learn much about our angel in a fur hat. We didn't know if he would be waiting to help us the next time we stopped at the train station in Minsk, but one thing was for sure, we would never forget him.

God's answers to our supporters' prayers made this January/February trip one of the most encouraging yet. We continued to see God answer prayer every day for more laborers, for finances, for equipment, for teaching materials, and for His direction in decisions to be made.

Chapter 34

NEW OPPORTUNITIES UNDER WAY

Marriage Seminar — January 1992

I (Betty) was so hoping it would be warm today, January 24, but not so. We needed to travel by bus to Sigulda for a marriage seminar. I had to wear my warmest clothing and add extra layers.

The big red bus was a welcome relief after the "squeeze, push, and shove" transports of the inner city. Al and I located some seats and waited while the rest of the passengers got settled into their places. I was excited! This would be an opportunity for a firsthand look at marriage relationships in Russian culture.

Wally, our fellow laborer in Christ from Finland, invited us to attend a weekend with him in his special area of ministry. As he was ethnic Russian, God had given him a burden for the Russian people and how they related to one another in marriage. We were about to witness the transformation taking place among young married couples as they came to understand the Biblical concept of marriage.

We reached the hotel, located in a lovely, wooded area with a river flowing right below our fourth-floor window. But as was so typical here, there was very little heat. It was dark and dreary and freezing in the lobby, and in our room, we could see our breath.

The rooms were quite primitive and dirty, and there was no hot water. And this in January! We crawled into our bed fully dressed to try and keep warm while we waited for the seminar to begin.

Somehow, none of these inconveniences or discomforts seemed to bother these couples. There were those who had traveled on rough, cold trains from as far away as Tashkent, St. Petersburg, and Moscow. Some were thousands of miles from their homes. But so exciting and so momentous was the possibility of improving their marriages that no amount of sacrifice was too great.

In one of the discussion periods, a lady spoke up and said, with great emotion, "I've suffered in my marriage for over five years now, and no one told me there is a better way of relating to one's mate."

These dear people were eager, teachable, and so hungry for the truth, especially the women, who had been treated much like work horses who were available for breeding and taking care of the family needs. To be married was most often a cross to be borne. So, we tried to communicate the Biblical foundation of the family and how success could be obtained only when we included God in our union.

The seminars were based on Biblical principles, illustrated with personal experiences. They were openly transparent in sharing even the most intimate areas of marriage. Anything to do with such a private issue as marriage was pretty revolutionary for people here. For the most part, these things were simply not addressed. This was especially so for things having to do with sex and family planning.

Even with these more progressive thinking couples, when the seminar topics were listed and the one on physical relationships was mentioned, it brought much snickering and blushing and embarrassment, and probably a lot of guilt. Not only had their traditions and "Christian" beliefs forbidden any form of family planning, but they had also been taught that never, NEVER was the physical relationship in marriage to be enjoyed by the women. It was to be used only for procreation. So, it was extremely moving, as well as heartening, to see these young couples get into openly sharing about the things they struggled with in their marriages.

Sitting in on some of the small group interactions, we witnessed painful suffering that made it difficult for us to go to sleep at night. With tears welling up in her eyes, one lady burst forth with, "I've suffered so long! And no one told us there is a better way!" Yes, they truly had suffered, especially the women, as this had been the prevalent attitude for centuries. The marriage union here had been quite aptly described as "hell for women."

For one thing, there was pressure from all sides to get married and bear children. Many churches taught that a woman was saved through childbearing. For those who were already married, there was pressure to have babies, to be fruitful. If more than three months lapsed between pregnancies, then the pastor would come around and question their "spirituality"! Many of these families ended up with ten to fifteen kids and very little means with which to raise them.

For those who chose not to have a baby every year, the means for family planning were not even an option, so the average woman in the former Soviet Union would have six abortions during her childbearing years. And some had many more. Could you imagine the guilt, the self-loathing that this kind of life generated? To say nothing of the risk and physical pain involved in a society where hospitals and clinics were still backward and primitive.

Al and I retired to our room after a long, intense session with the groups. We were tired and cold, crawling into bed without even any warm water to clean up prior to sleeping. We piled on the blankets and covered up over our heads to try and stay warm enough for sleep to come. The next day's seminar was scheduled to be on the topic of communication in marriage!

Over the course of the weekend, we were delighted to see new insight and understanding penetrating the relationships of these eager learners. We prayed for these couples—that they would have the courage to introduce a Scriptural concept of relating and loving as husband and wife. There was fear, and rightly so.

The risks were many, and they stood to lose a lot in taking such a stand. For example, they faced the possibility of being excommunicated by their church, disowned by their family, shunned by friends, all for rejecting the traditional views of marriage relationships and the role of women.

We had much to mull over in our minds and hearts after sitting in on the seminars with these Russian couples. We returned home to a cold flat, but were thankful to be here. Wearing extra layers, including caps, we managed to get comfortable enough.

Preaching in My Pajamas

Many people have had dreams where they were in a public place and suddenly realized they were wearing their pajamas, or maybe fuzzy bedroom slippers. I (Al) had the real-life experience in February of wearing my pajamas while preaching at the church in Riga.

The outdoor temperatures at this time sunk to well below freezing. Since many churches did not have a functioning heating system, the temperature inside was often not much warmer than outside. People would sit in church all bundled up with many layers of clothing, heavy coats and mittens, and of course, the Russian fur hats that most people wore.

We had already heard reports that the heating pipes at this church were frozen and burst open. Instead of hot steam, this heating system featured piles of ice beneath the broken pipes. When the pastor invited me to his church to preach, he referred to this situation as a "small problem." We knew it wouldn't cause them to shorten their normal lengthy worship service, complete with three sermons. Consequently, getting dressed for the occasion called for wearing as many layers as possible. To be safe, I decided to add my pajamas as an extra layer. Of course, I also wore other layers, topped off by my suit and tie and long winter coat.

Did we keep warm? No! Our bodies still ended up being a bit numb from the cold, but our hearts were beautifully warmed by the worship experience with our Russian brothers and sisters. Their worshipful singing, warm welcome, fervent prayers, and simple faith made the cold weather truly a "small problem." We wish each one of you could have been with us to share this beautiful experience.

News Headlines — February 5, 1992

Volatile political scene in the headlines today. Russian leader, Boris Yeltsin, threated with a coup as the people want changes fast! Al and I discussed plans should we need to leave quickly, trusting our car would be working with gas in the tank. The trains and planes would be packed.

Economic problems and the instability of the new government were, however, still big concerns for everyone. Christians had a purpose in their days, but unbelievers scrounged wherever they could without getting caught. Crime was escalating at an alarming rate. People were desperate, and now illegal drugs were entering the picture too. We'd taken every precaution we knew of—deadbolt locks, chains and padlocks on the windows. Now all we could do was pray that things wouldn't occur when we were at home!

Thank You, Father, for keeping us from experiencing this desperateness. No matter how impossible the world gets, You are watching over us.

There was a lovely covering of white snow this beautiful February morning, the kind that covered all the filth and dirt. *Thank You, Father, for this pleasant scene as I look out our kitchen window.* I did need to get outdoors and walk, though, per my doctor's orders. There were some hills in the forest and tons of walking trails. How wonderfully the Lord provided for my need to walk.

Train to Estonia for Seminars

Our next scheduled seminars took us to Tallinn, Estonia. My (Betty's) least favorite part of the whole trip was having to make our way down to the dark and dingy train station so late at night.

Our train didn't leave until nearly midnight, the time when most criminals were out and about. It was a dangerous time, so we committed our commute to the train, as well as our flat, to the Lord's hands.

Our time went fast while we waited for our train with so many "entertaining" individuals all around us. We boarded the train, learning that we would share a compartment with two other guys. One was nice and clean cut, but the other was a burly, stinky, crude man who snored so bad we could hardly stand it.

All night long, the rocking, rattling, shaking train made its way into the frozen north. As I watched the dawn break over the horizon, the lonely, desolate, barren icy land gave me such a feeling of isolation. A few scattered farmhouses dotted the countryside, all with low thatched roofs, as they were not typical sized houses. Slowly the lights appeared in some of the houses.

The next morning, we had our first seminar, then another in the afternoon, and a third group at 6:00 p.m. for our final four-hour seminar of the day. Al taught the evening seminar on Old Testament Survey. Each student present had a story and a need. Dimitri shared how he had an opportunity to teach in the public schools, but he needed materials and help preparing to teach. He also needed certification from a recognized school certifying he had completed an approved program of study for the Ministry of Religious Affairs. Alex and Nicholai traveled over two hours each way to attend this seminar. The commitment and dedication in these men was inspirational. They had full lives and schedules, so the amount of coursework assigned overwhelmed them. The enemy loves to discourage those doing Kingdom work.

At the close of the seminar, we had a time of prayer together. I was so touched as Oleg and Vasily in tears cried out to the Lord on my behalf for healing in a true lesson in fervency and care. I made a feeble attempt to tell Raisa how impressed I was at her meals and the amount of work she put into preparing it all. Her response was simply that it gave her great joy to serve us. I wondered if I'd ever get to that point of loving service for the Lord.

With seminars completed, we gathered our things and headed on down to the train station. There was not a speck of heat in the station or on the train! In spite of the sweat and urine smells and the grime of the ancient bedding in the compartment, I was able to sleep. This told me how exhausted we were.

It was so good to get back home again. We spent several hours reading and devouring our mail, which had been brought in during our absence. I always have plans of saving some of my mail for later days, but was far too anxious to learn whether everything was alright with loved ones back home to do that.

Opening of Riga International Bible Institute

Monday, February 10, 1992

Today is the opening of the Riga International Bible Institute (RIBI). That whole story is so fantastic! Al helped plan, develop,

First Class — Riga International Bible Institute — February 10, 1992

strategize, and fund this venture, and today, they will hold their first classes. We get up early and make our way downtown for this miraculous event.

The first five-day intensive study course is Evangelism and Discipleship, taught by Ed M. The atmosphere brings back memories of my days at Oak Hills Bible College. Except for the more austere and frugal surroundings, it could very well be a school back in Minnesota.

There's quite a mix of students. One from the Republic of Georgia. Others from Russia, Ukraine, Estonia, etc. It's a pretty awesome responsibility to be involved in teaching these twenty-five dear brothers and sisters. These are exciting times, and I'm so thankful God is allowing us a small part in His work here in Riga, Latvia. Most are young, but they love God and take seriously the ministry He has given them.

The excitement and eagerness of the students is contagious. They are here to learn, and nothing seems to deter them—not the long hard lesson assignments; not the absence of chorus books with the music they're singing. They sit and laboriously copy the English words and the music, note by note, into their workbooks. And they do it with such delight.

All are committed to using their training for the glory of God as they now begin to apply what they're learning in their first course. Additional teaching this first week has included lectures on Christian ethics and church history. They also have two hours of English instruction each week.

I introduced our students to some freshly popped corn for their snack, and it was a precious thing. It went over very well and was funny at the same time. The cook thought I would pop the corn in the oven! I had brought some popcorn with me from the States, so it was a big surprise and such joy to see them all experience something new and different.

The classes aren't finished yet, so this poor little old lady who does the cooking is bending over a little stool, peeling veggies.

There's no sink, no cupboard, no table, just a stove and a few dishes. But do they complain? NEVER! There are about thirty people for whom they prepare meals three times a day. But they are just so grateful for this opportunity for learning that they are willing to put up with the lack of conveniences. Meals, of course, are not what Americans would expect, but filling to the tummy, and no one's complaining. Breakfast consists of bread with sardines, maybe a cookie, and some coffee or tea. It's the first food for many since yesterday afternoon, so they dig in heartily.

Tuesday, February 11, 1992   Mild – Cloudy

Al went into the school at noon to observe Ed teaching. But Ed couldn't be there, so Al ended up doing the teaching. Ed's hotel room was burglarized last night. His camera, undershirts, and sweater—all the gift items he'd brought—all of it gone. So Ed was reporting all of this to the police while Al filled in for him at the school.

Al is so worn out tonight. It's been a good day for him at the school, but the students, translator, etc., all have stories of grief, and it gets pretty heavy to counsel and empathize with all the problems. There are economic problems, problems concerning the instability of the new government, concerns over the still-evident KGB surveillance, and of course, some being ostracized from their church just because the pastor doesn't like the charity organization they were working for. Others share the difficulty of living in a small, three-room flat with two other families, including lots of children. So Al felt rather drained, even though we're all very excited about the opening of the new school and potential it holds.

Friday, February 14, 1992

The tears stream down the face of one young woman. Others in the classroom are fighting to hold back their tears as they sing in Russian "How Great Thou Art." About thirty people are crammed into this tiny classroom as we bring to a close the first week of classes at the new Riga International Bible Institute. Since the Soviet Army invaded Latvia in 1940 until now, there has been no such opportunity. This first group of students seems to recognize the privilege God has given them. This is why there are such strong emotions this Friday afternoon as they praise God for giving them a part in this new Bible Institute.

Chapter 35

WHAT DO I (BETTY) DO ALL DAY

Someone asked me (Betty) recently what I did all day long. As I thought about it, and started making a list of items that ate up my time, I thought maybe it would be interesting to others as well to know a bit more about what it was like for me here.

Routine housekeeping and shopping: These kept me pretty busy, because it wasn't just routine here—at least not compared to the American way of life. Every day found me checking out the nearby stores at least twice to see what was available. It was almost imperative. When anything worthwhile came in, it disappeared so quickly that if you didn't check often, you just didn't get anything. Checking out included standing in line when there was something to buy.

We had several possible resources as far as shopping went. There were three little stores near our flat, two more a fifteen-minute walk from our place, and then the big farmer's market downtown. Let me just share an excerpt from my journal on one of our trips downtown. "This was market day. It's not like going to Hornbacher's Supermarket, but I must say it's far more interesting. Standing in line for food is hard. However, one is usually quite entertained by the happenings all around: the 'carrot man' who insists on emptying his baskets and piling it up on the stack, in spite of the fact that most were falling on the floor and the clerk was yelling and shaking her fingers at him to stop; the 'cabbage lady' screaming at people for handling the merchandise; the lady breaking line and wanting to get waited on before her turn and having everyone getting mad at her; the delivery of potatoes and people pushing and shoving to get their share; the farmer filling his jars with fresh(?) milk from the bucket; his wife unwrapping her homemade cottage cheese from the yukky looking cloth holding it together; the Mongol-looking Asian polishing his half-rotten apples in hopes of making them more appealing; merchants sitting in their stalls, shivering and blowing on their half-frozen hands. The whole scene is like something out of a story book, but it's all too true and all too real."

If one was fortunate enough to find food, then the next step was to get it home, which wasn't easy on public transport (I was glad when we had our vandalized car windshield fixed), cleaning it all thoroughly, and preparing it for use. That meant checking for roaches, washing and scrubbing, cutting and grinding (if one found meat), and then collapsing with a thankful heart for having found some useful items.

Cooking: There were no ready-to-fix mixes so that meant making everything from scratch. Recently, I collected enough of the necessary ingredients to try making pizza. We were SO hungry for that, but by the time I had made the crust, made something resembling pizza sauce, found some meat and fried it thoroughly, shredded the cheese, coaxed my very uncooperative oven into a reasonable temperature, I wasn't even hungry for it anymore. I spent many hours a week washing, peeling, cutting, and shredding potatoes, carrots, cabbage, and whatever else I could find for our basic meals.

Laundry: This was another challenge. I was really thankful to have a washing machine, although the drying was a real hassle. I draped things over doors, on radiators, and small clotheslines over the tub in my bathroom, but EVERYTHING had to be ironed when drying this way.

Cleaning: I'd always liked keeping a clean house, but here, it was pretty essential to try and keep up with all the dirt in view of the roach problem. Even though hiring help would be ridiculously cheap, we didn't feel it prudent to have a national in our flat. Word seemed to get around that we had Western products and belongings, so it would just be too much of a risk.

Consequently, I had five large rooms plus two toilets, two hallways—one very large—and three balconies to keep up. We were thankful for the space, though sometimes it didn't seem to be enough, but it was a job to maintain. I especially found rooms with area rugs hard to keep up; they seemed to require twice the work. Then there were the linoleum floors to scrub. With all the dirt and pollution here, there was a lot of grime being tracked in all the time.

So now that you feel plenty sorry for me, let me share some of the more exciting (and there are some!) things that I do.

Correspondence: I truly loved to write to people, but the Lord brought so many wonderful people into our lives, and I wanted so much to interact with each one. Unfortunately, there just weren't enough hours to go around. Al did some of the correspondence too, and I guess maybe I needed to learn to report like he did, instead of rambling. For Al, writing letters was a job that needed to be done. For me, it was great therapy and a genuine joy to visit with people this way.

Traveling: I sometimes traveled with Al to the other countries on our circuit and was involved with the seminars and the people, which was such a blessing and another one of the things where I invested my time.

Interaction with others: Preparation of gifts, creative ways of interacting with people of another culture and language, planning on how best to encourage and strengthen them, especially the women, was something I enjoyed doing. Many of them said that just the presence of another woman, one from the West who desired to identify and share with them, was a big help and a great support. Although I wonder sometimes just who was learning from whom!

Last week, we traveled to Tallinn for a couple of seminars. We stayed with a single woman, perhaps in her fifties who lived alone in a one-room flat. Her profession was as an engineer, but the stability of her work was very insecure. She expected to be laid off by the end of that month. Therefore, she had been taking in BEE World people to supplement her income. She didn't want much—even balked at five dollars per person, per night, plus meals—but considering the great inconvenience it was to her (she would sleep on the floor in her small kitchen), and all the work and effort and time invested in securing foods for guests, the hardship of doing all the laundry by hand, and the humbleness and attitude in which she served and took care of people, there was simply no way one could pay her enough.

Nor was there any way in which I could really identify with her. Most of these dear sisters had such a low image of themselves, and it was such fun to see some light come into their eyes, to see their heads come up a little straighter, to see some worth and respect enter their thinking as I praised them for their cooking (and generally it was great, especially when one realized how hard it was to get things). I marveled at their ability to make their flats nice and comfortable.

While attending the seminars, I was impressed by the attendees' commitment, dedication, and deep, genuine desire to learn and become equipped in serving our Lord. I was also deeply humbled by their personal caring. One of the first questions when we arrived was always in regard to my health, as they shared how they had been regularly praying for me. Then during the prayer time, to have them cry out to the Lord on my behalf, with tears streaming down their faces, I realized anew that the Lord had brought many into my life to share the burden.

In Brest (Belarus), a pastor in one of the groups publicly thanked me for not only permitting my husband to travel and bring them teaching, but also for accompanying him and encouraging them with my testimony. It was just such precious experiences that made it all worthwhile, and I was so grateful to the Lord for giving me these glimpses of fruit to spur me on and gladden my heart in the work He gave us.

Among other things I did when we traveled was take pictures of the groups. We'd explain our desire to intercede for them and that pictures helped us to remember each one individually as we prayed. I recorded pertinent data, taking note of special requests and questions that needed answering. It was so exciting to listen to some of the feedback in these seminars. The opportunities were bountiful. They shared how they needed materials and teaching in how to share the Bible with students in the schools. Would this ever happen in America?

Having guests in our home: People came from Vienna, regularly. We were also trying to concentrate on developing relationships with the nationals in Riga. There were some other Americans living here now too, and it was fun having them over. Because our flat also served as our office, Al often had people here for meetings. I tried to make these a time of refreshment for them as well as accomplishing intended goals for the ministry.

Helpmeet to Al: And then, of course, one of my very deepest desires and goals was to be a strength, support, coworker, companion, and friend to my husband. People have asked me about what it's like to be together almost all of the time.

On our bedroom wall, we had a Precious Moments poster showing a little girl on her trike and a boy dressed up in a policeman's suit writing her a ticket. The caption was, "The Lord must have brought us together."

I looked at that poster many times throughout the day and never ceased to give the Lord thanks for how He knew all along what our lives would be like in serving Him. In His wonderful knowing ways, He gave Al and me personalities, desires, and goals that were so compatible and complimentary. So, to answer that question—I LOVE IT! I can't really speak for Al, but for me, I truly appreciated and enjoyed having him around a lot of the time. We had the woods nearby, and when I needed time alone, all I had to do was go for a walk and be refreshed by the smell of pine wood burning in a little house in the distance and the loveliness of God's creation.

> *Praying at the same time for us as well,*
> *that God will open up to us a door for the word,*
> *so that we may proclaim the mystery of Christ...*
> *that I may make it clear in the way I ought to*
> *proclaim it.* –COLOSSIANS 4:3-4

Chapter 36

MEDICAL CARE IN FINLAND

Betty chronicled our visit to Finland for follow-up medical care in the journal entries below.

Friday, February 21, 1992   Cold-Sunny-Clear

We're preparing for our upcoming trip to Finland for my cancer checkup. The way God worked all that out is a story in itself. He gave us a "connection" just about the time we were wanting to make arrangements, and this fellow has made all my appointments, arranged lodging with a little old lady near the clinic rather than in their extremely expensive hotels, and answered lots of questions regarding travel arrangements as well. How good the Lord is!

Since our train doesn't leave until near midnight tonight, we went out for a walk this morning. It made for a refreshing outing in the woods before the long trip to Finland via train to Estonia then ferry to Finland. It was both a physical and emotional respite from the anticipation of cancer testing waiting for us in Finland. It was a lovely day. Lots of grey and black Siberian crows are making a big racket. As we walked to the store, we could smell the wood-burning stoves throughout the forest trails. It's cold and crisp with ice coating the tree branches.

Our dear friend Michael helped us secure our tickets. And another dear friend, Nicholai, gives us a lift to the station. His solid, lusty voice rings out in songs of Russian, Ukrainian, Finnish, German, and Belarusian as we made our way through the late evening traffic on our way to the train station. His joy for the Lord is truly strengthening, and new courage replaces the fear in our hearts.

The train is sitting several blocks from the main terminal, but Nicholai helps carry our bags along the dark, icy path. We make it on board with a few minutes to spare. Our compartment appears to be a bit on the cool side, but it isn't long before it becomes absolutely stifling. The heat makes all of us miserable. The sweat is pouring off the lady in the next bunk. She's a real heavy-set woman and is sleeping with a thick, wool sweater and polyester slacks that don't breathe. In my attempts to find some place cool, I place my palms on the glass window and try putting my head near a draft from the outside, but none of it lasts for long. I take off as many clothes as is decently possible and try to ignore the horrible jostling, rocking, chugging of the train along the ice-encrusted tracks.

Will this night ever end? My head is aching, my body is drenched, and the vertigo is making my already queasy stomach feel even more unsettled.

Meanwhile, Al is contending with the joys of sleeping on the top bunk, which is even hotter than mine below! His "partner" up there reeks of alcohol and body odor and is snoring so loud that none of us get much rest. Unfortunately, this is not an uncommon experience on these trains.

Saturday, February 22, 1992   Cold-Snow

At 3:00 a.m., the Estonian passport officers come on board and get everyone up. Despite everything, we do get a little sleep and, at 8:10 a.m., arrive in Tallinn, Estonia. John, a dear brother in Christ, is waiting for us on the platform and helps us get over to the ferry area. I am constantly amazed at how the Lord always provides. John is such a blessing; he is willing, helpful, kind, and sensitively looking for ways to serve. We stand in awe of God's goodness through His many "assistants." We fuss and worry and wonder how it is all going to work out, but God knows. Once again, we can see His hand go before us.

We weren't really expecting any problems in boarding the ferry to Helsinki. But, as is so often the case, the unexpected enters in. Our passports are thoroughly examined and scrutinized, while we are made to wait in this long line of people waiting to be called to look at our passports. All the while, Al and I are standing there trying to look calm and unconcerned. It seems they were very leery of the additional pages we had added when we were in the US. It did make it look kind of fake, and these guys aren't taking any chances. Finally, they accept what they see, put their stamp of approval in our passport, and let us go on board. Whew!

We take our bags and walk through this long, enclosed corridor to the ship—similar to the tunnel-like things leading to airplanes. The sight of things on this Finnish ferry is a breath of fresh air! Everything is nice, clean, and comfortable, and the staff are even cordial. What a contrast from our previous surroundings! There are about seven levels to this huge ship, and the best part of all is that the bathrooms don't even stink!

Sirkka, the little, eighty-four-year-old lady we'll be staying with here in Helsinki, is a dear, precious saint of the Lord's. Her flat is so interesting! It's filled with beautiful, antique pieces, every bit the image of old-world charm. The bed feels terrific. No rocking and swaying and no border officials to wake us in the middle of the night. It is paradise for us!

Wally, the Lord's "connection" for us in Helsinki, takes Al out to the store nearby, where he picks up some fresh celery, green peppers, bananas, and bread. We have a wonderful feast for our supper. Oh, how good it all tastes!

Monday, February 24, 1992   Cold–Windy

We leave the flat at 7:20 a.m. and walk the eight blocks to the cancer clinic, where I have my appointment. Everyone is very pleasant, but it's still hard not to be anxious. The tests begin with blood work, and then the mammogram. I read once that if a mammogram doesn't hurt then it was probably not being done correctly. So, this one must be VERY CORRECT! The doctor read the exam. I lie there on the cold, steel table trying to read the doctor's expression as he runs the scanner over and over my chest. It seems like he'll never finish.

Finally, he looks up and says, "I think, perhaps, would be good to do biopsy." *Oh God, not again. Please, dear Lord, don't let the cancer return.* My body begins to tremble, and then to shake violently. I can barely utter the words, "Please have my husband come in." Al appears almost instantly. I tell him what the doctor wants to do, and we decide to go ahead. As I'm being prepared, Al moves to the head of the table and takes my hand.

The biopsy procedure doesn't take very long, but it seems like forever. The doctor goes deep into my body with this big needle and suctions out tissue for the exam. The deep probing with the big suction needle finally ends. They have the specimen, but now we must wait.

We won't know until later in the week what the results are, but the doctor assured us that it didn't feel like a tumor. This is so different from back home. There, we knew immediately what the results were. I will learn quickly that the waiting time is always the hardest.

After pulling myself together, we leave the clinic and go on as though it were any other ordinary day. But it's not. *Will I be found to be carrying cancer in my body again, Lord?* As we walk the streets of Helsinki, I am vaguely aware of all the affluent people—in furs, expensive jewelry, genuine leather—scurrying back and forth, intent only on accumulating more and more. Is this all there is to their lives? *Oh, precious Father, give me a chance to share with the lost.*

Wednesday, February 26, 1992

Both Al and I have a restless night. What will the verdict be? What does the future hold? We talked into the wee hours of the night of what we would do should the tests prove positive. We pray for God's mercy before leaving our room. And we pray for God's strength for whatever He has for us.

The doctor—a tall, slim, Finnish man in his fifties—speaks some English, but not fluently. I'm not terribly impressed by his rather ho-hum attitude. However, he reports that the mammogram, ultrasound, and biopsy are all O.K. *Oh, thank You, Father!* Al and I are both rather numb. It's been a very stressful time—a time when we've had to face the possibility of some traumatic news and all the consequences that would have. But I've been granted a reprieve! A "pardon" for a time.

We walk out of the doctor's office, go through the motions of paying the bill (about $300.00) and getting our coats on, and leave this clinic in a strange land with a strange language. The reality of what has just happened begins to filter into my paralyzed mind. Al puts on his hat, looks down at me, and says, "Well, now what?"

The elation of the news we've just heard is pouring in full force now! The initial numbness wears off, replaced with gratitude. We still have no answers for the mouth sores I struggle with. All the doctor could say was, "stress, depression, and poor diet." I guess I can concur with that, considering all the changes we've faced in recent months. After we get our feet somewhat back on the ground, we look at one another, and I suggest we get some pizza. Al's quick response is a big smile, and he says, "My sentiments, exactly!" There are times when even missionaries need to celebrate.

Now we were actually ready to face life in Riga again. It would be a sudden culture shock as we reentered the Baltic states, but at least, the prices for what was presently available were far more tolerable.

Fortunately, the waters were relatively calm the day we boarded the ferry, so I (Betty) was able to control the motion activity in my stomach. We were on the Baltic Sea, with Helsinki fading farther and farther behind us. Finland was interesting, and I was thankful we were able to go, but it was a very affluent country. The normal attire was fur coats, leathers, and name-brand clothing. The clearest and most vivid distinction from other places in the world was that the toilets were immaculately clean. What a treat that was!

Our dear friend Johannes was waiting for us when the ferry pulled into Tallinn, Estonia. We were back in a world of grey, gloom, and grody conditions. The station was such a dump. It was dimly lit, with cracked and worn seats already occupied and people sleeping or chewing on their dry bread. The whole scene was like something out of a medieval movie. What a change from the clean, modern, bright setting of Helsinki.

Later that day, Johannes and our mutual friend Raissa took us to the train, which would transport us back to Riga, Latvia. We said good-bye to our dear ones and tried to settle into this dirty, smelly, over-heated cabin, but sleep did not come easily. Finally, our train arrived in Riga at 7:25 a.m., and we were able to get a taxi home right away.

We tried to take a nap and a little walk when we got home, but unfortunately, the "vermin" came out of their dens once the weather was milder like today, so the streets were full of drunks, druggies, and bums. It was rather frightening to be outdoors, even during daylight hours.

I did a little cleaning in my kitchen. The American missionaries from the States who kept an eye on our flat while we were gone were a bit less than careful in keeping things clean. I moved a canister with some rice in it, and the thing all but walked off on me! It was alive with roaches, and if not roaches, then with roach eggs. There was constant potential for bugs all over the place, since one brought these things home from the market.

It was cold today, March 3, but we decided to check out a nearby flea market. All these people were sitting or standing in the raw and bitter wind in hopes of selling their meager wares. It was incredible how they could stand it. Many were obviously sick, coughing and hoarse, hands and faces red and chapped. They sold everything from rusty nails to old dried-up fish. It was quite an experience to go to this flea market.

This society was so grey, dirty, colorless, and un-feminine, that it was difficult to ever feel like a woman. *Father, give me the grace to be the woman You would be pleased with and enable me to be an example to those around me, an example that draws others to Yourself. If it pleases You, Father, reveal Yourself to me on those days when I really need encouragement. Strengthen my faith and keep me focused on a life with eternal values and objectives.*

Chapter 37

A WALK THROUGH THE WOODS TO THE STORE

Within a thirty-minute walking distance of our apartment complex, there were probably a dozen or more "stores." Now the image that came to your mind was probably something like the large supermarkets so much a part of everyday life in America. But the stores here were anything from a large, square, ugly looking cement structure to the more commonly seen tiny, newsstand-type booth, where one walked up to an opening on the side and shopped through the "window." Then there was the small, two-aisle, neighborhood type. In the dozen or so stores available in our area, there were some of each, from the small to the large and those in between, but the merchandise was basically the same in all of them—simply larger quantities of the same items in the larger stores.

The stock turnover, however, in these stores took place almost daily, somewhat dependent on the season, but more dependent on what the government happened to get their hands on or what the individual merchants were willing to do to obtain goods for resale. Since the goods appeared and disappeared as quickly as a magician's rabbit, it was greatly advantageous to check each store several times a day.

The mindset of the peoples who lived under the former Communist system did not change quickly, and stockpiling when available was still the way they shopped. If they saw anything on the shelf worth taking home (meaning anything edible or resalable), then they bought as much as they had rubles for or were allowed to have at any one time.

Just because you saw row after row of pickles or cheese or cabbage on one day didn't mean there would be any there the next! In fact, they most likely wouldn't be.

My (Betty's) almost daily check began with securing all three locks on the flat as I left. I made my way through the sour, urine-smelling entryway and exited the front door of our complex. My first sight as I left the building was the line of people queuing up across the street in front of the large green tank of the Alus (beer) truck. Even though it was still early in the day, the pathetic sight of all the neighborhood derelicts was hard to ignore. But ignore them I must. Keeping a low profile was nothing more than prudent, especially for us, as Westerners.

The next sight was the row of babushkas, with their wares displayed for sale in front of the little store across the street. A crowd of people gathered around their tables to buy green onions or radishes (when in season), tiny little pumpkin or sunflower seeds, garlic, or crocheted items. But the biggest seller, and the most available, was the grand array of flowers. Each little grandma, using whatever means she could, tried to catch the buyer's eye and entice them into purchasing her particular floral arrangement.

The flowers were beautiful, fresh, and vibrant, and many of these fragrant, decorative bouquets were purchased for a few rubles and taken home to brighten up a dark corner of a tiny Latvian flat.

Walking no more than a city block, I came to the entrance of a wooded area that had been a precious oasis to both Al and me. In this otherwise noisy, drab, dismal, grey, and troubled society, this little patch of God's beautiful handiwork had been nothing more than a Balm of Gilead for us. In spite of the evidence that spelled a lack of care, it was still a natural beauty that only God could create. There was never a time we walked here that we didn't give God thanks for His provision in this particular way. The trails were thick with old, dead leaves, pinecones, pebbles, and a lot of garbage, but the natural smells of trees, flowers, and fresh air came through all of that, as we soaked up this little bit of country in a city of nearly a million people.

Along the paths of these woods, one saw a lot of others enjoying the outdoors as well. Lots of little old, wrinkled, hunched over, kerchiefed grandmas shuffling along through the woods, leaning on their canes as they made their way to the store. Lots and LOTS of young mommies with toddlers in tow, with a baby in a carriage and another one due soon.

In contrast to the elderly peasant-looking babushkas, there were the short-skirted, high-heeled, rather brazen-looking gals that took full advantage of their freedom, making up for all those years of plain, dull, ill-fitting clothes of the Communist era. They most likely had paid a full month's wage or more for even just one item of their contemporary wardrobe. But to them, it was far more important than bread or potatoes.

The styles in the state stores were still very limited and offered little choice in size, fashion, or color, but now there were some new hard-currency stores that offered a better selection. More puzzling to me than the question of how they could afford all this was how they managed to navigate through the woods on these rough dirt trails with those high, spiked heels.

The state tried to improve the trails through the woods, but only made them worse and more difficult to navigate. In their attempts to fill in the low spots and even out the dips, they brought in countless loads of dirt. The problem was that the "dirt" also had a lot of broken glass, rusty strips of metal, chunks of porcelain bathroom fixtures, and pieces of sharp, splintery wood. So, it was not only a challenge for those in high heels, it also took all of my concentration to navigate this part of the walk. As I came out the other side of the woods, I noticed how dusty and dirty my feet were and was reminded again of Jesus's servanthood when He washed His disciples' feet.

My next stop was a little state-run store that sold mostly dry goods. Sometimes, I found such treasures as handmade handkerchiefs that old ladies sold on consignment. Sometimes, I'd see a piece of amber jewelry that had been made by some local entrepreneur hoping to increase their meager income.

Afterwards, I'd check out the food stores. Each one was a little different, but they were all basically the same in what they offered for sale. Usually, there was bread. It might be dry and hard, but if you came at just the right time, it could be fresh and still warm. In addition, they always had their well-stocked aisle of Coke or a watered-down version of juice, always in large two-liter glass jars. The juices might vary in color, but they all tasted the same—blah. There would probably be a few cans of fish or some little jars of Russian mustard. Sometimes, there were small jars of canned peas. All in all, the variety was extremely limited, and the quality of goods was very poor.

As I made my way along the broken-up sidewalk to the next store, I saw a man wearing flannel pajamas as his street wear. Things like this were no longer so shocking. It was easier to understand why people wore what they did once you saw what was available to them.

After making an exciting discovery of cucumbers at the veggie booth, my last stop was the local deli and coffee shop. It wasn't that the coffee was so great or the atmosphere so pleasant, but I liked stopping there and spending a little time just observing people, their ways, their dress, their methods of relating to one another. It was a great course in cultural differences and human relationships. Sometimes, the Lord gave me an opportunity to do some sharing and encouraging with those who were concerned about the future.

The ladies serving the customers were usually pretty brusque and grouchy, but they had been quite patient with me in my fumbling attempts to use Russian. As I joined the queue for service, I had time to watch the man sleeping off his vodka at a nearby table and the busgirls with their sweaty brows, wearing worn-out shoes and dirty aprons, clearing away the badly chipped and stained, glued-together cups in time for the next customer. And then my eye fell on the fresh lilacs in tiny vases placed on the tables. How precious of the Lord to give such beauty and such fresh, crisp color to this hot, wilted, dirty atmosphere. *Thank You, Father, for this symbol of life.*

The line was short today, with only about ten ahead of me, so I was soon able to order my coffee. The cost was six rubles (about four cents), but the shortage of kopecks makes it impossible for the gal to give me correct change. We agreed to go to the closest ruble. As I made my way to a little wobbly table, I was again impressed by the infinite variety of people represented here—everything from the poorly dressed old, infirm, and blind to the nicely dressed, more Western-looking younger ones. The thing that stood out today was the swarms of little children. In a society where birth control was non-existent (except via abortion), the little ones were in great abundance. Most were dressed simply, their clothes either too large or too small and their shoes little more than cardboard or bedroom slippers. Many had home-knitted outfits that seemed to be warm and able to stretch with the child's growth. No one worried about matching. They wore what they had.

On my way out of the coffee shop, I took a quick look in the deli. The dark, dingy, unlighted display case had a few dirty dried-up carrots in it, a scrawny blue chicken (still with head and feet), some butter, and some pastries. There was also some cottage cheese in a large tin bucket, and I could smell the fish still flopping in the wooden barrel. I decided that sliced cukes and some rice would be our lunch for today.

Walking back through the woods, I marveled at how the dandelions and long scraggly grass seemed attractive to me. Compared to the sights and smells of the stores, the freshness of a natural setting was such a lift. I looked forward to tomorrow's walk in this corner of God's creation, thanking Him with a full heart for revealing Himself to me in this way and for this precious provision so close to our flat.

Chapter 38

SPRINGTIME IN LATVIA

Springtime in Latvia — April/May 1992

Brrr! Springtime in Latvia was a chilly experience, with morning temperatures sometimes in the mid to high forties! That was in our apartment! Outdoors, it was colder. Due to severe fuel shortages, the Latvian government turned off the heat completely in the whole city of Riga on April 13. We didn't expect there

Cold Latvia Springtime

would be any more heat in our apartment until mid to late October, if then. In the meantime, in this cold, wet climate, we were quite a sight, bundled up with all our heavy clothing, even in bed. We were thankful for two small electric heaters that we brought with us from Vienna. With them, we were able to provide a little heat in one room at a time. We were getting by, but the cold was definitely having an adverse effect on our health and on our work. Warmer temperatures would be welcomed!

Our living conditions left much to be desired at the moment. Nevertheless, we continued to be richly blessed by seeing the wondrous works of the Lord among His people. Most of our students were showing rapid spiritual growth and were being used by the Lord in very fruitful ministries. The results we'd seen gave us confidence that God would have us take another step forward—to begin the transition to having our students become the teachers in their denominational training programs. In fact, many of our students were already teaching courses in existing church training centers, Bible schools, and seminaries.

Beginning that summer, we focused our ministry on intensive training for a smaller number of students, namely those who had been selected by their denominations to become their training directors and teachers. We prayed that by the autumn of 1993, they would do virtually all of the teaching that we now did in the various denominational schools and training centers. Even as they were teaching, they would continue their studies with us, completing the BEE World base curriculum and moving into the advanced theological studies program.

Literature Translation/Publication/Distribution: New Russian language print runs of Series 2:7 and Galatians/Romans workbooks and facilitator packets were printed in the former Soviet Union for the first time and openly distributed to our groups throughout the newly independent former Soviet republics. Especially interesting was the fact that the leader of one of our study groups had contacts at a Soviet army base and was able to get them printed on the army base! The Riga storage depot seemed to be working well, with a good storage room and good inventory control. The only drawback was having to hand carry thousands of books up and down five flights of stairs, since there were no elevators.

Student Statistics: Key statistics showed that the number of students on our circuit had grown from 278 in 1989/90 to 600 in June 1992. During this same time period, students in the BEE World program taught by national teachers we'd trained grew from 165 to 414. Since our goal was total indigenization, it was encouraging for us to see this progression. Praise God!

> *I will give thanks to the Lord with all my heart;*
> *I will tell of all Your wonders. I will rejoice and be*
> *jubilant in You; I will sing praise to Your name,*
> *O Most High.* –PSALM 9-2

EASTER SUNDAY — 1992
Worship on Soviet Basketball Courts

A steady drizzle came down as throngs of people made their way through the heavy wooden doors of the "Temple." Aesthetically, this structure couldn't really be described as beautiful or ornately pretentious as one would imagine a temple to be. It was a huge, rectangular structure, five stories in height, with the most captivating tiny prayer tower stretching toward the heavens on one end.

But this temple symbolized God's presence and His eternal faithfulness in Riga. Many thousands of people came to a saving trust in Christ here, to serve Him and to ultimately make Him known to the surrounding peoples. This building came into being as a result of a great revival that took place here in the 1920s.

The Salvation Temple, as it was called, was taken away from the believers by the Communist officials after the Soviet army takeover of Latvia in 1940. It was turned into a sports center, and in fact, the basketball hoops, painted lines on the floor, and bleachers all remained in the auditorium. The only things salvaged by the believers when the Soviets took over was a huge painting of Jesus's baptism, which used to hang over the altar area and was now across town in Revival Church. Everything else in the Temple was either destroyed or converted into its present use as a sports hall.

Al and I were swept along with the buzzing crowd as we entered the Temple, making our way up the broad old stairway to the second-level auditorium where this first Easter service in many, many years was being held. An aura of great excitement permeated the crowd as last-minute preparations were being overseen. People were finding a few empty spaces left on the hard, backless benches stretching from one side of the great room to the other. Faces were radiant. Handshakes, hugs, and "holy kisses" were warm and genuine. Oh, how good to be with God's people!

Helene spotted us coming in and quickly and enthusiastically ushered us to the front. She insisted we take this place as their special guests.

Their faith was a testimony of great confidence. Already much work had been done in repairing the damage done by the Soviets over the past fifty years. There was total trust that God would indeed reclaim this property for HIS glory.

The endless red tape and official requirements never dampened or deterred their spirit. They simply forged ahead, trusting God to clear the obstacles and provide the funds to restore the building to serve His purpose for the people of Riga.

We had a few minutes before the service began, so Al took me up to the prayer tower. It was one year ago now, in this very tower, that God confirmed and made it plain to Al that this was where He would have us serve. Goosebumps flooded over my being as we climbed the narrow winding steps, up, up, up to the landing where Riga's skyline filled the whole of one's visual capacity. God's Spirit was present. We bowed in humbleness as we claimed, anew, Latvia and this part of the world for His glory. We committed ourselves to be used as His instruments in whatever way He felt was best, whether that be to continue here or in some other part of the world.

During their years of freedom (1918–1940), men were stationed in this prayer tower to pray twenty-four hours a day. The awesomeness of standing here on "holy ground," where godly men of decades past stood and prayed, and then later were executed or forcibly shipped off to Siberia and most likely gave their very lives for the cause of Christ, seeped into our souls. What did the future hold for us? For Al and me? What price would we be asked to pay? We didn't know, but we knew Who held the future—this we could rely on.

The service began. Everyone stood as Genadij proclaimed, "Christ is risen!" The crowd zealously responded, "He is risen indeed!" Time and time again over the next three hours, this shout of affirmation and joy went out over this vast auditorium. Each time, the people jumped to their feet and responded with spine-tingling conviction.

Every place was filled—all available seats were taken and people pressed together along the outside walls, all leaning forward in anticipation of this time of worship. The choir music filled the huge hall; the sound of instruments echoed off the high ceiling; and Jesus was praised for being a LIVING LORD! No longer among the dead but risen from the grave to redeem His people and prepare for them a place in glory, a place where there will be no more tears, no more food lines, no more government hassles, no more needless suffering. Oh, what a day that will be!

Five different preachers, many choir anthems, various recitations, music ensembles, two different altar calls, and three hours later, we were all still totally enthralled by what God was doing! The hope and intent of the service was that it be evangelistic, touching the hearts of non-believers. We witnessed the convicting power of God's Spirit as dozens of people came forward, falling to their knees in repentance and claiming God's forgiveness. We knew, without a doubt, that God honored our desire for this service. On this Easter Sunday, He called many people to a saving knowledge and trust in Himself.

SLAVA BOGA!! SLAVA BOGA!! PRAISE GOD!! PRAISE GOD!!

Easter Worship Service at Salvation Temple — April 1992

The Alus Truck — May 9, 1992

From the kitchen window, I (Betty) had a good view of all the activities going on in front of the little store across the street.

This morning, the line was already forming, and it was only a little after seven in the morning. People were queuing up. They had their jugs, plastic pails, jars, or bottles. There were little old ladies with wrinkled faces and men of every size and shape. Some appeared neat and clean, but most were disheveled, dirty, and a little bit shaky. We'd come to recognize many daily customers and had given them names. For example, there was Olive Oyl (so named because of her resemblance to the character in the long-running *Popeye* comic strip). Others we'd named Dirty Jeans, Yellow Sox, Bird Lady, and Obnoxious. All gazed expectantly down the road

Riga Beer Wagon Scene from Our Kitchen Window

for the green truck towing a large tank on wheels, which made its daily appearance in the front of the bread store across from our flat.

Were these people waiting for bread? Or was it milk? Did their families anxiously anticipate their return home with the daily rations? Unfortunately, it was none of these. The green truck brought an item that was much more in demand than any of those. It was the Alus (beer) truck. All day long, rain, snow, sleet, or hail, people stood out there drinking from the "community cup" and filling up their containers from this crude, tank-truck set up.

It was popular because it was cheap. For the many that came, it offered companionship for their lonely hearts, gave "purpose" to their empty days, dulled the pain of the past, and dimmed the uncertainty of the future.

A few hours into the morning, the crowd started getting quite noisy, and many no longer knew (or really cared) where they were. The unpleasant circumstances that surrounded them seemed to them a bit more tolerable. The rotten cabbage in the stores no longer looked so ugly. And the long lines for bread and milk seemed more acceptable and easier to handle.

The man in the white coat distributing the dark, murky liquid seemed to enjoy his job. He joined in with his customers enough to be sociable. But he seemed to maintain his sobriety, visiting with each new customer as if he were a hundred-dollar-an-hour psychiatrist.

What did he share with all these people? Was it more than just the discussion over the increased prices? Was it more than speculation on the precarious political scene? Was it sympathy with the many whose wives were pregnant once again, knowing they couldn't afford to have more children? Or was it concern over the many who had kids with serious handicaps and no help available to them? Perhaps none of these things, or perhaps all of them and more. Whatever it was, he certainly had a magnetic attraction that drew people out and had them waiting in line each day for his arrival.

I wondered whether my message was as attractive. Did my life, my work, my words of Christ draw and challenge as the man in this green truck? Did the comfort and counsel I offered help and give release to pain?

Chapter 39

YOU MUST CONTINUE!

Summer 1993 Meetings with Baltic and Belarus Church Leaders

Bishop E., head of one of the Latvian denominations, shook his head emphatically and said, "No! No! You must continue!" I (Al) was meeting with the bishop and the director of their new seminary. I had just explained that we did not have enough people to continue meeting regularly every month with their young church leaders, which prompted his response. I explained that we were not planning to abandon them. As the Lord provided people and funding, we would continue working to provide the BEE World curriculum in Russian for their seminary. As quickly as possible, we would support the work of translating it into the Latvian language. I reminded them that we wanted them to select pastors or men from the seminary to become equipped as their teachers, and we would then focus on preparing them to teach our curriculum to their young church leaders and in their other regional training centers.

Thursday evening, after my third day with only a couple hours of sleep, I met with the leaders of another denomination. I knew they had many contacts with Western mission organizations, so I thought maybe they would not miss our help if we were not able to continue. Not so! The response was the same as that of other denominational leaders; they wanted more help, not less! So, before

I left, I promised to meet with eight or ten of their leaders for a full day in September to help them develop their training program for pastors and lay leaders.

The next day, I traveled to Estonia, and at every stop, through the Baltic countries and into Belarus, the response was the same—"You must continue!" Finally, my last stop was the city of Brest, in Western Belarus, on the Polish border. Traveling there from the Baltics was a brutal, exhausting marathon with several unpredictable border crossings. We'd been meeting monthly in Brest for several years with a group of pastors, mostly relatively new believers themselves, who had started churches in Western Ukraine and Western Belarus.

I was prepared to tell them it was simply too difficult for us to continue going there, and if they wanted to work with us, they would have to send someone from their group to meet with us in another city more convenient for us. I told them at the beginning of our seminar that I would not be able to come there regularly anymore, but maybe we could occasionally come. Their first response was, "If you can't come, you must send someone else." Each of these men then told me how important it was to him that we continue teaching them.

As I listened, I was ashamed that I had wanted to spare myself (and my teammates) the hard trip involved in getting there. I suggested that maybe they would like our help in developing a regional training center in Brest. Their eyes brightened, their enthusiasm virtually lit up the room and moved me to promise that I would come back for a full day in September to work out plans with them.

How did I feel after all these experiences from Tallinn to Brest? On the human level, I was physically and emotionally exhausted, totally overwhelmed by all the pleas to continue with more help than in the past. They needed so much more attention than we could give them. We loved them all and wanted to see each one abiding in Christ, being conformed to His image and serving the church faithfully and lovingly. We wanted to see their churches grow and multiply.

All these things, of course, couldn't be forced by human efforts; only God could provide the resources for this task. Only as the Holy Spirit moved His people to do His work would we see the desired results.

As we faced these seemingly insurmountable challenges, we asked our prayer partners in America to pray for God's help as follows:

- That our focus would not be on buildings and books, nor on programs and activities, but rather on God as He worked through us, using these "things" as His tools.
- That God would give me wisdom and insight from Him as I prepared "proposals" for effective training in each situation.
- That God would send more laborers—men and women who were more than academic scholars; people who also know Jesus Christ, our Lord, so well that they couldn't help but be excited about their relationship with Him and would be able to help others know Him in that same way.
- That the doors would remain open wherever God had plans for us to continue working. Already, the Belarus parliament and the Russian parliament had passed laws that threatened the present freedoms we enjoyed.

Fall Report—1993

(Newsletter sent to American supporters from USA.)

Climbing to the top floor of this five-story building left us breathless! It was not only the 106 rough, broken steps leading up to our destination this morning that took our breath away, but also the total contrast from darkness to light. All along the way we saw only dim, dingy, run-down hallways, but the fifth-floor landing led to bright, clean classrooms and radiant faces. Simple and stark by Western standards, this place nonetheless exuded an excitement and exhilaration that went far beyond external environment.

The school was located on the fifth floor of a huge, old, brown cement building on the west side of Riga. As we climbed past the first four levels of this building, we saw various things, including locked steel doors on the fourth-floor landing. It appeared that a children's "hospital" was located behind this door. Puddles of urine and odors of illness seeped out from under the doors and permeated the landing. We never saw any of the children, but from the sounds coming through the big iron doors, it appeared to be a place for badly handicapped kids.

Finally, we arrived at the top landing where we saw a bright, shiny, copper plaque identifying the Riga International Bible Institute in three languages—English, Russian, and Latvian. The doors opened to a long, narrow, L-shaped hallway from which all the classrooms, etc. were located. The hallway floor was painted cement, and a few of the rooms had inexpensive linoleum. Fresh curtains were on the large, double windows looking out on the skyline of Riga. Brand-new paint and wallpaper covered the walls and ceilings. The color combinations might not win any decorating awards, but they'd used whatever bits and pieces were available in the stores. Everyone was thrilled with the radical change in these premises from February 1992, when the first classes met in this building.

There was one room set apart for office space where we met with the director and board members, along with the secretary, to plan and pray. This room housed a few simple hardback, wooden chairs, two very simple desks, and an old, manually operated typewriter. The phone rang almost constantly. Word had gotten out of the existence of this school, and many longed for the opportunity to receive good teaching.

The kitchen was small and dark, but had an apartment-size stove, a couple of crude, homemade cupboards, and a small utility table. There was a pass-through opening into the tiny dining room where simple tables and chairs were already setup for the morning break. The students received three meals a day here. The morning meal might include "manna," some bread, and tea. If food was plentiful, there might also be open-face sandwiches with canned fish. At noon, there would probably be a meal of Russian borscht soup accompanied by bread and a weak Kool-Aid-like drink. The late afternoon meal would probably be tea, open-face fish sandwiches, and occasionally, some sweets. Dishes were rinsed under cold water in a big sink near the toilet right across the hall from the kitchen and immediately replaced on the tables for the next meal.

Returning to this day, the temperature outdoors was below freezing. Unfortunately, there was no heat coming from the huge radiators in the classroom. The damp cold was penetrating, but there were fifty-eight students, warmly dressed in heavy sweaters and scarfs and tightly crammed shoulder to shoulder into a room designed to comfortably hold no more than twenty! Chairs were squeezed together as tight as could be, leaving absolutely no walking space.

Today, they started an intensive course called The Christian Life. They had already been taught the foundational courses: Galatians/Romans, Evangelism and Discipleship, Old Testament Survey, and New Testament Survey. Now came the time to look specifically at their own personal spiritual growth and how all this took place in their lives.

Biblically speaking, holiness speaks of being "set apart"; that is, different in appearance and purpose from one's surroundings, a living example of God's grace, provision, and guidance. With the goal of holiness, these students came, humbly seeking to grow more Christ-like in their daily walk, grateful for the training and discipleship we provided to them.

The school secretary, Tanya, rang a little hand bell to signal the beginning of class, and a reverent hush fell over the entire group as they gazed intently toward the front of the room where the teacher stood. Al opened the new session by introducing, through a translator, the teacher for this course, Pastor John Hutchinson from Florida.

RIBI Growth by September 1993

Pastor Hutchinson stepped forward and asked the students to introduce themselves and tell where they came from. There were names like Sergei, Natasha, Helen, Alexander, Svetlana. They came from various countries—Estonia, Lithuania,

Latvia, Georgia, Belarus, Ukraine, Russia. Anticipation and eagerness were clearly written on their faces.

The student body at the Bible Institute in Riga grew from 25 in February 1992 to 184 in September 1993. As John began to teach on the meaning of spiritual maturity, I was struck by the responsibility God had given us. It was awesome and humbling to consider the far-reaching impact as these people went back into their home countries and passed their teaching on to others. Millions were searching for the path that would lead them out of their dark past of atheistic Communism into the light of God's truth. *O Lord Jesus, give us the insights, the wisdom, the understanding, to share the truths You would want to use in developing these students. Help us to lean not on our own understanding, but in all our ways to acknowledge You.*

Chapter 40

AFTERWORD 1993–2024

While this book is primarily about our years of underground work with the churches in Communist Eastern Europe and the Soviet Union (1983–1990), I've (Al) also included how God led us in the years following the major political changes that allowed for open ministry.

This closing chapter includes something of our lives in the ensuing years.

Baltic Church Planter Trainees — 1997

By 1993, we needed to spend more time in the USA due to aging parents needing our help and the need to devote more time to mission organization leadership. Betty's cancer and other health concerns also meant more doctor appointments. Therefore, we decided to make our primary home in the USA as of April of that year, but we kept an apartment in Riga until 2004. Other team members could stay there while we were gone.

In Chapter 15, I told the story of the "fifty red dots" (the plan to train men to start fifty new churches in Latvia) and how that led to the start of the Riga International Bible Institute. By 1996, a further decision was made to begin a separate training program specifically for church planters.

God blessed that work, and I believe at least fifty new churches were planted as a result.

In January and February of 1996, Betty and I made a trip to the Baltics to do the monthly seminars. While in Riga, we made a visit to Pastor G. and his wife, Helena.

Mafia Threatens Survival of the Bible Institute — February 1996

Pastor G. came to pick us up at 1:00 p.m. He hugged us both. As a woman, I (Betty) wasn't prepared for a hug from a Russian pastor. But G. was special, and I guess he thought we were too.

Helene was at home, waiting for us with open arms. Oh, how precious to see these dear friends. They were truly God's people, and it was a privilege to know them. She served a nice, delicious meal, and after lunch, we shared family photos. Pastor G. asked what we felt the future of the Bible Institute was, and then we asked him to explain what had been going on there.

Pastor G. began his story, which started last fall, with the notice of a rent increase from the new owner—from $560.00 per month to $1,500 per month. Plus, they were asking for back pay of at least three months! When G. refused to pay, the mafia began showing up and threatening him, telling him he would also have to pay protection money! Pastor G., in his faith in Christ, refused. However, the mafia continued to hassle him with multiple phone calls, visits to the Bible school, and many threats to harm him if he didn't pay. Finally, he reached out to some other pastors for prayer and counsel.

Pastor B. and a pastor from Estonia came to pray with G. and to try and help him. Many people in Latvia and in America prayed as well. However, the Estonian pastor got some of his "friends" to come, and as it turned out, these so-called friends were also mafia! It seemed this Estonian pastor was in the car selling business (buying them in Germany) and got involved with the mafia far deeper than he'd ever expected.

As time went on, the mafia became more and more insistent that Pastor G. pay. They took him out in the forest several times, ready to "change his mind," but he again refused to pay, saying he trusted the Lord as his protector, not the mafia. Then the mafia backed off again.

G.'s friend Yuri, a man who had stood up to the mafia in the past, came to G. and said he would take his place with the mafia. Yuri was ready to sacrifice himself. The mafia took him up on it, smashing his face with a heavy piece of iron, crushing all the small bones, his jaw, his teeth, etc.

But the mafia didn't let up on G., insisting that he not only pay the exorbitant rent, but also the high rent for the past six years! The mafia claimed he was hiding the funds he had to work with, which, of course, was ridiculous.

Pastor G. finally went underground. But the mafia came after Helene, going to the flat and trying to break the doors down several times. It was then that Helene received an invitation to the USA from a friend, and she flew out in November.

After some time of being underground, G. decided to move out of the building housing the Bible Institute. While they were taking furniture out, a man came to him and said he was the new owner. It turned out he was a Christian Latvian who wanted Pastor G. to stay, saying the Bible Institute was a good thing for the country. He would negotiate the rent, plus take care of the mafia! It also turned out that this man's job was assistant prosecutor, focused on going after the mafia! Who but our great God could have arranged something like this?

Not that the problem was all solved, but G. now had an ally. This new owner was brutalized by the mafia, beaten up, abused, and sent naked back to town. He had no love for the mafia. He claimed the whole city was controlled by them, but he intended to do something about it.

This new owner planned to appeal to the Latvian government for rent subsidy help. He gave the Bible Institute January rent free and only half-charged for February. The new negotiations would most likely result in rent about two times more than before, but that was simply the rate of inflation.

Pastor G.'s heart was truly that of a pastor. His burden was for trained leaders. He said, "The best have left Latvia for other lands, so we must train new ones." But what a challenge!

Al spoke about possible financial ways to support the Institute, like teaching people how to operate and manage a business, which in turn would support the RIBI. But of course, none of the things which sound so logical and easy to us were without complications for the Russians living in a land where they were not wanted. We shared this situation with our mission office in Fargo and with our prayer and financial support partners. They responded generously as long as their help was needed, and the school is still serving the people of Latvia and other countries.

Time Marches On and Brings Changes

Later in the summer of 1996, I made a teaching trip with a pastor friend through Estonia, Latvia, and Belarus. All along the way, we were greatly encouraged by the reports about how God had used our training to equip men who had been sent out as evangelists, pastors, church planters, etc. and how this would not have happened if we had not been faithful in coming to them with our Biblical Education by Extension training over the prior seven years. What a blessing for us to hear them say these things! Since the early 1990s, of course, many other organizations and individuals had followed our early efforts with their help.

By the year 2000, Betty's cancer had advanced to Stage 4. The next thirteen years, until her passing, were filled with constant chemotherapy and a number of hospital stays. In 2004, we worked with her primary cancer doctor to give Betty the approval to make one last trip to Latvia, which she deeply desired to do. We were able to make that trip, and the Lord gave her nine more years after that before taking her home in August of 2013. These last years were especially difficult because of her failing health, but she was blessed to have many good times with family.

Shortly before her passing, she was asked to describe her life in one word; she chose the word, "overflowing." She explained that she had been blessed by the Lord with such a marvelously abundant life, and she prayed that it had overflowed into the lives of others through her service to Him.

Betty requested Philippians 1:21 be inscribed on her tombstone, "For me to live is Christ; to die is gain."

Since her passing, I've had the privilege of serving in leadership of two mission organizations. In January of 2022, I became one of the founders of Serving Workers for the Harvest, which I continue to serve as president in 2025. Over the years, I've had the joy of working with ministries and enjoying relationships in dozens of countries on six continents all around the world.

I continued to make international visits to our ministries in Europe, Asia, and Africa after Betty's passing, including a number for special occasions. In 2014, I was invited to Riga to speak at the Latvian Biblical Centre graduation and again in 2017 at the dedication of the renovated building that became their new home. In 2019, I was able to attend two separate forty-year reunion gatherings (Thessaloniki, Greece and Vienna, Austria) of the ministry we served with back in the 1980s and 1990s. As you can imagine, those were incredible opportunities to revisit old memories and catch up on the current lives of many I hadn't seen for decades.

During the 1980s and 1990s, special events were held in Fargo at various churches and other auditoriums to report on our ministry and to raise funds for ministry projects. I especially remember one event where two songs with special meaning to us were sung as part of the program.

The first was the familiar hymn, "Amazing Grace," which included the line, "Through many dangers, toils and snares I have already come." Betty and I could relate all too well to these words and to the picture of God's amazing grace in our lives.

The second was the song by a guest singer entitled, "May All Who Come Behind Us Find Us Faithful." That song continues to be my prayer as younger generations follow us to mission fields around the world.

Only the Lord knows how much longer I have to serve Him in my remaining earthly life. My prayer for whatever time He gives me is from Psalm 71:17-18:

> *God, You have taught me from my youth,*
> *And I still declare Your wondrous deeds.*
> *And even when I am old and gray, God, do not abandon me,*
> *Until I declare Your strength to this generation,*
> *Your power to all who are to come.*

ABOUT THE AUTHORS

Al and Betty as Farm Kids in Minnesota and North Dakota

I (Al) was a WWII baby and grew up in a rural middle-of-nowhere Minnesota farm community with a Norwegian immigrant background, where my parents' generation still spoke mostly Norwegian in everyday life. During my eight years in our small one-room country schoolhouse, I eagerly devoured the content of all the books in the school library, including encyclopedias and the dictionary! I was especially enchanted by tales of the early European seafaring explorers who discovered all kinds of previously unknown lands around the globe. While doing my everyday chores on our small family farm, I daydreamed of traveling someday myself to see and explore the jungles and mountains and islands and peoples and cultures they described. One warm spring afternoon, as

Al as One-Room Country School Student

I was walking home alone from school on our quiet dusty country road, I was struck by a strong sense that it was actually going to happen, as impossible as it seemed at that time.

My world in my early years on our family farm included kerosene lamps instead of electric lights, a battery-operated radio on a shelf in the kitchen for news and entertainment instead of TV and internet, trips down the path to the little outhouse at the edge of the woods, and Saturday night baths in a galvanized washtub next to the kitchen stove.

Farm Work Began at an Early Age for Al

International travel was simply not a realistic dream. Stories by my parents' generation telling of the Great Depression and WWII were a big part of my world in those days—and have had a lasting impact on my life to this day. This background greatly helped me relate to those we served years later in Europe. In fact, most conversations with Europeans during the 1980s included vivid WWII memories told by those who had personally experienced them.

Meanwhile, Betty's early childhood years were centered around her family's "little house on the prairie" in a largely German-speaking farm community of rolling hills featuring pastures and grain fields in rural North Dakota. It was a quiet life with her parents, older brother, and younger sister, helping them care for the cows, horses, and chickens, and also attending a small one-room country school.

Since her grandparents had immigrated to the Dakotas in the late nineteenth century from German settlements in the old Russian empire, her familiarity with the history, foods, and customs of that region greatly aided our acceptance and bonding with those we served in the 1980s.

Betty as Student at One-Room Country School

Betty's North Dakota "School Bus" — 1940s

Leaving the Farm

My (Al's) teen years were difficult as I left the one-room country school after completing eighth grade and entered a large freshman class in the nearest city high school. In that setting, I was a total misfit, as my "citified" classmates were so much more "sophisticated" and comfortable in their well-established cliques. I coped by hanging around with other misfits and joining them in drinking, smoking, and petty crime.

Entering college four years later, I soon found myself in a much better position socially, but I made the bad choice of "majoring" in drinking, parties, and many sinful relationships.

However, by the mid 1960s, the Vietnam War buildup was underway, and like so many of my generation, I soon found myself in a military uniform undergoing training for war (weapons training, jungle combat training and survival, etc.).

Then shortly before boarding the plane that would take me to wartime military duty in Vietnam, I was standing in line for a hamburger at a military base concession stand in California. I began to picture myself coming home from Vietnam in a coffin, which was

Al with M-16 in Vietnam War — 1969

what ultimately happened to fifty-eight thousand young men like myself. Suddenly, I was hit hard by the realization that I did not know the Lord's salvation, and if I were killed in Vietnam, I would spend eternity suffering in hell. I virtually broke out in a cold sweat with that prospect staring me so boldly in the face. Like nearly everyone in our community, I had attended church regularly in my early years, so I knew something of the Bible and its teachings, but there was never any personal saving faith involved. Sad to say, it was another ten years before I did anything about it and chose to receive His freely offered salvation. However, God, in His mercy, spared me from coming home in a coffin. Instead, He brought me home alive to return to school

After returning safely from Vietnam and completing a degree in business management, I served ten years in the business world. This experience included positions as a senior vice president in one international business, and then as general manager of another company startup, which later also became an international business. These jobs provided good business experience, which proved to be helpful later in life and ministry, but at the time, were just filled with more travel, more drinking, and more sinful relationships.

Meanwhile, Betty was also not part of the "in" crowd at her high school. She enjoyed her role as majorette leading the band for school and community events, but mostly kept a low profile. However, her classmates apparently sensed something adventurous in her as well, because in her high school yearbook class prophecy, they saw her becoming an international correspondent in Europe for the *New York Times*.

After high school, it was Betty's heart's desire to train in the medical field. However, both of her parents had experienced lengthy and difficult illnesses, which meant large medical bills and limited ability to work. There was no money for further schooling, so instead, shortly after turning eighteen, she agreed to what was pretty much an arranged marriage. Her dreams of a career in the medical field evaporated. Instead, her home became a twenty-six-foot-long mobile home, and she became a stay-at-home mom, eventually raising three children. By 1973, after nineteen years of a very difficult and painful marriage, she concluded that divorce was necessary and biblically justified. She then completed a course at a local business college and took a job to provide for her family.

Just two years later, I saw her across the ballroom floor at a dance. We experienced an immediate mutual attraction. We danced a waltz together, and she very willingly gave me her phone number. (I realized many years later that she had kept the long light-blue evening dress she was wearing that night in 1975 as a memento of our meeting; it's still hanging in my closet.) I had recently ended a relationship, and she soon ended the relationship she was in at that time. We started dating and became a couple very quickly.

Love Changes Our Perspective on Marriage

Prior to meeting Betty, I was more interested in parties and multiple relationships than in marriage, while Betty's hellish marriage experience had led her to swear that she would never ever again consider marriage. However, after six months or so, our growing love for each other changed our perspective, and in July of 1977, we very seriously and emotionally exchanged our wedding vows. Our first Christmas gifts to each other as man and wife included my gift of a set of luggage to Betty, and her gift to me was a beautiful globe. I guess God knew the plans He had for us even though we had no clue.

For a time, we enjoyed the "good life" most Americans strive for. We enjoyed a two-part honeymoon—first, a time at a Minnesota lake cabin following our summer wedding, and then a beautiful relaxing and memorable December/January in Hawaii.

We both had well-paying jobs; we were financially well off with a beautiful home, a new Buick Regal, and promising and prosperous potential in the business world, but God was soon to reveal His different plans for the rest of our earthly lives.

ABOUT THE AUTHORS

Al & Betty Wedding Photo — July 16, 1977

Decision to Receive Free Gift of Eternal Salvation in Jesus Christ

For by grace you have been saved through faith; and this is not of yourselves, it is the gift of God.
–EPHESIANS 2:8-9

After a couple of years of typical American work and family life, God began to change everything for us.

Life was leveling out for me (Betty) and my kids after many difficult years. Mike, especially, had been through some very troubled times involving drugs and alcohol, etc., but he came home one day for a chance to visit and spend time together. While Mike had been away, he'd been witnessed to by his aunt, and had found grace in the eyes of the Lord. He embraced this new-found faith in Christ with arms wide open and desired, whole-heartedly, to share it with us.

For the first time in my life, I finally understood the gospel. That it is a gift, not something to be earned, but that Christ secured this gift for us through His death on the cross, and that all we had to do was believe and accept it. Upon recognizing my sinful nature, asking God's forgiveness, accepting the love of Christ and His desire to see me walk by faith with Him, I then gave my heart to the Lord and have never looked back.

It's always so fascinating to me to see who the Lord uses in reaching us. Now who would ever have suspected He'd use my own son to make the gospel clear to me. Perhaps that's why it was so easy for me to respond, since I didn't have any defenses in place. Mike then invited us to go with him to an evangelical church where he knew the pastor.

It wasn't long before Al, too, was wrapped in the goodness of God's love, and he also experienced the "new birth" (John 3:3–6) during a Sunday morning worship service. The Lord used the preaching of this pastor, who would some years later have a strategic role in our ministry in the Baltics, to draw Al into the Kingdom. I feel so small when I consider the Lord's mighty ways. He is great—and good—in every way.

I remember so well how the dear people from this church pulled us into fellowship. It wasn't long before we felt comfortable in formally joining this body of believers, and we were baptized in the backyard swimming pool of one of the church elders. The kindness of many who reached out to us, invited us into their homes for meals, or took us along to various activities made all the difference in how welcome we felt. The warm friendship we experienced there gave us a sense of the Savior's love, and we were thrilled to have this group as our church family.

Al was soon asked to lead a midweek home church group for prayer and Bible study. When challenged with this role, we at first just laughed, as we were new believers and not at all equipped for this responsibility. However, others in the group were also new believers, so we agreed to try it. Over the course of a year, we carefully and thoroughly studied our way verse by verse through the book of Romans together.

This year of immersion in Romans was not only a beautiful time of growing in God's Word, but we also shared many other aspects of our lives with one another as well. Try as we might, we've never been involved in such a group since then. God gave us a special time during that year with a select group of people. It was one we have looked back on with great fondness many times over the ensuing years.

You can visit Al online at SWHarvest.org/al-baanna.

ACKNOWLEDGMENTS

God has blessed us with faithful board members and with a host of faithful prayer and financial supporters for the past forty-plus years. They have all been an essential part of the ministry service I (Al) describe in this book.

Our many administrative and missionary teammates and international ministry partners over the years have also been an integral part of the stories I share in this book. I only wish I could include more about them and the parts they've played in our lives and ministry—but it's just not possible as there have been so many.

I specifically want to acknowledge those who have spent many hours helping me in the preparation of this book. Mary D. and Val K., especially, invested countless hours into converting Betty's hand-written journal entries and our old prayer letters into MS Word so I could edit them and use them in my writing.

Printed in Great Britain
by Amazon